FOOTSTEPS

OF

OUR LORD AND HIS APOSTLES

IN

Syria, Greece, and Italy:

A SUCCESSION OF

VISITS TO THE SCENES OF NEW TESTAMENT NARRATIVE.

BY W. H. BARTLETT,

AUTHOR OF "WALKS ABOUT JERUSALEM," "THE NILE BOAT,"
ETC. ETC.

LONDON:

ARTHUR HALL, VIRTUE & CO.

25, PATERNOSTER ROW.

1851.

LONDON :

PRINTED BY RICHARD CLAY,

BREAD-STREET-HILL.

Arch of Titus.

ILLUSTRATIONS.

Engravings on Steel.

WOODCUTS, BY BRANSTON.

ERRATA.

Page 9, *for* Consolato, *read* Consulato.
    67, *for* Mount St. Cymon, *read* the mountain.
    78, *for* Adona, *read* Adana.
    91, *for* Solis, *read* Soli.
    119, *for* Juxtonilla, *read* Juxtanilla.
    183, *for* Japhet, *read* Saphet.

MAP TO ILLUSTRATE
THE
TRAVELS OF OUR LORD
AND HIS APOSTLES

The dotted line shows
the supposed track of
St Paul's voyage from
Cæsarea to Rome.

Scale of English Miles

London J Hatt Virtue & Co

CHAPTER I.

ALEXANDRIA TO JAFFA—WAR IN PALESTINE—ACRE—TYRE—SIDON—BEYROUT
—THE CEDARS—BAALBEC—DAMASCUS, &C.

SOME few years back, in the red and glowing haze of an
Egyptian sunset, a party of Frank travellers stood upon the sandy
shore of the harbour of Alexandria, surrounded by their heterogeneous packages, and awaiting the uprising of that evening
breeze which was to waft them to the coast of Palestine. In
those days Mediterranean travelling was very different from what
it now is, steam-boats were not yet introduced, and the impatient
pilgrim, with his imagination eagerly fixed upon the sacred
localities of his religion, or the wonders of Egypt, had often to
waste many weary days, or perhaps weeks upon the way, before he
could attain the desired object. Such had been the case in the
present instance. After long waiting to no purpose for an
opportunity of proceeding to Jaffa, our party, in pure despair,
had at length chartered a vessel to that port, and laid in a stock
of provisions sufficient to last them the passage. With every
preparation made, and impatience at its utmost stretch, the Arab
captain still found each day some pretext, real or imaginary, for
delaying his departure. Sometimes the wind was positively
contrary ; sometimes it was fair, but then either too strong or else
too light; and it was only at a propitious juncture, when the
steady land-breeze promised to carry us fairly to our destination
in four-and-twenty hours, that the dilatory Reis at length arose,

B

took the pipe out of his mouth, tightened his girdle, shuffled on his papooshes, screamed madly to his ragged sailors, and definitively prepared to embark.

Of the party of five, squeezed with their baggage into the ship's little crazy boat, four were Englishmen, and one American, and even amidst the grotesque variety of character and costume which salutes the eye at Alexandria, they were justly regarded by the natives as something out of the common way. They were, for the most part, men of good family and means, who, at home, would, some of them, have been remarked for nothing save aristocratic propriety and *retenu*, and fastidious attention to the minutiæ of fashionable costume. They had just returned from a cruise up the Nile, their countenances were—not bronzed, according to the usual phrase, but they were literally *baked* into the dark red colour of Egyptian brickdust, and their unclipped beards and moustaches had grown into more than oriental amplitude and savagery. Their costume!—that beggars all description for its reckless *abandon*, and proud indifference to public opinion. One wore the wreck of an old plaid shooting-jacket, with capacious pockets, stuffed with powder and shot, his waistcoat had long been discarded as worse than useless; what had been once a shirt, now scarcely more than a waistcoat, flew wildly away from the open brawny chest; and in lieu of braces, a thick red sash, stuck full of pistols, was girt around his loins, serving, doubtfully, to uphold a pair of trowsers in the last stage of disorganization. His head and feet were à *la Turque*, the former being surmounted by a huge turban, the latter thrust stockingless into a pair of pointed red papooshes. Others preferred rather to reverse this process, wearing broad-brimmed straw hats over a sort of fancy oriental costume selected at random from the bazaars; in all, the incongruity was equally ludicrous, and all were equally and utterly callous about it. So cool and yet so crazy looking a set baffled the speculations of the orientals, who looked up to them with something of that reverence accorded to those whom a mysterious Providence afflicts with mental hallucination.

On boarding the rugged sides of the ship, and gaining its deck, the wisdom of our captain's precaution became somewhat disagreeably evident. The Arabs, we know, were the first to brave the perils of the deep, but they have not kept pace with the gradual improvement in navigation. Our vessel was just like the old models in nautical cabinets of ships in the middle ages, high tilted at the poop and stern, and with masts, spars, and rigging of curious and antique fashion. So far so good—to a lover of the picturesque; but this was not all; the craft was perilously crazy, the seams yawned as if the shrunken planks were about to come asunder, the ropes and sails looked as if the first stiff breeze would snap the one and split the others to shreds and tatters. There was neither chart nor compass on board. It was, in fact, just a sample of the Arab coasting vessels, the wrecks of which so picturesquely bestrew the shores of Syria. But then it was the height of summer; the azure sea, ruffled by a light breeze, and reflecting the serene blue of heaven, was pleasant to look upon, and delicious was the coolness of the humid air, after the hot atmosphere and glaring sands of Egypt. Jaffa was but two hundred miles, and if the breeze held, we might hope to reach our destination in four-and-twenty hours, and be up at Jerusalem in time to witness the ceremonies of the Easter week.

The interior of the vessel was as primitive as its build and tackle. It was simply decked over from stem to stern, the interior being totally hollow, and looking, with its naked planking and rough ribs, like the interior of some monstrous skeleton, and smelling as if the process of desiccation had been imperfectly accomplished. There was no level boarding at the bottom, which was covered with sand and shingle, by way at once of flooring and ballast. A portion of about one-third of this dark den was partitioned off as a cabin, into which, we descended, and from which, we ascended, by the gymnastic process

of clambering up and down an upright post, having notches cut
into it for the feet. Our carpets and baggage were arranged
upon the sand. Sand is said to breed fleas, and our experience
fully tended to corroborate the opinion. Nothing, in short, but
nasal and ocular evidence could convey to the reader a correct
idea of the interior of this worm-eaten old ark, or of the
"creeping things innumerable" that took up their habitation
within its uncleanly chinks.

With the usual amount of frenzied gesticulations and unearthly
howling, our Arabs hoisted their tattered sail to the breeze, and
with a turbaned old pilot to direct our way between the perilous
sunken rocks that impede its entrance, we flew rapidly out of the
harbour of Alexandria into the open sea. We had lighted upon
a period then loudly vaunted as that of the "regeneration of
Egypt." That ancient land, fallen from her ancient glory into
the condition so emphatically called in prophecy the "basest of
kingdoms," was supposed to be on the point of springing into
new life at the bidding of Mehemet Ali. Wherever we looked
around, we saw the evidences of his marvellous energy; new
lighthouses appeared, palaces and arsenals bordered the harbour,
and huge three-deckers and frigates studded its bosom, while the
number of merchant-ships bore testimony equally palpable of
increasing commerce. The ambitious designs of Mehemet Ali
were then in full and successful development. Acre had recently
surrendered to his power, and the whole of Syria had submitted
to his sway. Ibrahim Pasha, we knew, was then in that country
with his army, engaged in compelling the reluctant acquiescence
of the petty chiefs to a new and regular system of government;
one of the first results of which would be the entire security of
travellers, and the certainty of their being treated with every
consideration both by the pasha and his officials. We had
wisely provided ourselves with firmans, enjoining the latter to
aid and assist us, and might reasonably anticipate a triumphant
progress through the length and breadth of the land. With

anticipations thus pleasurable, we beheld the low shores of Egypt, the Pharos of Alexandria, and the tall masts of the men-of-war, gradually lessening from our vision, until after one of those solemn sunsets, to which no description could do justice, they vanished in the obscurity of night.

Our old craft skimmed prosperously over the gently rippling sea, which, as she moved along, was churned into a wake glittering with phosphoric splendour; the stars in countless hosts were above our heads, the night, in short, was splendid, but this could not withdraw our thoughts from the discomforts of our situation. The idea of going below was horrible; we preferred to have our mattresses spread upon the deck, dovetailed as well as the limited space at our command permitted, and then covering ourselves with cloaks, lay down for the night, emphatically under the guidance of Providence, and Providence alone.

When we awoke and had rubbed our eyes next morning, the sight that saluted us was most disheartening. The breeze had almost died away, coming only in occasional puffs, the sea was calm as glass. We had hoped to see the evening's sun shining on the walls of Jaffa, but we had evidently made but little progress, and whether that progress was in the right direction, was painfully problematical. Our Arab captain evidently had but one plan, that of the boy lost in the wood, to go straight on till he came to the end of it—somewhere, and this was the way in which he expected to make the coast of Syria, unless, indeed, it should happen to be that of Cyprus, or peradventure that from which we had just departed. But we were determined not yet to croak; we had a good stock of fowls, plenty of rice, and with the aid of these " vivers," worked into a capital *pilau* by the skill of our cook, we contrived to get through the first day in tolerable good humour. But alas! there came a second, and a third, and a fourth, and still the same unvarying blue sky and sickly-gleaming sea, upon which we seemed to be enchanted, for while we were almost always sailing towards the land, we never somehow could contrive to make it, though we knew we must have gone double the distance. Provisions, too, were rapidly running out, and it was with the most melancholy feelings that we beheld the cook drag forth from his coop our last surviving fowl, and behead him upon the bulwark for a last *pilau.* But on the fifth morning all our troubles were suddenly dissipated. As the light vapour, which hung like a veil over the sea, was lifted by the rising sun, there came into view a long blue range of distant mountains, at first resembling a bar of clouds, and mistaken more than once for it, but at length, as the light increased, and our vessel advanced nearer, it was evidently land, and, as we hoped, the Holy Land, to which our pilgrim steps were directed. Our Reis, who had been on the coast before, was confident, from its general configuration, that the coast of Palestine was before him, but at the same time he gave us to understand with equal clearness, that he knew not what particular part of it we were abreast of. Out therefore came all our maps and guide-books, and an animated discussion took place, at which the captain and all the crew assisted, with a noise and volubility proportioned to their ignorance of the matter. On which hand was Jaffa? should we stand north or run south for it? that was the question. A northerly breeze which happened to spring up, inclined, or rather compelled us to the latter alternative, and approaching within a mile of the coast, we continued to follow it to the southward.

Hour after hour thus passed, and yet no signs of Jaffa appeared. The country, at first green and pleasant, seemed to grow more desolate and abandoned as we advanced, we saw no signs of life, and consequently no inhabitants of whom we might inquire our whereabouts. Two eminences rising above the undulating range of downs arrested our attention as we passed along, but it was not till afterwards that we learned that they bore the famous names of Askelon and Gaza.

Slowly the evening came on, and all of us, even the captain, were seriously disquieted. At length, while speculating as to

some method of bringing our uncertainty to an end, we
suddenly descried a solitary Arab slowly wending his way along
the sandy beach, distant about half a mile from the ship. A
brilliant idea flashed across the brain of the Reis, his eye
twinkled with sudden inspiration, and he gave instant orders to
lower the ship's boat and give chase to the individual whom
Providence had sent for our succour. The order was obeyed with
unusual alacrity, and in a few moments the boat, manned by two
sailors, was dashing towards the shore, while leaning over the
bulwark in a row, we awaited the result with intense interest.

For some time after the boat left the vessel, the Arab continued to pace on slowly as before; but as he saw it get nearer
the shore, he suddenly paused and regarded it with evident
uneasiness. It touched the beach at last, and one of the sailors
leaving it in the care of the other, jumped ashore and advanced
in the direction of the chase. At first, not to startle his man,
he walked on gently; but finding that the Arab quickened his
pace in proportion, he suddenly broke into a run, at the same
time shouting and waving his arms towards the fugitive, who,
his suspicions being now fully confirmed, started off at the
utmost speed of which he was capable. In fact, the terrible
conscription, dreaded above all things by the Syrians, was then
in full operation, and the man supposed that our object was to
kidnap and carry him off in chains as a recruit. He dashed
on, then, furiously, madly, as if the avenger of blood was behind
him, while we watched the result of the race with an anxiety
produced by the conviction, that possibly our very lives depended
on his capture. The same conviction seemed to animate the
legs of the pursuing boatman, who after almost superhuman
efforts at length came up with the fugitive, and after running
neck and neck with him for some minutes, bawling all the while
to him to stop, but bawling in vain, finally clutched his hand
upon his shoulder, and adroitly tripping him up, sent him
rolling over and over in the sand. On jumping to his legs, the

man was about to defend himself, when the explanations of his
captor seemed to satisfy him, for he came to a stand still, and
after a quiet parley resumed his onward way, while the
boatman retracing his steps, regained the boat, and both plying
their oars with vigour, in a few moments more were climbing up
the side of the vessel.   There was a general rush—and "where
are we?" was the eager demand.   The captain's long face seemed
longer and yellower as he learned the fact, communicated to ourselves by the dragoman, that we had been running all day away
from Jaffa, of which we must have been nearly abreast in the
morning, and that had we but continued our southward career
during the night, we should by daylight have been off the
Pelusian mouth of the Nile, and in a fair way to regain the port
from which we had started.   With such a system of navigation,
and with no harbours to run for besides, one ceases to be
startled at the number of wrecks with which the coast of Palestine
is studded.

There was of course nothing for it but to get back again to
the latitude of Jaffa as quickly as possible, which we happily
contrived to do about noon on the following day.   As we drew
near, the gloomy old city, encircled by its heavy wall, stood out
upon its hill-side, overlooking one of the most ancient sea-ports
in the world, so old that Noah is traditionally supposed to have
selected it for the building of his ark, and a more miserable place
he could hardly have chosen for the purpose, since it is exceedingly confined, and imperfectly defended from the sea by only a
natural ledge of rocks, over which the surf, in heavy weather,
breaks with tremendous violence, and only approachable through
a passage between them.   Several distressing casualties have
occurred in effecting the entrance in small boats, and many a
ship has been dashed to pieces upon the perilous shore.   Within
this ledge we perceived what seemed an unusual number of
small boats, and we were no less surprised at the quantity of
tents pitched among the thickets and gardens that environ the

town. As a pilot-boat came off to take up the passengers through the reef— for the vessel remained outside—we ascertained the meaning of these unexpected appearances. The whole country, we learned, was in a state of insurrection. The hill chiefs of Palestine, accustomed, under the old standard of the sultan, to enjoy virtual independence, were not disposed to bend to the yoke of Ibrahim Pasha; and taking advantage of the general disaffection occasioned among the inhabitants by the conscription, had raised the standard of revolt, occupied the mountain passes, and prepared for a desperate and sanguinary struggle. At that moment Ibrahim Pasha was encamped with a small body of forces in the vicinity of the town, awaiting the arrival of succours from Egypt before venturing to measure his strength with the rebellious chieftains.

This information threw a sudden cloud over the bright anticipations of spirits highly excited with the expectation of reaching Jerusalem in a few hours. Nevertheless, embarking our effects and taking leave of the old captain, we descended into the boat, pushed through the reef, crossed the harbour, and jumped upon the shore of Palestine, amidst a crowd of vociferous Arabs and yelping dogs, the latter race, hereditary persecutors of Frank travellers, raising a tenfold clamour at the sight of our grotesque habiliments. Preceded by our dragoman, we hastened through a maze of dark and tortuous alleys to the abode of the British vice-consul, to seek from his authentic lips the confirmation or denial of the evil tidings we had just heard. We speedily reached his house, which differed little from the dilapidated edifices we had already passed; but having over its sombre portal the welcome inscription, " Consolato Inglese," with some rude attempt at an imitation of our national arms. We were ushered into a room furnished, although rather meanly, with divans and mats; but from its latticed windows, overlooking the port with its picturesque jumble of shipping, its rugged reef, and our old vessel, riding at anchor on the bluest of blue seas, canopied by a cloudless sky of similar intensity of colour, gemmed by a few barks with huge white sails, flitting birdlike across the outstretched expanse,—the scene, simple as were its elements, was lovely, the sea-breeze blew freshly into the apartment, we had got rid of the old ship, and in spite of sinister forebodings we could not but rejoice at feeling our feet on terra firma, and on the threshold, at least, of the land which we had come so far to see.

Our reflections were interrupted by the entrance of a figure even more grotesque than our own, who saluted us with an infinity of airs and graces. He was a tall, gaunt, hairy individual, invested in a long purple gown of state, which had grown exceedingly shabby, hurriedly and in honour of our visit thrown over an under garment, which had once been white; his naked hairy legs were partially invested in a pair of dirty socks, terminating in yellow buskins; while in his hand, as he bowed and bowed again, he waved theatrically to and fro a tarnished three-cornered cocked hat, which had been bestowed on him, as we understood, by Napoleon Bonaparte. After a ceremonious interchange of obeisances between .ourselves and this dignified representative of our country, we plunged at once "in medias res," and earnestly inquired of him, through our dragoman, if the report we had heard was indeed founded in truth. As he assured us it was, our hearts sank within us. We had come three thousand miles, through all manner of hindrances and impediments, to see Jerusalem, and found ourselves balked when almost within sight of the place. Compassionating our distress, Signor Damiani (such was the name of the vice-consul) proposed that we should wait upon the pasha, and learn from himself the actual state of affairs, at the same time offering to act as our guide and interpreter, not sorry, perhaps, to have an opportunity of displaying his dignity as agent to a nation with which he well knew, as in fact we did all, the pasha desired to be upon the best of terms. We closed instantly with the proposal;

the vice-consul mounted his three-cornered hat, and with a mock heroic dignity escorted us into the street, along which, headed by himself and his dragoman, as well as our own, we filed in solemn procession, to the evident satisfaction of the grinning *gamins*, and the fearful irritation of the canine part of the population, who followed at our heels three deep in howling chorus to the outskirts of the town, in spite of objurgations both loud and deep, and notwithstanding a volley of stones and brickbats, with which we attempted to give effect to them.

The streets along which we passed, were like those of most modern oriental towns,—nests of filth and nurseries of plague, close, fetid and gloomy, bordered by stone-built houses with small latticed windows and heavy portals, and in some places covered over to exclude the glaring sun. The town is of small extent, and in a few minutes we reached the gate and emerged into the open country. The change was so perfectly magical that we all uttered involuntarily an exclamation of surprise.

Indeed, the scene before us was one that could never be forgotten. A range of long billowy swells of deep red earth arose from the verge of the blue Mediterranean, which was rimmed by a border of fine white sand, upon which the crisped waves, as they chased each other to the brink, broke into long lines of silvery spray, lighting up the whole landscape with their flashing brilliancy. The wavy surface of deep ochre was every-where dotted with gardens and bosquets of the most vigorous verdure, in which the palm, fig, olive, pomegranate, carob and other oriental trees were matted together into a mass of deepest green. Roses and jasmines of rare beauty, "the rose of Sharon," adjacent to Jaffa, being mentioned in Solomon's Song as the very type of beauty, trailed at will among these verdurous clumps, and perfumed the air on all sides. But it was not alone the face of nature which attracted us, for everywhere, perched upon little monticules or half-hidden among the bowery thickets, were reared the white and green tents of the Egyptian army.

Horses were picketed, arms piled, groups of soldiers in the picturesque white dress and red caps of the Nizam, were thickly scattered about; while their officers, in dresses of the same cut, but gorgeous in crimson, blue, and gold, were smoking and reposing themselves among thickets of palm and pomegranate. From the universal air of enjoyment that prevailed, one would hardly have imagined that the soldiers were on the eve of a bloody campaign, from which half of them, at least, were never destined to return. But a few months since and the greater part of these men had been peasants on the Nile, dragged from their homes by arbitrary power, and marched in chains to Cairo, where they had been drilled by French officers, and sent into Syria to carry out the ambitious designs of the pasha. Yet to all appearance they seemed quite to have forgotten their troubles, and from the victims of a degrading tyranny, to have passed easily into its readiest instruments.

On a sandy hillock slightly dominating the whole encampment, a small mosque or tomb, surmounted by a dome, was pointed out as the head-quarters of Ibrahim, and to this we accordingly directed our steps, receiving many cordial salutes from the Egyptian or Frank officers as we threaded our way through the scattered tents. On reaching the spot, a sentinel made known our arrival to an aide-de-camp, who at once conducted us into the interior of the building, in which a few divans and carpets had been hastily arranged. Seated upon one of these was the redoubtable conqueror of Syria, whose name, like that of Cœur de Lion in the days of the Crusades, thrilled like a spell of terror through the hearts of his adversaries. There was something, we thought, of the pride of conquest in his flashing eye, which redeemed what was otherwise a rather vulgar and butcherly aspect, as he bowed in return to our respectful salutations, and beckoned us, with an ill-suppressed smile at our sublime conductor, to be seated on an opposite divan. Sad to say, on this occasion, upon which he had been calculating for a display of his eloquence, poor Damiani found his occupation gone, and himself reduced to a mere dummy by the presence of Omar Effendi, an aide-de-camp, and intimate friend of the pasha's, who had been sent to England when a youth by Mehemet Ali, who spoke our language with surprising fluency, and whose deportment exhibited not a little of the polish of European society. With him therefore, to the vexation of the poor vice-consul, we entered at once upon the business that had brought us to the place.

After complimenting the pasha upon the success of his arms and the vigour of his administration, in terms which we were well assured lost nothing by being translated to him, inasmuch as they elicited a gracious smile and bow, we inquired more particularly the chances of our being able to visit Jerusalem. In reply, the effendi assured us that unless we went in the train of the pasha, the thing was simply impossible, the mountain passes, through which the road runs, being strongly guarded by the insurgent Arabs, who, as he informed us with a satirical smile, regarding the Franks as the natural allies of Ibrahim, and especially as known to be the advisers of the detested measure of the conscription, would not fail to pick us off from their lurking-places, as first-fruits of their grateful regard. Ibrahim's eye was upon us as this announcement was made; he observed our blank and disappointed expression, and with great animation and heightened colour, addressed a few words to the effendi, which the latter immediately translated for our benefit. "Why," said the pasha, "should they not march up with us, and witness the discomfiture of the rebels, who will fly like chaff before the face of our victorious troops? Even at this moment the sails are in sight, which bear the expected succours sent from Alexandria; as soon as they are landed we shall march without delay; the campaign will be short and vigorous, and the English effendi will speedily enter Jerusalem in triumph. Horses and tents shall be freely furnished, and every necessary provided, as is the pleasure of his Imperial

Highness, our father. What say they?" We looked in each other's faces, but reading therein nothing like unanimous assent to this gracious proposition, and conscious that the present was not the place to enter upon a discussion of its merits, we arose, and bowing our respectful thanks, with a promise to decide before the army should be ready to march, we retraced our steps towards the city.

As we passed through the camp in returning to the town, we found the air of listless enjoyment had given place to one of serious preparation. Several ships of war were seen in the offing, and crowding all sail, with a fair wind, were rapidly nearing Jaffa. The place itself was all in a bustle, an embargo was being laid upon every boat in the port, for the purpose of landing the approaching succours. In the midst of this scene of confusion, we returned to the house of Signor Damiani, who hospitably placed before our numerous party such refreshment as the place afforded, over which we held serious consultation touching the pasha's proposal, at which our worthy host was present to assist us with his counsel. From his knowledge of the state of the country, and such information as he had picked up respecting the force of the insurgents, he had reason to believe that the struggle would be more severe and protracted than Ibrahim was pleased to imagine; and should this prove to be the case, and his arms sustain a reverse, our position as his allies would be extremely critical. On the other hand, should the pasha's anticipations of victory be fulfilled, and the country be reduced to obedience, nothing could be easier than to return again to Jerusalem by another road through the interior. We therefore decided—*nem. con.*—on taking a boat and visiting the coast, which was then entirely tranquil, until the issue of the quarrel should be decided.

It was too late to obtain a boat and depart that evening, as all were wanted to land the troops, and moreover, we so much enjoyed the lately acquired liberty of our legs, that we had small disposition to deprive them of it. Leaving all arrangements therefore till next day, we accordingly sallied forth, determined to make the most of the time upon our hands.

Jaffa, or Yáfá, the ancient Joppa, is one of those places which owes more to its venerable associations than to anything else; "Vox et præterea nihil,"—the name is here everything. In this antediluvian sea-port, as the Phœnicians considered it, Noah, as before said, is supposed to have built the ark. Classic tradition here chains Andromeda to one of the grim rocks of the port, from which she was delivered by Perseus. Leaving the regions of fable, we know for certain that the cedar wood from Lebanon, hewn by the skilful Sidonians, and intended for the erection of Solomon's Temple, was floated hither from the Tyrian shores, and conveyed by land to Jerusalem.

By far the most interesting fact connected with Jaffa, however, is that here was the house of Simon the tanner, to which St. Peter, after being warned by a symbolical vision, that the barrier between Jew and Gentile was broken down by the new dispensation, repaired from Jerusalem, to learn the memorable lesson, as yet ignored by the world, that of a truth "God is no respecter of persons." As tradition is never at fault in Palestine, the identical house of the pious Simon is still devoutly shown, and as devoutly believed in. Nor is Jaffa without a niche in modern history. Hardly any one needs reminding that Bonaparte here put to death, in cold blood, a part of the garrison, on the ground of a breach of parole, during his short, and, thanks to the valour of our countrymen, disastrous attempt upon Syria. As Jaffa is the port of Jerusalem, from which it is distant only about forty miles, it has always been, too, the chief landing-place of the innumerable pilgrims who have repaired to the Holy City, from the earliest times even unto the present day, when large cargoes annually arrive. As the road lies through a narrow pass, affording excellent opportunity for levying a tax upon these unfortunates, the native chieftains little relished the abolition of such a system, and the rendering the road secure by Ibrahim Pasha. "Hinc illæ lachrymæ!" One might walk all over Jaffa, and never dream that anything important could have happened there, so dull and insignificant is the place, and so destitute of anything in the shape of monumental interest. In our western towns a prison is a thing apart; here the whole town is a prison, and one only feels free in emerging from its gloomy gates. In our perambulations on the following morning, we met with one of the American missionaries of Jerusalem, who having left his wife and family there, had come down here on business. He now found himself unable to regain his home, with the knowledge, besides, that it would inevitably become the seat of hostilities, while he was unable to return and protect his exposed household. Nor were his apprehensions at all without foundation, and we had reason to congratulate ourselves that we had retired from the seat of war. It was not, of course, until some months afterwards that we learned the issue of the struggle. Ibrahim Pasha had marched up into the hill region of Jerusalem, but so far were the inhabitants from scattering like chaff, that they cut off some of his regiments, and nearly succeeded in capturing their redoubted leader himself. Some of the Arab chieftains meanwhile obtaining ingress, it is said, by creeping up through an ancient sewer or water-course, the channel of which had become dry, surprised and sacked the city, and when, at length, the unfortunate missionary was able to return, he found his home desolated, and his wife in a state of insanity. It was only after receiving considerable reinforcements, that the pasha succeeded at length in overcoming the resistance of the insurgents.

On the next day, although hardly escaped from the tedium of a week's voyage, we were again huddled on board a small Arab coasting bark, which, with our servants and baggage, we completely filled; in the hope, however, that five-and-twenty hours at the utmost would carry us to our destination. This time the fates were propitious, for going on board as the night breeze sprung up, we made such rapid progress that, passing at a distance the ruins of Cæsarea and Castel Pellegrino, we doubled Cape Carmel the following noon, and running across its famous bay, shortly after landed at the foot of the ramparts of Acre.

This far-famed city, the bulwark of Palestine, so often and so obstinately contested, had but just passed through one of its most memorable sieges, and presented at that moment a vivid picture of the devastation that follows in the track of war. The whitening bones of camels lay scattered on the strand, and the ground near the walls seemed heaving with the ill-concealed heaps of festering corpses. On entering, by the Jaffa Gate, this unfortunate town, we found it shattered to pieces from one end to the other; whole streets lay in ruins, the roofs of the mosques were broken in, the fountains dry, and even the huge and gloomy fortress built by the ferocious Djezzar, with walls fifteen feet thick, had been laid open to the light of day by the showers of bombs directed against it during a six months' siege. Such of the wretched inhabitants as survived, had just began to patch up again their tottering houses, and some little show of traffic was beginning to appear in the ruined bazaars. Mehemet Ali, with his usual energy, was rapidly repairing the fortifications which his cannon had just been battering to pieces, and at vast expense rendering this stronghold of his power in Syria impregnable, as he fondly flattered himself; with what success, we shall hereafter see.

In the midst of all this, our only refuge was the Catholic convent, which had to some extent escaped the general destruction. The poor monks willingly put the building at our disposal, and offered us such hospitality as they could. But the confinement of our quarters, and the scarcity of provisions, developed an alarming evil—confusion arose in the camp. Like Abraham and Lot in olden time, we found the land was not wide enough for ourselves, our servants, and our cattle, and we were ready to exclaim to one another, like the patriarch to his

brother, " Separate thyself, I pray thee, from me: if thou wilt
take the left hand, then I will go to the right; or if thou depart
to the right hand, then I will go the left." The difficulty was
rendered insuperable by the quarrels of our dragomen for place
and precedence. In Syria, where there are neither inns, roads,
nor conveyances, and where, moreover, the traveller is generally
ignorant of the language, he finds it absolutely indispensable
to carry a servant with him, and soon discovers that while
nominally the master, he is really in the power of his dragoman,
who feeds him how he likes, and when he likes, makes him pay
double price for every article purchased, and often runs away and
abandons him in the moment of danger. To manage, therefore,
one of these fellows, requires a constant exercise of firmness, and
is a perpetual trial of temper; and where several of them are
together, the difficulty increases like a series in geometrical
progression, as, with the low cunning peculiar to them, they
generally contrive to involve their masters in the disputes that
arise among themselves. Such unfortunately was the case in the
present instance; and it became evident that we must break up
our party, and pursue different paths.

Another cause of division arose. The East has always been
the land of exaggeration; the imaginative turn of the orientals
leading them to magnify perils, and multiply numbers to an
indefinite extent. We got at last to be quite used to this, but
at first it was rather alarming. We had fallen upon a time
" of wars, and rumours of wars." I was taking a turn through
the bazaars, when an individual accosted me with an air of
mystery, and declared that it would be unsafe to prosecute our
journey. Thousands of insurgents were in the vicinity of the
town, ready to pour through its ruinous breaches, and wrest it
from the possession of Mehemet Ali at the news of the slightest
reverse sustained by Ibrahim. The roads, he averred, were all
beset, and to proceed would be the merest insanity. I ascended
the ramparts and looked abroad, but not a soul was to be seen;

yet what motive could the man have for deceit? On returning home, I told my companions what had happened, and a difference of opinion immediately arose as to our plans, some maintaining that it would be running a foolish risk to go on to Beyrout by land, when we could proceed thither by sea. Our servants took up the question; and my own, who, with a swashing and a martial outside, was really one of the whitest-livered cowards the sun ever shone upon, earnestly requested me to let him go by sea. Should we be attacked by robbers, he pathetically pleaded, they might content themselves with stripping the masters, but the throats of the dragomen they would infallibly cut. The discussion terminated, at length, by the greater number of our party deciding to go by sea, and my giving my cowardly dragoman leave to accompany them, and take charge of my baggage; while the American and myself resolved to pursue the land route by Tyre and Sidon at all hazards, and with a single attendant.

Before separating, however, we resolved to make a visit together to Mount Carmel, which stood out boldly on the other side of the bay, projecting its lonely hallowed ridge into the sea, and crowned with a white convent, which had a particularly inviting look. The distance being only ten miles by the sea-shore, we did not start till late in the afternoon, and owing to the perils with which we were said to be environed, we hired a small escort, which, with our own party, made up a body of twenty men all armed to the teeth. We sallied out by the Jaffa gate, and kept along the shore, pushing our horses through the spray, and keeping a sharp look-out upon the jungle of prickly bushes and palmetto shrubs that bordered the sandy beach, in full anticipation that a body of Arabs might suddenly dash through and dispute the passage; but we met with nothing looking half so robber-like as ourselves, and pursued our ride without the slightest let or impediment.

In rounding the bay we forded two rivers of historic interest.

The first, an insignificant stream not far from Acre, was the
Belus, upon the banks of which, according to tradition, glass
was first made by the Phœnicians. The second, which rolls
into the bay near the foot of Mount Carmel, is "that ancient
river, the river Kishon," which once ran into the sea purpled
with the blood of the hosts of Sisera. It comes down through
a sedgy jungle, and when swollen by rains is deep, and dangerous to ford. Another mile or two on, is the little town of
Caipha, the roadstead of which offers but uncertain shelter to
barks driven into the bay, as the ribs of many a coasting vessel,
half-buried in the sand, and with the sea breaking wildly over
them, sadly testify. We rode through Caipha, the inhabitants
all coming out to stare at our numerous cavalcade; and passing
through a venerable olive wood, ascended the rugged steep that
leads up to the top of Carmel.

On the summit of this holy mount we seemed to breathe
another atmosphere than that of the turmoil which had pursued
us since our landing. From the top of the promontory on
which we stood, its rugged sides descended almost perpen-
dicularly into the sea. Westward, the vast expanse of water
was bounded only by the aërial horizon, towards which the sun
was solemnly descending through a sky of undisturbed serenity.
The low monotonous roar of the waves, which fretted round the
foot of the crags, just ascended faintly to our ear. Northward,
the eye followed the sinuous outline of the bay we had just
rounded, and resting for a moment on the white walls of Acre,
jutting into the sea on their stony reef, traced the distant coast
surmounted by the snowy ridges of Lebanon, faintly melting
into gorgeous haze. Southward, stretching from the foot of the
mount, were the level and desolate plains extending towards
Jaffa. The rocky surface of the mount was thickly covered with
wild shrubs and flowers, which, as we crushed them in our
passage, gave out a pungent and aromatic odour, that, combining
with the freshness of the sea-breeze which plays over this lofty

crest, carried healing and refreshment to the senses. There was no disappointment, no discrepancy with preconceived expectations; the actual beauty of the site fully answered the most poetical idea one could form of it.

In the meanwhile some of the party had entered the building, and the servants had conveyed our baggage upstairs. The Convent of Mount Carmel is a large and handsome edifice, neatly constructed of white stone—a shining landmark to mariners far out at sea. One or two venerable monks came out and conducted us to the suite of rooms appropriated to our use, and evidently enjoyed our expressions of agreeable surprise. There was nothing at all monastic about them—none of that fusty odour of sanctity, redolent of lamp oil and incense, that pervaded the gloomy corridors and cheerless cells of the convent at Acre, with their iron-barred windows and wooden pallets. The rooms were spacious and well lighted with glazed windows, and the curtained beds were scrupulously white and spotless, looking most irresistibly tempting to men whose ribs ached, and whose skin was tatooed with the misery of their recent nightly quarters. The good monks raised our satisfaction to the highest pitch by the production of an excellent supper; and such was the tide of mental exhilaration and the sense of bodily comfort, that it became a question whether we had not better take up our abode with them altogether until the country was reduced to a state of tranquillity. That night we revelled in clean sheets, and rose next morning like giants refreshed with sleep. The land and sea were glorious, and we could have gazed untired " the morn, the noon, the eve away," but for the go-a-head propensities of certain of our number, who insisted forthwith on " doing " the mountain, and then returning to Acre. Accordingly, under the conduct of our monastic guides, we visited a large apartment deeply cut into the rocky hill side, and denominated " the School of the Prophets ;" nor were we at all disposed to cavil at a tradition so apposite to the *genius loci*.

The solitudes of Mount Carmel, we know, were the favourite
haunt of Elijah and Elisha, and here occurred the striking scene
of the destruction of the prophets of Baal. Nothing has since
invaded the primitive wildness of the place except the solitary
convent. It remains in a state of nature, and one may range
for hours about its thyme-covered summit, still haunted by the
wild boar and the eagle. There is something exceedingly grand
and elevating in the commanding isolation of a spot linked with
so many and such interesting memories.

Before noon we took leave of our hosts, with whom we left a
little offering towards the completion of their edifice, which, like
the other Terra Santa convents, is under the protection of
France. Putting our steeds to their mettle, in less than two
hours we regained Acre, and betook ourselves to our convent,
which seemed more dismal than ever by contrast with the unwonted luxuries of Carmel. Myself and companion now hired
horses, and prepared for our departure to Beyrout on the following morning, maugre the thousands of insurgents, who somehow seemed to keep themselves most carefully out of sight.

I had straggled about the interior of the ruined city, but had
not yet made the tour of the walls. Accordingly, ascending to
the breastwork by a flight of steps, I traced its whole circuit
so far as the gaps and breaches would admit. Next the sea
they were but little injured, being protected by a reef of rock,
on which there is a constant surf, and which tended to keep
vessels at a respectful distance. On the land side, where there
is a deep ditch, the work of havoc had been most tremendous.
Few ramparts can boast of such associations as these. Extending inland from the foot of these walls was the plain which had
trembled under the fiery onset of the Crusaders; here Richard
of England had pitched his camp, and here, in later times,
Bonaparte had taken his stand to urge his columns into the city,
which, already reduced by the rules of war, still kept up a
desperate resistance from day to day by the valorous efforts of

Sir Sidney Smith, until the Gallic invaders were forced to a disastrous retreat. Upon this defence the fate of empires may have turned, since, if Bonaparte could have obtained a footing in Syria, the tide of his ambition might have flowed eastward instead of westward.

On the same spot Ibrahim Pasha had recently encamped, during the siege which had left behind it such fearful traces; and on the plain which had so lately been trodden down by his army, he was even now making preparation to introduce an

WALLS OF ACRE.

improved system of agriculture, by the compulsory labour of the peasantry, already oppressed by all sorts of exactions, and demoralized by incessant warfare.

On further research among the ruins, we lighted on a large building of the era of the Crusades, when within the narrow circuit of the walls of Acre were crowded together the military orders and representatives of every Christian power; when every street had a feud with the next one; every building was a separate fortress, and immorality and corruption were at a fearful height. It was from Acre that the Christian knights were finally expelled, after a murderous slaughter of the Templars; the Hospitallers retreating to Cyprus, and thence shortly after

establishing themselves in Rhodes. The edifice we discovered
is supposed to have belonged to this order.

Early on the morrow my companion and myself took leave
of our friends, whom, unless we fell into the hands of the
Philistines, we expected to meet again at Beyrout, and sallied
forth into the open plain. Our *cortége* was insignificant enough,
consisting of a single servant, four horses for ourselves and
baggage, and the mukharey, or groom, who had the animals in
charge. We took care to carry but just piastres enough to bear
our expenses for a few days, and were hardly worth the powder
and shot of any wandering troop of marauders. So far from
meeting with any, the plain seemed more than usually solitary.
Its fertile expanse lay half uncultivated, and a straggling peasant,
visible at wide intervals, only added to the oppressive solitariness
of the landscape. It is a sad consequence of oriental despotism,
that the rich and level tracts are comparatively neglected, while
the rugged mountains are carefully terraced and cultivated;
since, in the former, the greedy extortioner can so much more
easily pounce upon the unhappy peasant, and deprive him in an
instant of the fruits of a year's labour.

Leaving the plain, we ascended a steep road leading almost
close to the shore, and carried over the edge of a rugged precipice, called, from its appearance, " Ras el Abiad," or the
" White Promontory ;" and here at nightfall we encamped in a
solitary khan. By this time we had obtained ample evidence
of the falsity of the rumours which had somewhat disturbed us
at Acre. In fact, notwithstanding the presence of war in Judea,
such was the terror inspired by Ibrahim's arms, and such the
vigour with which his determination to make the roads secure
was carried out, that we soon came to feel the most entire
security, nor did we meet with one solitary instance of annoyance in the part of Syria we traversed.

On the morrow, coming abruptly to the edge of the precipice,
at a point where it sunk down sheer some two hundred feet into

the sea, the territory of old Phœnicia spread out before us,—the cradle of ancient commerce and navigation, and which has played so important a part in the history of mankind. It is a narrow strip of plain, rarely extending above a mile or two from the shore, and backed by ranges of mountains piled tier upon tier to the snow-covered crests of Lebanon. Jutting out at about three miles off, was seen the desolate-looking island of Tyre, connected with the mainland by a broad causeway of sand; while some broken lines of aqueduct, and a little hill crowned with a small mosque, are dotted about the adjacent plain; far different from the scene which must once have burst upon the spectator from this height, when caravans converging from all parts of the East unloaded their riches at the port, which was filled with the thousand sails destined to waft them to the remotest coasts of the known world. But it was not the time, nor was it the place to moralize on the spectacle of fallen grandeur before us, our utmost attention being bestowed on the preservation of our precious necks, as we stumbled and slid down one of the most dangerous stone pathways in the world, gaining dizzy peeps down upon the sea chafing among the " unnumbered idle pebbles " at our feet. This road, said to have been made by Alexander the Great, is no doubt as old as the city itself, and bears the suitable appellation of " the Ladder of Tyre."

From the foot of this pass we galloped over the broad plain towards the city, making a temporary halt at the extensive cisterns called " Ras el Ain," works of very ancient date, and conveniently attributed, like so many others in eastern lands, to the potent agency of Solomon. The original city of Tyre stood somewhere on the mainland, probably on the ground we had passed over on the way from the " Ladder," and these cisterns no doubt had some connexion with it. At a short distance we struck upon the broad sandy isthmus, which time and tempest has heaped over the stone causeway made by Alexander when he levelled the glory of Tyre in the dust, and hurled her towers into the midst of the sea. At the end of the causeway is the wall encircling the modern town; the blood-red flag with the white crescent hung idly from its staff, and a couple of sentinels, in the costume of the Egyptian army, kept watch at the unfrequented portal. Passing through this, we entered the small mean town, which occupies an angle of the original site, and made our way to the remains of the past. The sea broke against a few ruinous fragments of walls, upon which, in literal fulfilment of Ezekiel's prophecy, the fishermen had found "a place for the spreading of nets," while one or two of their small barks lay within at anchor. We took a boat and rowed out a short distance to obtain a view of the island, which is of small extent, and presents to sea-ward a rugged line of rocks. The mouldering ruins of the cathedral, built in the middle ages, and the few buildings of the modern town, thinly sprinkle over the desolate site. In the distance towers the range of Lebanon, and to the south of it, the isolated snow-crowned summit of Mount Hermon. A boatful of fishermen were plying their occupation, and one or two ships of small burden lay at anchor off the port,— sole representatives of the ancient glories of this world-renowned emporium.

We slept that night at a khan near Tyre, and on the following day pursued our way along the confined Phœnician plain, toiling through the deep sands, and over the rugged stony horse-tracks; and, passing over the site of Sarepta, where Elisha restored the widow's son to life, reached, about noon, the luxuriant gardens that surround the modern Saida, and came to a halt before entering the city gates.

It now became a question how best to dispose of ourselves for the night, inasmuch as, besides the khans for the reception of travellers, there was a Catholic convent at Sidon, as well as consuls both English and American, who, if we went to their houses, would probably receive us with hospitality. These agents are generally natives of some consideration, who serve

without pay, glad of the immunities and privileges attaching to the office, and eager to show respect to travellers from the countries they happen to represent.

My American companion, on whom I was now exclusively dependent for society, was a very creditable sample of the sons of the West ; but he possessed two of their peculiar characteristics in a preeminent degree, that of going a-head, and that of bragging as to the infinite superiority of everything transatlantic. The objects we met with seemed a perpetual text-book to remind him of something better at home. Especially did he delight in comparing the new with the old country, to the infinite disparagement of the latter. The American girls were the handsomest in the world; the ponies beat all creation at a trotting match; the houses in New York were far finer than those in London ; even the pumpkin, or, as he would have it to be according to Walker, pünken pies of America were unequalled by any other earthly delicacies attainable in England. Happily, if the Americans sometimes exhibit the pardonable vanity of a young people, nothing can exceed the indifference of John Bull as to what people say or think of him. I listened, and sunk into insignificance; and as my fellow-traveller had been long enough in the East to grow a beard, allowed him to take precedence, and make all the necessary arrangements.

Now it so happened that he was in theory a devoted vegetarian, and had strenuously urged upon myself the propriety of abstinence from animal food during the journey, as a gross diet breeding the most pernicious humours, altogether unsuitable to the burning climate of Syria. To this I had agreed, and rice with *lebn*, or curdled milk, and such bread as we could obtain at the khans, had constituted our sole diet since leaving Acre. It was suspicious for the stability of this self-denial, that my American on this occasion was taken with a sudden desire to pay a visit of respect to his consul, and was not disposed to proceed at once to the convent, represented to us as a perfect House of

Famine, but where at all events we determined to take up our
abode for the night.   However, I said nothing, but promised to
meet him at the convent, after surveying the exterior of the city ;
whereupon he speedily dived through the gate and disappeared
with surprising alacrity.

The spot where we parted was an extensive cemetery interspersed with immense plane-trees, coming up to the city wall,
which is massive and strong, and joins on to a castle on a hill,
erected by St. Louis in the time of the Crusades.   In order to
obtain a better view of this building I made my way across the
turban-headed broken tombstones, and sat down in the shade not
far from a tent pitched in a sequestered spot, at a distance from
the road-side, apparently the temporary home of some wandering
traveller who, like myself, had chosen this place for the seclusion
and quiet it afforded.   This impression was confirmed by seeing
the curtains of the tent softly opened, the glimpse of a female
figure within, and a pair of braceleted arms put forth and waved
mysteriously to and fro, as I supposed, to warn the dog of a
Christian that he was thrusting his contaminating presence too
near to the privacy of a Moslem lady.   Fully expecting that the
summons to depart, if disregarded, would be summarily enforced
by the cudgel of her indignant lord and master, I hastily retreated
to a more respectful distance, and averting my vagrant optics
from the forbidden precincts, fixed them with an intensity of
gaze upon the crenelated battlements of the gothic chateau of St.
Louis.   On a casual divergence from this line of vision, which
I had maintained for some time with undeviating rectitude, I
perceived that the inmate of the tent seemed more disquieted than
ever, and the clapping of her hands continued with unabated
activity.   I rose to depart to a still wider distance, when lo ! the
tent door suddenly opened, and the lady herself,—*proh pudor!*—
without the muslin sack and yellow buskins in which Turkish
women usually protect themselves from unhallowed eyes,
advanced straight through the tombstones to the very spot where

I was standing. In another moment she stood before me, in a Syrian dishabille of so peculiar a nature that her character and object could be no longer misunderstood. Looking towards the tent, I then observed a man, the proprietor of this unfortunate creature, intently watching the result of the manœuvre. I waved my hand with an expression of dissatisfaction, and the child, for she was no more, returned mechanically to the tent of her heartless master, who no doubt lived upon the wages of her shame. A strange incongruity, to pitch the tabernacle of guilty enjoyment amidst the festering remains of mortality.

After this adventure I left the cemetery and found my way to the Catholic convent, the misery of which fully answered to the accounts we had heard of it. A young Italian monk stepped forward with an air of genuine cordiality, and welcomed me to such accommodation as his poor home afforded. His mien and countenance were strikingly noble, and he seemed a being far superior to the generality of Terra Santa monks. There was absolutely no refreshment of any kind in the convent, and in rummaging my saddle-bags for some miserable fragments of bread wherewith to stay the cravings of an appetite sharpened by several hours' ride, a small pocket Bible fell out, which the young monk seized with curiosity, and immediately made my possession of this prohibited article the text of a warm discussion in Italian upon the merits of our respective creeds. Famished as I was, I felt my mental energies unequal to sustain the honour of Protestantism with any chance of success, and was trying to beat a retreat, when my companion suddenly entered with a radiant expression of visage that cut me to the very quick. His cheeks glowed and his eyes twinkled with such unusual satisfaction and lustre, I felt sure that something peculiar had taken place. My suspicions were aroused, and I eagerly demanded whether he had not been guilty of a breach of that abstinence which he had so rigidly imposed upon me. " What could I do?" he replied, his eyes fixed on the floor; "after taking so much pains to welcome a

stranger, it would have been churlish to refuse them the pleasure
of seeing me eat. I was obliged to break through my rule for
once; but to-morrow we can begin again, and carry it out with
renewed strictness." It was evident he had been imitating the
practice of Dugald Dalgetty, and laying in a stock of *provant*
when the chance turned up, sufficient to bear up against a week's
starvation.

The great object of my friend was now to go up into the
mountain, above Sidon, to pay a visit to Lady Hester Stanhope,
and I was perforce compelled to accompany him.

Everybody knows that Lady Hester Stanhope was for many
years as great a "lion" to Syrian travellers as the Holy Sepulchre
or the Temple of Baalbec, and that no book of the many that
were annually published was deemed complete without a peep
within the walls of Djouni, and some fresh details about the
strange and eccentric life of its possessor. Those who were
fortunate enough to be admitted to a brief interview often came
away with hasty impressions, which when wrought up for effect
gave but a distorted view of the original. Others, who were
unsuccessful in their object, avenged themselves, naturally
enough, by taking the most unfavourable view of her character;
and thus the idea most generally formed of Lady Hester
Stanhope was that of a half-crazy misanthrope, who, disappointed
in her pursuit of power at home, brooded over her imaginary
wrongs in this wild solitude, till, her mind becoming unhinged,
she with malicious pleasure loved to refuse to her own countrymen that hospitality she so profusely extended to all besides.

With this persuasion, unfurnished besides with any credentials,
and absorbed in the splendid and novel scenes of which, with all
their associations, every day of Syrian travels furnishes a new
stock, it may be supposed that an humble artist could not have
the least idea of intruding upon the seclusion of the lady of
Djouni. In fact, nothing was further from his thoughts, and
even his wishes; but chance, in spite of himself, brought about

what all the contrivances of others had so often failed to effect.

My friend had provided himself with a letter of introduction, and was in a state of the highest exultation—greater, probably, than on any other occasion during his tour; and, as we toiled up wild hill after hill, looked out impatiently for the lone abode of the mysterious lady. In fact, it was high time, for his reception was yet uncertain, and we might still have to seek some other shelter for the night: it was therefore with great satisfaction that from a sudden rise we caught sight of the white walls of Djouni, on the crest of a steep hill, in the midst of a wilderness of rugged ravines and impracticable looking crags, crowned with the snows of Central Lebanon, which glowed with the last rays of sunset. Here we determined to await the answer to my friend's missive, despatched by his servant, before making a nearer approach to the walls, from whence after all we might have to make an inglorious retreat.

I say we, because, although I myself had sent neither a card nor message, yet was I not without a lurking hope that I might obtain, under cover of my companion, though not a sight of her ladyship, at least, what I more valued at the time, a supper and the shelter of her roof. The truth is, I had slept the night before on the ground, in a miserable khan, and was both fatigued and famished; it was getting quite dusk, the neighbourhood was wild and insecure, the mukharey did not know the mountain, and there was a bitter cold wind sweeping over the heights of Lebanon, sharpening the painful sense of my interior vacuum, and giving zest to the anticipation of a soft couch and savoury fare.

This blessed anticipation was dispelled by the return of the servant, who after long delay came back at a gallop. "Her ladyship," he said, "had made especial and pointed inquiry if his master were really an American; as such she should consent to receive him, but not if he were an Englishman in disguise."

My Yankee friend was in raptures, while I was indignant at

this strange and unfeeling caprice, this degrading preference of
a transatlantic tuft-hunter; so, after hastily arranging to keep a
look-out for the favoured individual in order to meet him on the
following day, I turned aside in dudgeon to find some other
shelter for the night.

My wrath, when I found myself alone, with bed and board to
seek, was extreme, but it was nothing to that of the mukharey,
who gave way to the most furious imprecations upon a degree of
inhospitality unknown among Arab hinds. We were really at
a loss,—the paths among these precipitous mountains, by day all
but impracticable, are actually perilous on a dark night; we had
only the lights of scattered dwellings to guide us, and, in attempt-
ing to make for the nearest group of them, were descending almost
headlong into a ravine, where we were soon brought up among
tangled rocks and bushes. I urged the mukharey forward: he
became furious, and pointing to the lights above us, significantly
drew his finger from ear to ear; but whether to intimate that he
intended to cut my throat, as being the cause of his troubles, or
that we were both in risk of such a treatment at the hands of
some fancied robbers, I could never discover. With much
difficulty we scrambled up again, and feeling our away along the
more level ground, came at length to a small village, welcomed
by the clamorous onset of a pack of Syrian curs.

We stopped at a cottage; the wrathful mukharey explained
our treatment and our troubles, at which the peasant significantly
smiled. They did not invite us to enter, but spread our carpet
for the night on a raised platform of hardened plaster, beneath a
wide-branching mulberry-tree, and soon after, a fine comely girl,
in the beautiful costume of Lebanon, with bracelets around her
arms and ankles, brought forth a large bowl of milk and a little
Syrian bread, which appeased our hunger, and restored our
exhausted frames: after this, wrapped in cloaks and coverlets,
we lay down like Sancho among the saddle gear, and slept
soundly.

I awoke quite chilled with the keen air of the mountain, and with anything but a pleasant feeling towards the mistress of Djouni, the walls of which inhospitable abode I now perceived to be divided from our nocturnal bivouac by an almost impassable ravine. Before noon I saw the fortunate Yankee issue from the portal, with a led horse and some servants, upon which the mukharey saddled my steed, and we joined him at the bottom of the valley.

His manner was provokingly triumphant and patronising,— "My dear fellow, you are to come to Djouni,—I explained it all; her ladyship was *so* sorry that you should have gone to that village, and would have sent for you last night, but that the path was dangerous, (from which I gathered that intelligence of my movements had been conveyed to Djouni,) and now, after visiting some convents to which she has given me a guide, it is her wish that I should bring you to see her."

There was much within me that rebelled against this sort of invitation, but my bones were sore, and my spirit humbled; I had no wish to sleep a second night on the peasant's dais; moreover, the whole thing struck me as so ridiculous, that it was unworthy of any feeling of serious resentment. I therefore gulped down my remaining chagrin, resigned my miserable hack to the mukharey, and mounted instead the caparisoned steed appointed for me.

I shall not give any further details of the ride than to observe that we visited a large convent, and also a nunnery, in somewhat suspicious proximity, and on presenting ourselves at the latter, where as we approached we could see the sisterhood peeping at us from the lattices, we were received, not as we had expected, by a lady abbess, but by a goodly personage of the opposite sex, who seemed to have the spiritual direction of the fair recluses. About three o'clock we reached the walls of Djouni, and were at once ushered into the presence. The building, or rather maze of buildings, enclosed within the old convent,—for

D

such had been the original destination of Djouni,—were for the
most part erected by Lady Hester for the reception of those
whom she imagined would, at the great epoch of trouble that
would precede the coming of the Murdah, repair to her for protection; and were so cunningly devised and intricate, as to create
a feeling of mystery in the minds of strangers.   Through these
we were conducted to her reception room,—sunk in a subdued
shadow, befitting the grave and imposing appearance of the
robed and turbaned sibyl who professed to read in the stars the
destinies of nations and of individuals.   She certainly possessed
—partly, no doubt, from nature, but principally from long and
penetrating habits of observation—an almost preternatural power
of divining the characteristics of those subjected to her gaze,
especially those least obvious to the common observer, but of
which the conscience of the startled delinquent secretly recognised the truth.   No one, from prince to peasant, escaped
the keenness of her scrutiny, and without respect of persons,
his good and bad marks were instantly scanned, his star revealed,
and the decisive and irrevocable judgment pronounced upon him.
" It was this comprehensive and searching faculty, this intuitive
penetration," says her biographer, " which rendered her so formidable; for, under imaginary names, when she wished to show
a person that his character and course of life were unmasked to
her view, she would in his very presence paint him such a
picture of himself, in drawing the portrait of another, that you
might see the individual writhing on his chair, unable to conceal
the effect her words had on his conscience."

My American friend, who, to do him justice, was really a
handsome fellow, had met with her unqualified approval.   Her
decision on my character and fate now came, and it must be
confessed that, after all, it sounded very much like vulgar
palmistry.   Born under a good star, a fortunate career was
promised; and amidst the cares and troubles of life it is consoling to think, that one's future advancement rests upon the

secure and satisfactory basis of astrological prediction. Such good things were not, however, bestowed without the accompaniment of some humiliating but truthful disclosures, of which she playfully declared "she could let out more if she would." Satisfied apparently by her scrutiny that my star was neither hostile nor malignant, she led the way into her garden, struck with the beauty of which, the fresh green of its turf and alleys, kept, especially for so sultry a climate, in the nicest order, I could not help remarking that it reminded me of England. This remark, though it might afford a secret pleasure, was by no means graciously received. "Don't say so," she exclaimed; "I detest everything English;" yet the semblance of this feeling with which she was so often reproached, was no doubt but the affected hatred expressed by many when disappointed in gaining an object secretly beloved. For Lady Stanhope was fond of recalling her English life, and if we are to credit her biographer, it was the want of a provision suitable for her rank and pretensions that first drove her from her native land, while her experience of the hollowness of the great, and the forgetfulness or perfidy of friends, with an exaggerated estimate of what was due to her who had once played so conspicuous a part, contributed to add disgust to disappointment.

Her appearance struck me as remarkably majestic: her tall and stately figure was robed loosely in a simple Arab dress, a turban of mystic and indefinite outline overshadowing her high, pale, Roman features, which, if they were not classically correct, had a nobleness of contour and an expression of mingled dignity and sweetness. She seemed fitted at once to awe and fascinate those around her. She bore a strong resemblance to the great Lord Chatham: this instantly occurred to me, when, some years after seeing her, I was turning over a volume of portraits, and lighted suddenly upon that of the above-named statesman; and on reading her memoirs, I was gratified to discover that this was also the opinion of her friends and biographer.

A black slave now summoned us to dinner, which was prepared for us in a comfortable pavilion, her ladyship always dining alone. The dinner was truly excellent, setting aside the additional relish given to it by a fortnight's penance upon bread and eggs. We were especially grateful for an inimitable apricot tart, in which my last lingering bitterness was buried, and which my Yankee friend with enthusiasm declared might vie even with the "pünken" pies of his own country. We little thought at the time that its composition, as well as our other comforts, might have been presided over by the priestess who had just revealed our characters and destinies; for the restless spirit of Lady Stanhope was accustomed to allow nothing to pass without her superintendence, from the fate of nations to the garnishing a dish of vegetables; and besides, she could not bear to see her guests neglected—although she often declined to see a visitor, from her utter inability to receive him as she wished. These difficulties are revealed in a most amusing manner by her biographer. " Now, doctor," she would say, " what can be got for their _déjeuner à la fourchette?_ for there is nothing whatever in the house. Ah! yes, there is a stew of yesterday, that I did not touch—that may be warmed up again, and some potatoes may be added; and then you must taste that wine that came yesterday from Garyfy, to see if you think they will like it. The spinach my maid must do;" (and, by the way, we ourselves had some for dinner;) " Dyk (the cook) does not know how to dress spinach, but I have taught Zezefôon, to do it very well. (Ding, ding, ding.) Zezefôon, you know how to boil spinach in milk, and you must garnish it with five eggs, one in each corner, and one in the centre." " Yes, Sytty," (my lady.) " And, Zezefôon, send the _yacknay_ (stew) to Dyk, and let it be warmed up for the strangers. They must have some of my butter and some of my bread. Likewise give out the silver spoons and knives and forks; they are under that cushion on the ottoman there: and mind you count them when you give them to

Mohammed, or they will steal one, and dispute with you afterwards about the number—a pack of thieves." Such precautions
may seem unworthy of a *grande dame*, but they were highly
necessary: in fact, her servants were literally what she called
them, and plundered her of her very wardrobe; and her un-
comfortable, and often destitute state, has been known to affect
her visitors even to tears.

In the afternoon we were again called, and, as it proved,
to a sitting of several hours, during which the conversation,
wherein her ladyship bore the principal part, never flagged but
while our pipes were being lighted afresh. It is common enough
in the East for ladies to smoke, but the mistress of Djouni would
indulge for hours, nourishing thus the dreamy and imaginative
mood in which she loved both to recall the scenes of her earlier
life, and then, by a sudden transition, to expatiate in wild and
mystic visions of futurity. This double and curiously contrasted
tendency it was that preeminently characterised her conversation,
and gave it so singular a charm. Few, if any, indeed, of her
sex, had in modern times been more conspicuous in the great
world: the niece, confidant, and even counsellor of Pitt, and at
the head of his establishment, she was profoundly acquainted
with the political as well as fashionable life of her time, and
being gifted with more than masculine vigour and penetration,
and endowed with astonishing fluency and vivacity of expression,
her anecdotes of state intrigue or private scandal, her racy and
graphic delineation of individual characters, her play of witty
remark, of light and lively satire, mingled with traits of grave
and sometimes pathetic recollections of long bygone incidents,
were, especially to persons who had lived in so totally different a
sphere, life-like and amusing as the finest comedy, and not the
less so, that her opinions mingled largely with her narrations. It
was easy to perceive that all her predilections were aristocratic—
race with her was everything; but this was, after all, far less the
vulgar prejudice of mere high birth and fortune, regardless of

correspondent elevation of qualities, than a feeling that these qualities depended upon purity of blood, and that it was utterly in vain to attempt making, as it is said, " a silken purse out of a sow's ear." " God created," she would say, " certain races from the beginning ; and although the breed may be crossed, and the cart-horse be taken out of the cart, and put to the saddle, their foals will always show their good or bad blood. The good or bad race must peep out ; high descent will always show itself." Yet here her notions were somewhat inconsistent, for elsewhere·she declares that " by low born she does not mean poor people ; for there are many without a sixpence who have high sentiments ; " and " although she was constantly drawing a line between the high and low born, good qualities in the most menial person bore as high an estimate in her mind as if she had discovered them in princes."

Like many of those who exclaim the loudest for the maintenance of despotic rule, she was herself the last to brook the idea of a superior power ; she preferred keeping up, among the solitudes of Lebanon, the empty image of supremacy, to being less than she was once at home ; and this feeling, which, with reduced means, led to her expatriation, nourished by solitude, and unchecked by opposition, became at length the ruling principle of her character. Even the shackles of " principle " were unsupportable and not to be mentioned, as she said, " to a Pitt," who *could* not act otherwise than royally by her own proper impulse, without being bound by the laws intended only for the restraint of meaner souls. In keeping with this, she was generous and princely, but arbitrary and exacting : she would exercise a ruling foresight over the well-being of all around her—would attend with her own hand to their necessities ; but then, she must be the arbitress of their most petty concerns, and woe to the recusant who stood upon his independence ! a network of *espionnage* was cast around him, and he would find himself in the meshes of an almost supernatural watchfulness and omnipotence of petty tyranny. Such are the painful inconsistencies of powerful but ill-regulated minds. But even this stern-spirited woman, if she could not walk humbly with her God, nor recognise the superiority of man, was not without her "hero worship." Pitt was her idol, and the ingratitude supposed to be evinced in his treatment and in her own, and felt more on *his* account than on her own, was the theme on which she, at least, never wearied, whatever might be the sensations of her visitor.

In the evening of the same day we reached Beyrout, the ancient Berytus, now the principal sea-port on the coast of Syria, and the head-quarters of missionary operations. The situation is splendid, at the foot of the snow-crowned Lebanon, and surrounded by the most luxuriant vegetation. But the air, affected by the quantity of sand in the neighbourhood, is hot and relaxing, and in summer almost insupportable, while the town is pestiferous and fetid. We found refuge for the night in a small inn, where we were almost suffocated.

Next day we visited the British Consul, Mr. Abbott, and also some of the American Missionaries, who inhabit handsome country houses at a short distance from the walls, and where, during our sojourn, we generally spent the day, returning at night to our horrible prison in the town.

Beyrout is the port of Damascus, from which city it is but two days' journey across the mountains; but as it was our wish to visit the Cedars of Lebanon, and the Temple of Baalbec, we were compelled to take the more circuitous road by Tripoli.

Our route lay along the sea-shore, at the foot of Lebanon, and proved, upon the whole, rather tedious; the only remarkable object on the way being the sculptures at the Nahr el Kelb, or Dog-river, a short distance from Beyrout. There, are to be seen tablets cut in the face of the rock, commemorating the passage of Rameses the Great on one of his warlike expeditions, and also that of some Assyrian conqueror, in his career, perhaps, towards Egypt.

On leaving Tripoli and its noble Gothic château, we set our faces towards the steeps of Lebanon, which we had hitherto only skirted, but were now to cross, in order to reach Baalbec and Damascus. The whole road, or rather horse-track, was a succession of pictures. At first, it passed over the rich plain, extending from the sea to the foot of the mountains,—the seat of the most exuberant productiveness: sometimes diving into the luxurious and perfumed verdure of an orange-grove, with its thousands of glowing fruit; or passing through a field of the tall rustling sugar-canes; or through the grey, refreshing shadows of an olive wood; or a more open plantation of mulberry, intermingled with trailing vines; or over an open, sunny stretch of waving corn.

On reaching the foot of the mountains, the track becomes narrower and more difficult, and thickets of dwarf round-topped pine and umbrageous carob dot the hill-side, which, wherever the abruptness of the ground requires it, is built up into terraces, and planted with mulberry-trees, for the silkworms, which constitute the principal wealth of Lebanon. We still continued to clamber, height after height, till when half-way over the mighty range, we paused to gaze upon the extraordinary scene around us. Our halt was on the edge of one of those tremendous ravines which, commencing among the topmost peaks of the snow-tipped range, rising overhead like a wall ten thousand feet up in the sky, gradually descend, by many windings, through the heart of the mountain, and open gradually as they sink lower and lower, till they debouch into the plain at its feet. In their lowest depths, and hung dizzily upon their sides, among little patches of corn and mulberry, appeared innumerable villages of white flat-roofed houses. We could trace paths from one to another, among the terraces into which the sides of the mountain were laboriously cut, and could detect here and there, in more sequestered nooks, or see proudly perched upon some commanding eminence, the white walls of the numerous convents with which it is everywhere studded. Far below these solitary abodes reposed the luxurious plain, gemmed with its numerous villages, and extending to the margin of the sea, which spread out westward till lost in empurpled haze. As we stood and listened, we could just faintly hear the roaring of the Kadesha, or Holy River, as it made its noisy way from the solitudes of the Cedars, past the village of Besherrai, at the foot of the precipice on which stands the convent of Canobin, the residence of the Greek Patriarch. In another gloomy cleft of the rocks appeared a solitary convent, that of St. Antonio, to which we now ascended by a rugged and dangerous pathway, upon the edge of unfathomable chasms. After resting for a short time at this sequestered spot, we still continued our ascent, and at sunset reached the village of Eden, one of the highest up the mountain, and within a short distance of its topmost crest. In one day's ride we had passed through every variety of climate,—first, the sultry enervating heat of the plain, then the temperate zone of the midway range, until now, at even, we were fairly shivering in the alpine elevation we had reached.

We lodged that night in the house of the Sheik of Eden, who treated us with the utmost hospitality; and at an early hour pursued our way towards Baalbec. It was but very recently that all this part of the mountain had been cleared, by the fervent heats of the summer, from the snow that buries it in the winter and spring; and large patches of it still glittered on the topmost crest, which rose but a short distance on the left, cutting into a sky of intensest and most lustrous blue; while the air was instinct with a keenness and purity perfectly indescribable. On a swelling mound at the foot of a bare green slope, tipped with snow, appeared a dark spot of verdure which, as we neared it, displayed the straight trunks and broad spreading branches of the famous grove of cedars,—the first we had hitherto seen, upon the mountain, which has given its distinctive appellation to this most majestic of trees. During the winter they are buried in snow, and even in spring are often inaccessible, from the deep drifts which accumulate in a hollow way that leads up to them. This was now clear, and, striking into it, our horses' hoofs fell noiselessly upon a carpet of turf; large cedars growing out of the sides overshadowed us as we passed, and, climbing the ascent under a thickening canopy of boughs, we dismounted in the centre of the grove, at the foot of those venerable patriarchs of the forest, which date, according to tradition, from the days of Solomon.

This famous cedar grove consists of a few trees, obviously of very great antiquity, and a host of young and flourishing offspring around them, that increase in size and vigour as their aged parents sink into ruin beneath the weight of years. From a comparison of the visits of former travellers, the number of the old cedars has been gradually decreasing, and very few of them are now left. Their enormous girth—their wildly-spreading branches, white with the ghastliness of extreme age—the disproportionate hugeness of their stems, and the scantiness of the foliage that crowns them—show that their vigour is decayed, their sap dried up, and that their huge and almost lifeless limbs are ready to fall upon the turf beneath.

Ten minutes from the cedar grove brought us to the top of the pass which crosses the highest range of Lebanon; and we immediately began to descend the opposite slope, by a path of fearful abruptness, into the broad plain of Cœle-Syria,—running between the ranges of Lebanon and the parallel but inferior one of Anti-Lebanon. At the further extremity of this plain appeared the temples of Baalbec, at this distance seeming merely a confused mass of stone-work glittering in the sun. We had lingered so long upon the way, that darkness overtook us before we could cross the plain, and not a single habitation could we discover, or even an eligible tree under which to establish our bivouac; and it was not until after much research that our servants found out a cavern, in which we sought shelter from the unwholesome vapours which, nevertheless, laid the seeds of subsequent illness.

I arose in the morning evidently unwell, and, in spite of the burning sun, which smote upon us as we crossed the plain, felt the chill and creeping sensation which heralds an attack of fever. Excited to the highest by the prospect before us, we pushed on eagerly for Baalbec, which at every mile assumed a more distinct appearance; and, as we approached, presented an aspect of astonishing grandeur. Over a huge wall, rising above the level of the plain, and composed of stones surpassing in dimensions anything we had yet seen, uprose the light and elegant forms of the ruined temples, surrounded by a wilderness of other constructions, of different ages and in different styles. Six lofty columns, of peculiar elegance, crowned with a gorgeous entablature, rose supreme amidst the general desolation,—so beautiful, that from whatever point, and under whatever circumstances they are viewed—whether the sun shines full upon the delicate chiselling of their white marble shafts, or whether they range themselves in shadow, spirit-like, against the glow of the twilight sky, impress the beholder with a mingled feeling of admiration and melancholy. But it is not my object to portray these temples, already so often described. Suffice it to say, that, after spending the whole day in examining them, we hastened, as the sun went down, in quest of a brother traveller, to whom we had a letter of introduction, and who was encamped, as we understood, at a spot called Ras el Ain, about a mile distant from the temples, and at the head of the stream which here murmured along one side of the wall, among heaps of prostrate columns and broken masonry, that had fallen from the building above.

Following the course of this stream, we arrived, in about ten minutes, at its source,—seemingly, a small oval pool, bordered with grass and sedge. A large tree bent over it, and the ruined arches of a Christian church stood round about its borders. At a short distance from these were pitched two large tents, which

had a most inviting look of snugness and comfort. Lights were
seen within, horses were picketed on one side, and the evening
watch-fire gleamed upon the faces of the Arab attendants. We
dashed through the rippling stream, and, dismounting, were
ushered into one of the tents, occupied by Mr. Catherwood, the
gentleman to whom our letter was addressed. He received us with
heartfelt cordiality; and thus, in that evening, under the roof of
a Syrian tent, commenced an intimacy which has been renewed
in many lands, and will, I trust, only terminate with life.

That night we passed in the encampment of our hospitable
friends. After I arose on the morrow, the fever with which I had
been struggling completely mastered me; and as the proximity
of the water was deemed injurious, I shifted my quarters, by
Mr. Catherwood's advice, to the dry and elevated plateau of the
temple itself. Adjacent to its northern portal is a massive castle
of Arabian architecture, long since abandoned to the owls and
bats. On entering its deeply hollowed portal, a broken staircase,
with fissures opening into the gloomy vaults beneath, ascended
to a large chamber, with walls of immense solidity, perforated
by slender lancet windows. The floor was, like the staircase,
full of yawning holes, and covered with the dust of many centuries. This was partly swept away, and my matting and carpet
were arranged on the stone floor, upon which I laid down, with
that horrible shudder in the limbs that ushers in an attack of
intermittent fever. To this shortly succeeded a heat altogether
as violent, and the fit terminated by a copious perspiration, which
left the frame in a state of extreme depression. With these
violent attacks of ague, which succeeded each other continually,
were complicated evident symptoms of cerebral disease; my mind
began to wander, and the most gloomy imaginings chased each
other through my perturbed fancy. Thus passed the first day
and night in this gloomy abode.

My uneasiness was greatly aggravated by the cowardice of my
servant, who had, much against his inclination, been obliged to

abandon the encampment, and follow me alone into this solitary ruin. His mind was tortured with real and imaginary dangers; first, lest we should be robbed and murdered by some assassins, who might easily conceal themselves among the neighbouring vaults; and, secondly, lest we should be disturbed by the Efrits, or Genii, which, according to Eastern belief, invariably choose such sites as their congenial dwelling-place. Accordingly, no sooner did the morning dawn, than he repaired to the encampment, and made out so lamentable a story, that Mr. B——i, who accompanied Mr. Catherwood, resolved to leave his comfortable tent, and come down and pass the night with us at the castle. Scarcely had he returned with this consoling intelligence, than I heard an unwonted noise of many footsteps at the extremity of the passage, and my friends of the night before entered, accompanied by a young English medical man, who had come from Damascus, to accompany a wealthy Turkish invalid. Finding me seriously ill, he proceeded to shave my head, and administer other remedies, which probably checked what would otherwise have proved a fatal attack.

Thus passed several days, which seemed interminably long, in a state of great mental and bodily prostration, deepened by the horrible solitude of the place. When the last red rays of the setting sun shot upward through the slender window on the ceiling, and the bats rising from the vaults below began to flit through the chamber, I used to hear the cheering cry of my friend B——i echoing through the winding passage, and the tramp and bound of his footsteps, and the clang of his sabre against the wall, as he sprang hastily up the broken staircase. And never did a sick child thrill more at his mother's voice than I, at the hearty, "Well, how are you, old fellow?" which issued from his lips as he burst into the dreary apartment. Then the lamps were lighted, the pistols primed, Antonio planted on his mattrass across the entrance, and everything made snug in case of attack.

At last I got well enough to crawl out of the fortress, when taking my post in its shadow, I would pore for hours upon the magnificent temple which rose directly in front, watching the huge brown lizards emerging from its chinks and crannies to sun themselves upon the hot stones; or marking the sinuous track of some glittering snake, as it wound its stealthy way among rich fragments of chiselled entablatures scattered around. By degrees I got about, and after a full exploration of the place, at last once more mounted my horse, and one morning before daylight wended my way alone towards Damascus. I was the last tenant of the Temple. My American companion had already started for that city; my friends had struck their tents and gone elsewhere, and I was glad to turn my back upon the scene of so much suffering.

From the ascent of the Anti-Libanus I took my last view of Baalbec, and tracing its narrow valleys, approached at evening the village of Zebdané, where we were hospitably received by the patriarchal sheik. Next day we followed the windings of a stream, which from its source in the highest parts of the mountains flowed downward to the plain of Damascus. The heights overhanging it were bare and white, and glittering painfully in the deep blue sky; but the verdure below was refreshing and luxuriant. Soon after noon, when the sun was still near its zenith, and the white parched soil dazzled the eye and scorched the face with reflected heat, the road, leaving the course of the valley, struck up the side of a bare hill, the topmost peak of which was crowned with a small kiosk. As we ascended, we heard the tinkling of bells, and the leading files of a large caravan came toiling over the top of the pass in the opposite direction. Beyond, stretching away into the haze of distance, as far as the eye could reach, was the immense plain of Damascus, a perfect sea of verdure, in the centre of which, marked by a line of white minarets, winding for some two miles long, and relieving most brilliantly from the intense green,

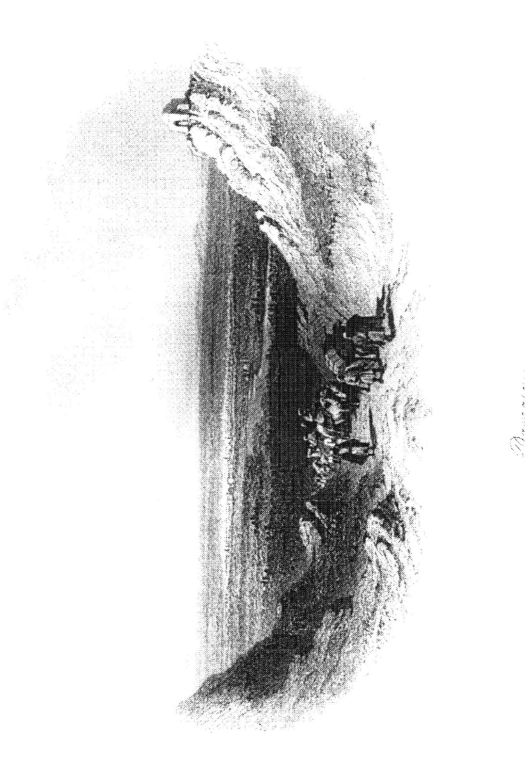

appeared that great city itself, with its immense suburbs. In the foliage around it only one opening could be discerned, this was a streak of velvet meadows, through which meandered the river Barrada, the same we had been all day following, in its course towards the city, where its waters are drawn off and distributed among the endless channels and water courses, which circulate, like silver veins, among the gardens, to maintain their perpetual freshness. Such as Damascus is at the present day, it was ages and ages ago. Since its foundation every empire of antiquity has fallen, and every great city been buried in the dust; the Syrian capital alone survives the wreck of time, without a wrinkle on its brow, flourishing and populous, and invested with eternal youth. Its position being indefensible, it has changed masters indeed, but only for a while; and, as Lamartine says, "is stamped upon the world's map, by the finger of Providence, as the site of a great city." At the foot of central Lebanon, on the edge of the great desert, midway between northern and southern Syria, and only two days' journey from the sea, all the commerce of western Asia converges to it as a natural centre. Such was the great city which now expanded before us at the distance of a couple of miles, and which Mahomet, taking his stand under the kiosk above our heads, declared to be the earthly paradise of the true believers.

To enter it, however, some little precaution was requisite. Its Moslem inhabitants, after those of Mecca, have ever been reputed the most intolerant in all the Turkish empire,—a feeling which the annual passage of the great caravan had greatly contributed to maintain. Accordingly, travellers had hitherto been compelled to put on the most rigorous disguise in venturing within its walls; a precaution which even Lamartine, who had very recently visited the city, thought it no more than prudent to adopt. Of all places in Syria, as we know, Damascus had submitted with the greatest reluctance to the conquering arms of Ibrahim Pasha; and although by an overwhelming display of

force he had succeeded in establishing his new system, by which
the Moslems were no longer permitted to tyrannise over the
Christians, yet it was with reason feared, that in the first
reverse that might overtake his army, the former would immediately rise and throw off his yoke, avenging upon the Frank
strangers as well as the native Christians (who, it must be
confessed, under their recent emancipation had behaved with
great imprudence) the indignities, as they deemed them, to which
force alone had compelled them to submit. Since leaving Jaffa,
our accounts of Ibrahim's proceedings had been fluctuating and
uncertain, and by many he was reported to have suffered severe
loss. It was not, therefore, without some uneasiness that
I prepared to enter the city, especially being invested in the
obnoxious coat and pantaloons.

I had a letter of introduction to an English merchant, which
had been given me by one of the American Missionaries at
Beyrout, and only that one; but I was aware that Mr. Farren,
the British Consul General for Syria, had been recently appointed,
and at once determined to call upon him, and learn what was the
state of the country; whether the war was over, and the road
to Jerusalem at length safe. As we approached the northern
suburb, called Salahiyeh, my dragoman ascertained from a passenger that the consul had a country house there, where he was
at that time residing, and that the house of the merchant was
only just across the road. A few moments brought us to the
gate of the consul's house. A fine young Syrian, of striking
personal beauty, set off by a very elegant dress, was at that
moment standing at the portal, and immediately led the way to
the interior of the country house. This handsome personage,
who then officiated as the secretary to the consulate, was the
same Asaad el Kayat who has since been so much lionized
among the ladies in England, and, after studying with a view of
introducing the art of healing among his neglected countrymen,
has recently been appointed our vice-consul at Jaffa.

Nothing could possibly be kinder than the reception given me by Mr. Farren. He corroborated the information as to the proximity of the house of Mr. T——, the merchant, who would no doubt give me a room; but as that gentleman, it appeared, always dined in the city, he pressed me to occupy a seat at his own table during my stay.

Our conversation immediately turned upon the state of the country, especially as regarded my own prospects of returning to the Holy City; and I soon found it was at that time both peculiar and critical. During the Turkish sway, the administration had gradually become exceedingly lax and corrupt; the pashas, and other officials, usually obtaining their posts by bribery, and indemnifying themselves by peculation and pillage. Thus, although the taxes paid to the Porte were nominally low, the people really groaned under extortion. The Christians and Jews were oppressed, the country was divided by feuds and factions; population declining, the roads were often unsafe, and travellers liable to insult and robbery. At Damascus, so rife was the bigotry of the people, that no recognised European agent had ever been allowed to establish himself within its walls. Such was the condition of Syria when Ibrahim Pasha rapidly overran it, and simultaneously with his conquests introduced a totally opposite system of government. Liberalism, as well as policy, had induced him to abolish all distinctions between the Moslems and Christians; local feuds were put down by the strong arm; robbers disappeared from the roads; and travellers were not only able to go about unmolested, but were received with distinction by the agents of government. The expenses of the pasha's administration were enormous, the taxes were raised, and although the government agents were no longer allowed to extort money on their own account, yet, not content with this heavy taxation, it was not long before Mehemet Ali, in order to fill his coffers, gradually began in Syria the same iniquitous and crushing system of monopoly that he had already carried out in Egypt. Even the improvements in agriculture that he introduced among, or, to speak more correctly, *enforced* upon, a reluctant peasantry, were only intended to minister to his own aggrandisement.

At Damascus, a profound discontent was known to be fermenting among the people, which was only restrained by the vigour of the administration and the formidable force then within the city. Let but Ibrahim sustain a defeat, and it was certain that nothing could prevent a rising. The European residents, who had recently ventured to establish themselves, felt as if upon a volcano that might explode at any moment. The consul had a house in the city, but never ventured to sleep there; and horses were always kept in readiness for escape to the mountains in case of need.

With regard to the war then raging in the hills of Judea, nothing certain was known, except that, though in the main triumphant, the pasha had sustained severe reverses; some of his regiments, it was said, being entirely cut off. Jerusalem had been taken and sacked by the insurgents, though soon recovered from them; and in the present unsettled state of things, it would be highly imprudent to attempt visiting that city. Further information as to the issue of the struggle might, however, shortly be expected to arrive.

In melancholy mood, I now repaired to the adjacent country-house of Mr. T——. In the evening, that gentleman—who, I should say, was agent in Syria for the Bible Society—returned from the city, and immediately invited me to establish myself in his house. He then introduced me to a young Jew, who, as he informed me in a whisper, had recently embraced Christianity, and was at present lodging in his house. His mien and manners were very prepossessing, and nothing that I afterwards saw, or heard of him, belied the apparent sincerity of his profession. The slow rate at which the conversion of the Israelites goes on, as compared with the expensiveness of the machinery employed, is so notorious, that a facetious journal has estimated the cost of each particular case as something quite enormous. Moreover, the majority of converts have done but little honour to their new faith, and there is too much reason to fear that interest rather than conviction has induced some to profess themselves Christians, as it did many of their forefathers to become Moslems, while really at bottom retaining a belief in their ancient faith. But it would be grossly unjust to allow this suspicion to influence us in all cases; or to regard the idea of converting the Jews with contempt and ridicule. One could not, at any rate, forget that it was in approaching this very city of Damascus, some eighteen hundred years ago, that Saul of Tarsus,—a Hebrew of the Hebrews, who had just held the clothes of the murderers, while Stephen was stoned to death, and who was then "breathing out threatenings and slaughter" against the handful of Christians concealed among its population,—was suddenly and marvellously converted to the faith he was persecuting; that here he narrowly escaped the infuriated bigotry of his countrymen; and that he received within these walls that impulse which led him to undertake his world-wide missionary enterprise. There was something, perhaps, in these associations, as well as in the manner of the young convert, that led me to regard him with a feeling of interest, afterwards increased into friendship by further acquaintance with him, and by the services which he rendered me during my stay. There was something that recalled the practice of Paul himself in his manner of life, since he gained his subsistence by his ordinary vocation, while labouring in private to influence the minds of his countrymen.

The conversation naturally turned upon the prospects of missionary labour in Syria, especially as regarded the Turks. My host, a man of earnest and over-enthusiastic temperament, maintained that my friends, the American missionaries, were doing no sort of good. Nothing, he contended, could be so utterly unapostolic as their proceedings. Instead of going from city to city without purse or scrip, and boldly preaching in the market-places to convert the infidels; they had built themselves the best houses in Beyrout, were in receipt of comfortable salaries, and formed a sort of religious aristocracy, like that of the Templars of old, except that instead of manfully fighting with sword and buckler, they preferred trusting to the efficacy of Bibles and tracts.

I reminded my worthy host that, as he well knew, it would be madness for them openly to preach Christianity to the Turks; since, if they did, they would be ordered to leave the country directly; that no consul would or could interfere to protect them; and they would, moreover, be torn in pieces by the first mob they were so rash as to address.

" And what of that?" exclaimed my fervid friend; " the blood of the martyrs is the seed of the Church. I have even offered to share the peril, and stand by them while they preach; but they had not faith enough to accept my offer."

" I cannot blame them," was the reply. " You are a single man, while they have, most of them, families. What would become of their wives and children in case of anything happening?"

" And what business," fiercely retorted my friend, " have missionaries with wives and children? Every weight should be cast aside when engaged in the service of Christ. Why can they not live unmarried, like myself and Calman? If they are incapable of such self-denial, they are unfit for the work they have undertaken."

I might perhaps have pleaded that a missionary, like an apostle, was not prohibited from leading about with him " a sister or a wife;" that the wives of missionaries had in modern times been sometimes found even more useful than their husbands, from their employment in the education of females. But the truth is, that I merely laughed, and thus cut short an argument in which I had no chance of convincing my opponent. The

" whirligig of time," however, " brought back its revenge."
Calling upon my friend some time afterwards in England, I
found that, like the missionaries, he had renounced celibacy, and
taken unto himself a wife; and as he introduced me to the lady,
(who certainly was interesting enough to apologize for any
inconsistency,) she little understood, I dare say, the meaning of
the malicious smile that played on my own lip, and of the sudden
colour that suffused the cheek of her husband.

The last rays of the closing day were burnishing the tops of
the trees, and the freshness of evening succeeding to the fierce
heats of a Syrian noon. Taking our pipes in our hands, we
ascended from the divan to the open verandah at the top of the
house, which looked over the intervening suburb towards the
city. The most intoxicating odours arose from the luxurious
masses of orange, citron, tufted fig, pomegranate, and other
fragrant trees, which so densely crowded the neighbouring
gardens, that it seemed as if you might have rolled a ball over
their tops up to the city walls. A few black cypresses shot up
their pyramidal cones into the sky. Here and there peeped out
in the vicinity the flat terrace and verandah of the contiguous
country houses, upon which we observed the stately forms of the
Turkish inmates gradually make their appearance also, pipe in
hand, and, sitting down, with a gravity and stillness perfectly
statuesque, smoke on in undisturbed tranquillity. Except the
distant howl of the Damascene dogs, which came in bursts, and
died faintly away upon the ear, the plaintive cooing of the doves,
swaying to and fro on the waving palm-trees, was the only sound
which broke in upon the dreamy and pensive quietude. The sky,
of a deep purple, and without a single cloud, seemed, as we looked
into it, to form a vast arch, terminating on the distant horizon in
a bar of pale orange-coloured light. The red sunbeams died off
the tops of the innumerable minarets of the city, from which
arose not a single curl of smoke; and beyond, the dark level plain
extended to the distant desert, across which the caravan pursues

its way to Bagdad. As the sun sank, the evening breeze, which
had been playing across the snowy heights of Lebanon, and over
the distant sea, came rushing down upon the gardens, which
were all in a rustle with waving orange and pomegranate
blossoms, mingled with jasmine flowers and rose leaves. Truly
Damascus might well be regarded as the earthly paradise of the
true believers!

At night I was conducted by my host to a large apartment,
which had formerly been the reception-room, but was now rarely
made use of. It was both spacious and splendid, paved with
variegated marbles, and with a fountain in the midst, lulled by
the murmur of which I gradually dropped asleep.

Next day was one of much bustle and preparation at the
consulate, Mr. Farren having settled to take a ride through the
city, accompanied by his lady, a guest, and myself, and attended
by the usual number of kavasses and servants. I have before
observed, that being the first consul ever appointed, the inhabitants in general had displayed much opposition; and even
now, although he had made many acquaintances in the upper
ranks of society, the mass of the people still regarded him with
a certain distrust. This was no doubt partly owing to his
resolution not to give way upon the point of national costume,
but to maintain, together with the dignity of his office, that of
the European hat, coat, &c. so repugnant to the prejudices, as
well as contemptible to the taste, of the magnificent Moslems.
The whole party were therefore dressed rigorously à l'Anglaise,
and looked the more strange and conspicuous by contrast with
the attendant janissaries, who preceded them in gorgeous oriental
dresses, and glittering with richly ornamented arms.

Issuing from the consulate, we passed along the narrow paved
road bordered with mud walls, overtopped by orange and fig-
trees, which leads from Salahiyeh into the city. On penetrating
its streets, there was nothing at all answering to preconceived
ideas of oriental splendour. They presented, for the most part,

only dead walls of dried mud, perforated by a few gloomy looking portals and iron-barred unglazed windows. Whatever magnificence there might be, seemed carefully concealed from view. It was not until we entered the bazaars that we could form the slightest idea of the immense populousness and commercial prosperity of the capital of Syria. A bazaar, in oriental language, means that part of a city exclusively devoted to business. The bazaars of Damascus are covered in, to exclude the rays of the sun, and lined with shops open to the street, in which the shopkeepers not only display their articles for sale, but also carry on their craft. Although, perhaps, even more crowded than those of any other oriental city, this does not form their most striking feature, which is rather the immense variety of character and costume, in a place where no European innovations have taken place, as at Cairo and Constantinople; at once rivetting the stranger's attention, and turning an ordinary street thoroughfare into a succession of splendid pictures.

First came the Turks themselves, not wearing the red Fez cap, and clipped costume, now coming so generally into use in these degenerate days, but with their grave brows overshadowed by turbans of prodigious amplitude and grandeur, with long majestic beards, and robes descending almost to their very heels, most graceful in outline, and costly in material, and infinitely varied in colour. All the different tribes of the Lebanon had their different representatives, each wearing a dress perfectly distinct from the others. There were the Aleppinnes and northern Syrians, in their fur-lined jackets; Armenians, who being mostly "Rayahs," or native Christians, and prohibited from using the same brightly contrasted colours as the Turks, had adopted and were generally robed in a sober garb of blue; while the Jews as usual, even when rich, in order to disarm envy, were sordid in outward appearance, and for the most part dressed themselves in black. Among the crowd might occasionally be seen natives of Persia, in the tightly fitting dress, with long sleeves, and the bell-shaped conical cap of black wool, somewhat resembling the figures on the Nineveh marbles. Arab sheiks, the heads of the Nomad tribes of the adjacent desert, were also there; and the common Bedouin, with his wild look, and his desert freedom of mien, also conducted his camel through the press of the more civilized crowd.

The bazaars were, as usual, divided into avenues, appropriated to different branches of trade. The manufactures of Damascus are less celebrated than of old; the famous "blades" with which such wonderful exploits were performed, are now no longer fabricated; yet, the stuffs, and silks, and horse-trappings, make a splendid show, and are highly prized through the surrounding country. Nothing seems more remarkable than the number of sweetmeat shops, the piles of candy, the delicate cates, and the delicious "kaklakoom," as it is pronounced; a word that, rolled upon the tongue, seemed aptly to designate the thing it indicates. The cook-shops, at which the savoury "kabobs" and other Arab dishes are served, are very numerous, and there are coffee shops at every corner. Some of the coffee houses are built upon the margin of the river Barrada, among groves of trees, and are the favourite resort of the orientals, who delight in the lulling sounds of running water and the rustling of foliage, almost as much as they do in coffee and tobacco.

In passing through the city we were not gratified by the discovery of any very noticeable edifices. The mosques are almost innumerable, but all built on nearly the same pattern; the only one remarkable, being that said formerly to have been a Christian church. The great court of the building abuts upon the bazaar, and we could catch here and there a glimpse of the interior, which but rendered us the more desirous of obtaining an indulgence, from which all Christians, as it may well be supposed, are jealously debarred—that of a minute and leisurely inspection. We passed also the castle, a massive building, then occupied by the Egyptian commandant with his troops. Owing to the excited state of the city, every one was on the alert, and every possible precaution taken to guard against a sudden outbreak of the populace. Having traversed the city, we emerged, by another gate, into the suburbs, and passing through an extensive cemetery, took a circuitous way back to the consulate. Our passage had not been signalized by any actual insult, but there was that in the sullen physiognomy of the Moslems which told us that our immunity from outrage was owing to force alone.

For several days I continued to explore the city, and to lounge about its bazaars. Here I once more met with my American friend and the rest of our company, who had all of them been "down" with the fever, so rife while the heats of the summer continue. During my rambles I never met with any annoyance, but as the European dress rendered me disagreeably conspicuous, I took into my head the sudden fancy of assuming the costume of the country; a project which, with the assistance of my friend C——, I accordingly proceeded to carry into execution. Eschewing the gorgeous and expensive dress of the Turk, I determined to adopt the more sober style of a "Rayah," or Christian. A turban of white muslin, edged with gold, wound artistically by the skill of my servant round a red cap, formed a complete protection against the sun; and heavy as it seemed, was, as I was assured, only half the weight of those often mounted by others. Over a loose shirt, composed of silk and muslin, and "very spacious breeches" of thin calico, was worn a long silk robe girt around the waist with a shawl; while a grave long gown of blue cloth, with ample sleeves, completed the entire suit, which was considered neat and becoming. As my face was burned the colour of brickdust, and, to save trouble, I had suffered my mustachios to grow to a respectable size, the transformation was so complete, that my own mother, had she met me in the street, would have passed me by without recognition. Instead of boots I wore two pairs of slippers, one pair all of soft yellow

leather, fitted tightly round the foot; the other of red, more
stoutly built, and with soles to them, but no heels, were worn
over the former, and intended to be thrown off and left at the
door, when calling to pay a visit. Having donned this garb,
and taken my pipe in hand, I plunged into the midst of the
crowd. My feelings were indescribably odd. The luxurious
looseness of my dress, so different from the tight garments that
I was accustomed to, and the feeling of almost impenetrable
disguise, produced a totally different set of sensations, amounting
almost to a doubt of my personal identity. When we arrived
at the house of a friend of C——, and kicking off my red
shoes at the entry, I shuffled into the reception-room, and
jumping up on the divan, squatted down cross-legged like a veri-
table Moslem (an operation impossible in tights), and the black
slave handed me coffee and a pipe, and I began to smoke dozily
away like the others, the feeling of illusion became altogether
bewildering.

The first practical result of this change of costume was but
little encouraging. In pushing carelessly through a file of
Egyptian cavalry, which was straggling rather than marching
across an open square, I was saluted with a hearty curse from
the nearest horseman, accompanied by a smart blow across the
shoulders with the flat of his sabre, an indignity he would
never have dared to offer to a Frank; but the comfort of it in
shuffling about the city, and the perfect incognito which it permitted, induced me to retain it in spite of my choler at this
untoward commencement.

I have already observed that Mr. Farren had succeeded in
gaining several acquaintances among the higher classes; and
while the mass of the people looked with dislike upon the hated
giaours who insulted their prejudices by wearing the offensive
hat and coat, some of these—as extremes meet—took a secret
delight in showing their emancipation from the prejudices of their
forefathers. This gave rise to an adventure, to which, having

narrated it fully elsewhere,* I shall but briefly allude here.
A venerable Moollah, who boasted of his descent from the father-
in-law of the Prophet, and was regarded by the people with the
utmost respect, having chanced to call whilst I was engaged in
sketching the costume of a female domestic of Mr. Farren's,
invited us to pay a visit to himself and his wife, in order that
I might take a portrait of her also.

We repaired to his house as invited, when as it happened, we
were not only introduced to his lady, but enjoyed a sight of the
remainder of his hareem. As I greatly desired to obtain a
drawing of the great Mosque, I begged that our venerable
entertainer would endeavour to procure me the means of doing
so. This he promised to accomplish, and according to his
instructions, I repaired one morning to his house, in my oriental
dress, among the folds of which I had concealed some paper and
pencils.

We took our way to a narrow and secluded street, at one end
of which was a small barber's shop, and immediately opposite,
one of the gates looking into the court of the great Mosque.
The Moollah then dived into the shop, and beckoned me to
follow him, but as only a very imperfect view could be obtained
from thence, I stepped out into the street, and after ascertaining
that no one was in sight, produced my drawing materials, and
advancing to the gateway, began rapidly to copy the leading
outlines of the mosque. Scarcely had I done so before I observed
the Moollah with his turban off, and his head and chin enveloped
in lather, wildly motioning me to retreat from the imprudent
post I had chosen. It was already high time; some people at
a distance in the court had observed me, and were laying their
heads together. Their gestures and glances betrayed anything
but satisfaction. A tempest was evidently brewing, the issue of
which might have been serious. I quietly thrust my paper into
the capacious bosom of my gaberdine, and after looking around

* The Nile Boat.

me with an air of innocence, walked over to the barber's shop, where I was received with a horrible frown by my conductor, who, as soon as the barber had finished his operations, retired precipitately from the spot.

I saw the worthy Moollah more than once during my stay in Damascus; and some time after my return to England, was favoured by the consul with a letter, which exposes the situation of Syria after Ibrahim Pasha had succeeded in crushing all his enemies, and introducing his system of monopoly.

" Two days ago," observes the writer, " I had the pleasure of seeing your Turkish friend, who is a lineal descendant of the first Caliph, Abou Bekir; and it strangely occurred that I have lately had as my guest for about three weeks, a descendant of Ali, the opposite branch of the blood of Mahommed, and one of the most sacred men in Persia, the Imaum of Meshid in Khorassan;—two lineal descendants of the great opposite lines of the royal and prophetic blood of Mahommed, meeting together at Damascus, the gate of Mecca, in the residence of a British officer! *Tempora mutantur.*"

" The resistance of the people has been overcome; hope and promise are now prostrate, and Mehemet Ali is draining and debilitating the resources of the country. I fear that under his government, if it continues, after a few years longer, it will be sadly reduced. I trust, however, that all these events are but the great means of Providence for breaking up the system which has so long bound and degraded the energies and morals of these countries, and for re-establishing the national, intellectual, and social character of the people on truer principles."

I shall say but little as to the statistics of this great city. It is supposed to contain a population varying from 120,000 to 150,000 souls, sometimes increased to 200,000 by the influx of Bedouins and Druses.* This is independently of the numbers congregated in its walls and suburbs during the passage to and

* Chesney's Euphrates.

fro of the great caravan from Constantinople to Mecca. The number of Armenian and Greek Christians is about 11,000, and of the Jews about 5,000. It will, no doubt, be in the recollection of many, that a persecution of the latter people, on the old and absurd charge of sacrificing a Christian boy at their festivals, took place a few years back, when Sir Moses Montefiore went over from England in order to obtain immunity for his brethren from similar outrages in future.

The most interesting biblical associations connected with this city are, that it is mentioned as already in existence when Abraham migrated from Ur of the Chaldees into Palestine, his steward being one Eliezer of Damascus; that here was the residence of Naaman the Syrian; that the Abana and Pharphar which he so patriotically deemed better than all the waters of Jordan, and whose names ring so euphoniously in the stately verse of our great poet,* here unite in the modern Barrada; and that, as every one knows, it was the scene of St. Paul's conversion at a period when Syria had fallen under the Roman sway. Tradition has preserved the memory, and has pretended to identify the localities connected with this critical period in the life of the Apostle. The alleged spot where he fell from his horse is pointed out, about two miles from the city on the direct road leading towards Palestine, and by which road he must almost necessarily have approached. One of the streets still retains the name of " Straight," a main avenue, but rebuilt very probably over and over again since the Apostle's days. There is here some degree of probability; but this ceases altogether when the houses of Ananias and Naaman are pointed out, and the place where Paul was let down in a basket from a house over-hanging the city wall. The " Arabia " into which he retired on this occasion was probably Haouran, the district eastward and southward of the plain.

I returned to Beyrout by a more direct road, through Barouk

* Paradise Lost. Book I.

and Deir el Kamar. The journey to Damascus had proved
extremely interesting, but the state of the country was still so
unsettled, that it was deemed exceedingly imprudent, especially
with limited time and resources, to attempt penetrating the
disturbed district. To give up Jerusalem when within a few
days' journey, was most distressing, but none of my companions,
nor any other traveller, had succeeded in getting there; and I was
therefore reluctantly compelled to renounce the long-cherished
hope of visiting it, with not the slightest expectation moreover
of being able to redeem such a disappointment at any future
period.

CHAPTER II.

HAVING decided, with many a pang, to turn my back upon the Holy City, and to proceed into the north of Syria, it was some indemnification, at least, for the bitterness of my disappointment, that the region I was about to visit was less hackneyed by travellers than the ordinary routes through Palestine. Antioch, the queen of the East, had been comparatively little explored. The city " where the disciples were first called Christians,"—the seat of one of the earliest churches, proverbial for the luxury of its inhabitants and the magnificence of its edifices, of which latter considerable remains were said to exist,—presented itself to my imagination in the most attractive colours.

Having hired one of the very smallest barks that ply along the coast, I took leave one evening of my kind friends at the British consulate, and, favoured by the land breeze, ran so rapidly along the coast, that long before noon on the following day we reached the little island of Ruad, many miles to the north of Beyrout, where, the wind entirely failing, we were compelled to wait until the evening. This island, under the name of Aradus, formed a part of the commercial confederacy of the Tyrians, and after the revolutions of so many ages, seems at the present day a humble maritime republic, in which all the inhabitants are seamen or shipwrights. Some small vessels were on the stocks, and a considerable number of fishing-boats at anchor; and we even hunted out an English vice-consul, who, but rarely troubled with the visits of travellers, gave us a hospitable reception; nevertheless, time hung so heavily on hand, that a boat was hired to row across to the neighbouring town of Tortous, or Tortosa, near which we could discern at this distance the remains of some considerable edifice.

Having reached the deserted strand, we found it was but a short walk up to the building, which proved to be the ruins of a large church, apparently, from its pointed arches, the work of the Crusaders. The spot had long since been abandoned; the roof was entirely gone, the walls rent, and a few goats were browsing upon the long rank grass that grew where once had been the altar. We then walked on to Tortosa, another ruin, with the remains of strong fortifications, also erected during the brief existence of the Latin kingdom. These memorials of the stirring and romantic ages of the Crusades can never, at least by me, be beheld without a feeling of peculiar interest. Tortosa was one of the last strongholds which yielded to the arms of Saladin, and here the Christian knights took their final leave of the land they had so long and so gallantly struggled to maintain.

We returned to Ruad, and, favoured again by a fair and pleasant breeze, set sail, and soon lost sight of that ancient commercial island, amidst the light vapours that rose after sunset from the cerulean sea. There were no berths in this diminutive bark; as before, a carpet spread upon the sand which served as ballast, saddle-bags for pillows, and a cloak for a coverlet, made up the accommodation; I slept soundly, and had the pleasure, on awaking, to find that we were proceeding with the same rapidity as before. The coast scenery was growing bolder as we advanced. Beyond the lofty headlands which dropped into the sea, was seen the stupendous cone of Mount Casius, isolated like Vesuvius, its summit bare and white, but its flanks, which rose directly from the waves, covered with magnificent forests, apparently in a state of nature. We flew rapidly along past this magnificent object, and in the afternoon entered the Orontes. At the mouth of this river is a bar upon which the surf was breaking roughly, and in crossing this, we were at one moment very near being capsized among the breakers, the next, our bark was in still water and quietly moored to the shore.

Near the landing-place, in a village called Suwadiyeh, or as Europeans call it, " Suadéa," is the residence of Mr. Barker, formerly our consul at Alexandria, who having retired from active life, has here purchased an estate, and devoted himself to his favourite pursuit of horticulture. A letter of introduction to this gentleman had been furnished me, which I sent forward while I waited; and soon, " on hospitable thoughts intent," a member of his family rode down, bringing a led horse upon which I was to accompany him to the house. Whether the having passed two nights in an open boat, or the evident cordiality of my reception had influenced me, I know not, but when I saw the white walls and shady verandahs of the building peeping up among luxuriant gardens, it struck me as the prettiest and most English looking place I had seen in the whole of Syria. Nor can I ever forget how I was welcomed by this estimable gentleman and his lady. In a word, I felt on this remote and unvisited corner of Syria, *at home*. There was all that goes to make up the precious significance of that word to a wayworn traveller in the manner of my host and hostess. That night I laid my head on my pillow with an unwonted feeling of mental and bodily luxury.

Next morning I was abroad before breakfast, with Mr. Barker, inspecting his gardens, in which he might well take pride. The soil of Syria is most prolific, but the art of gardening has long been forgotten, and the fruits obtainable in the country, grapes and figs excepted, are of poor quality. My host had introduced varieties of the apricot, vine, and other trees, and the products of which under his system of horticulture were so delicious, that I have heard a captain of a man-of-war on the Syrian station declare, that when once he had got into the garden he knew not how to get out of it. Up in the neighbouring mountains Mr. Barker had also established a plantation of potatoes and other vegetables requiring a colder climate, with complete success. He was thus not only indulging what Bacon calls " the purest of human pleasures," but bestowing a boon upon the country. Yet so deeply rooted were the indolence and apathy engendered by long habit, that when cuttings and seeds were given to the neighbouring peasantry, they seldom took the trouble of cultivating them. This luxuriance of production showed, at all events, what Syria once was, and what she might again be, under a government that should know how to stimulate, without crushing, as Mehemet Ali was then doing, the industrial energies of the people.

After breakfast, we mounted our horses, and rode over to see the ruins of Seleucia. This city, which bears the name of its founder, Seleucus, was the port of Antioch. When that city was in all its glory, so also was Seleucia; but, while the former

TOMB AT SELEUCIA.

city still subsists, although in a degraded condition, the latter has fallen into irrecoverable ruin. We reached its remains through a wild tract, overgrown with myrtle and oleander, which here flourish in the utmost luxuriance. The city stood on a plain stretching to the sea, backed by Mount Saint Cymon which served as its Necropolis; its precipitous cliffs being everywhere hewn into sepulchres, after the fashion of Petra, accessible only by flights of steps cut in the rock. Passing through a ruined gateway, we crossed the area of the city to the port, of which extensive remains may still be traced, sufficient to show that it was once capable of sheltering a considerable number of ships.

PORT OF SELEUCIA.

The sea was breaking desolately over its ruinous piers; and Mount Casius (upon whose top Julian sacrificed to the titulary deity of Antioch) lifted its magnificent cone in the background. Here, in the days of its former prosperity, when the harbour was crowded with shipping, and its temples hung with the votive offerings of grateful mariners, and the city alive with commerce, Paul embarked on his first missionary voyage to Cyprus; and here he landed and embarked again more than once during his numerous missionary journeys to and from Antioch. No spot on earth can now be more utterly desolate than Seleucia. That

it was formerly great and populous might well be seen from
its tombs and ruins alone; but it was not until we visited its
really wonderful excavations, forming, apparently, a convenient
passage from the city down to the sea, that we could form any
adequate idea of what the place once was. They are thus
correctly described by Colonel Chesney :—" The first part of
this extraordinary work is a hollow way of 600 feet long by
22 feet wide, and, in some places, about 120 feet high. The
second is a regular square tunnel, 293 feet in length by 22 feet
wide, and 24 feet high, which, like the preceding portion, is cut
through a compact tertiary limestone. To the latter succeeds
another hollow way, of 204 feet long by 22 feet wide, from the
bottom of which, at the southern side, whilst the excavation
itself descends more rapidly, a supply of water was carried along
a channel of 18 feet wide, preserving the same level till it
reached the exterior side of the hill, from whence it was carried
southward into the city. In this portion of the work, which is
110 feet high, (represented in the engraving) a narrow staircase
descends along the side of the rock, from the top of the excavation to within about 14 feet of the bottom, which, probably,
was the ordinary level of the water in this part of the cut.
Another tunnel, 102 feet in length, succeeds the latter portion of
the work, and then a hollow way of 1,065 feet, the eastern part
of which is crossed by a graceful aqueduct, supported by a single
arch. In a recess near the opposite extremity of this, are some
well-executed tombs, on the upper part of the rock; and a little
onwards, the effects of time are apparent, in the water having
forced a passage through the southern side of the excavation,
from whence it proceeds, along a steep rocky descent, into the
great basin. Thus far, the general direction is W.$\frac{1}{4}$S.; but the
excavation now sweeps gradually round, and at 322 feet northward, it is crossed by an arch, bearing some imperfect inscriptions. Finally, about 588 feet further, the hollow way, which
is in this part 30 feet high by 17 feet wide, terminates abruptly,

Ravine
at
Silenica

without any kind of steps, at nearly 30 feet above the level of the sea."

This detailed description will convey an idea of one of the most surprising works of its kind in existence. The effect strikingly reminds one of the ravine at Petra, although less wild and rugged, and principally, if not entirely, artificial.

The evening passed away most delightfully in the society of our host and his family circle, to which were added some young Syrian ladies, of an exquisite type of oriental beauty, with almond-shaped eyes of the most winning softness;—there was also a rich Christian merchant from Antioch, named Girgius Deeb, who invited me to take up my quarters at his house, while visiting that city.

Next morning, at an early hour, I set off with my servant on a temporary visit to Antioch, intending to follow as far as possible the windings of the Orontes, and also to visit the site of Daphne by the way. We therefore struck down to the banks of the river, not far from the spot where we had landed, and made our way along them by a narrow horse-path, worn through the thickets that came down to its brink. The scenery was wholly unlike anything I had previously seen in Syria,—strongly resembling that of the Wye, except that the vegetation was totally different; but though, for the most part, growing wild, it was luxuriant and beautiful beyond description. Tangled thickets of myrtle covered with odoriferous blossoms, and of bay, laurel, and other flowering shrubs, scarcely left room to pass. We had not proceeded far, when a mass of rich purple rocks, dipping their feet into the river, forbade all further passage along its brink. This romantic spot is called "the Pass of the Red Cliff." Here, then, we diverged from the stream, and, making a wide circuit around this precipitous obstruction, came down upon the river some miles further up, and ferrying across, ascended its right bank, up which the road passed steeply towards Beit el Ma, believed to be the site of that luxurious Daphne which corrupted by its fascinations the citizens of Antioch. The path to the top of the mountain overhanging the Orontes is through avenues of bay and myrtle-trees; and the air is redolent of most luxurious odours. At length, we lost sight of the river and descended into a secluded valley, overhung with lofty mountains, whence several streams, issuing forth from the fragrant thickets, dash wildly down its slope in numerous runnels and waterfalls, forcing their way through tufts of purple oleander and scented shrubs, and throwing out a delicious freshness. No temples now adorn the site, no sacred groves any longer exist; but the natural fascinations of the spot amply bear out the glowing accounts transmitted to us by its ancient panegyrists.

We pursued our way from Daphne through a mountain tract until, from the edge of a steep descent, we suddenly beheld Antioch, with the plain of the Orontes at our feet, and the distant mountains beyond. Its situation is one of the most striking imaginable. The valley of the Orontes, here exceedingly broad, is defended on the south by a range of lofty crags, from which the ground sinks gradually to the river. Extending along the top of this range of crags, themselves a natural fortification, had been drawn a line of wall which, descending the heights abruptly to the river, was carried along near its edge, so as to enclose the whole circumference of nearly seven miles. This wall had been flanked by an immense number of towers, of which many still lifted their stately heads before us. Of the extensive area enclosed within these bulwarks, an area which was formerly crowded with the magnificent buildings of the Syrian capital, the paltry town of Antakea, half-buried among gardens, occupies merely the north-west angle. We rapidly descended the stony pathway, and passing under one of the huge and tottering towers, entered the town by a breach in the ruinous wall, and in a few moments reached the comfortable abode of Girgius Deeb, who received us with the utmost cordiality. The house, mostly built of wood, was, as we found, erected upon the remains of the

Roman wall overhanging the Orontes. Girgius appeared a man well to do in the world; his household was numerous, and a constant succession of visitors shared his hospitalities. We sat down with a party of merchants from Aleppo to dinner, which was served in a divan, enclosed on three sides, and open on the fourth to the court. Before dinner a whet of *raki* was handed round. Upon a large stool was next deposited an enormous tray up-piled with a mountain of savoury pilau, into which the guests dived with their fingers, and, by a dexterous manipulation, managed to convey no inconsiderable portion down their throats. To this succeeded other Arab dishes, equally tempting, which were disposed of after the same fashion; and at night we had a comfortable shake-down upon the broad and cushioned divan, which, as in oriental houses, serves at once for a sofa by day, and a bed at night. Some of the pasha's officers joined us in the evening; and we got up a little music, intended to be lively, and, perhaps, really so to Oriental ears, but very dreary to those of Europeans.

Next day I was abroad early, and taking my dragoman, set off to examine the city. Beyond the walls hardly a trace of antiquity remains. Ancient Antioch has, indeed, been crumbled to dust, alike by the sudden convulsions of its oft-repeated earth-quakes, and the slow but certain operation of revolving ages. We passed through a few shabby streets, and by two or three mosques, and soon after saw a church, appropriated to the religious services of the Greek Christians, but found nothing to remind us that here the disciples of our Saviour were first " called Christians."

The present population of Antioch is under six thousand; that of the city and its port, Seleucia, being formerly, it is said, a million,—more than that of the whole of Syria at the present day. Of this a large proportion consists of Greek or Syrian Christians, and including in their number my host, Girgius. One of the entrances to the city still retains the name of

St. Paul's Gate; and not far from thence are the excavations
supposed to form part of the Church of St. John.

Leaving the town, we struck up through the gardens to the
slope of the hill, and, following the road to Aleppo, soon entered

WALL AT ANTIOCH.

a wild ravine, enclosed within the walls, and which was formerly
crossed by bridges, of which the foundations could still be traced.
Then we shortly came upon, perhaps, the most surprising part of
the ancient fortifications. The wall, descending steeply from
the heights above, is built across the ravine, up from the very
bottom, and then carried along the edge of a range of precipices
to the opposite height, whence they descend in the same manner

to join the wall along the river side. Perhaps there is nothing in existence that gives so striking an impression as this of the *daring* genius of the Roman engineers, and of the style in which they were accustomed to treat obstacles apparently insuperable.

One afternoon I left the house of Girgius to examine more particularly the splendid towers of the western wall, and, unfortunately, not only accoutred in my eastern habiliments, by this time rather the worse for wear, but also unaccompanied by my servant, to whose somewhat encumbering attention I had a dislike on such occasions; although, happily, my Alexandria firman was safely stowed away in the breast-pocket of my silken gaberdine. A walk of a few minutes through the streets of the town, and over a breach in the ruinous wall, had brought me to the foot of the towers; where, seated on a fallen fragment, I hoisted my umbrella, took out my sketch-book, and prepared to commit to paper one of the most picturesque subjects of the kind that ever tempted the pencil of an errant artist.

The towers that rose before me formed, without exception, the grandest specimen of Roman fortification I had ever seen, or that, perhaps, ever existed. To use the words of Col. Chesney, whose description, as a military man, must be much more satisfactory than any I could give :—"It was in overcoming the defects of the ground at the southern extremity of the city, that the skill of the Romans is most conspicuous. Owing to the steepness of the declivity, the ordinary platform surmounting the wall here, becomes a succession of steps between the towers, which are very near each other, and have a story rising above the wall, to protect the intervening portions from the commanding ground outside. The towers are of uniform construction, about 30 feet square, and project each way, so as to defend the interior side as well as the exterior face of the wall. The latter is from 50 to 60 feet high, and 8 or 10 feet broad at top, which is covered by cut stones terminating in a cornice. The towers are perfectly upright, and have interior staircases, and three loop-holed stages resting on brick arches, the uppermost having a stone platform, and a small cistern beneath. Low doors, or rather posterns, afford a passage along the parapet, so that these structures may be regarded as a chain of small castles connected by a curtain, rather than as simple towers." This description will be elucidated by a reference to the engraving. Of this chain of magnificent bulwarks, some had fallen in huge fragments around, overthrown probably by the earthquakes that have shaken the rocky·soil; one or two were undermined and tottering; but the principal chain still remains in an excellent state of preservation. There was an interest in observing the similarity of construction to that of the Roman remains in England, the bricks being of the same shape, and disposed in layers, with stone-work between them, like those of St. Alban's, Rich-borough, and Leicester; and in thus realizing the extent of that stupendous empire, which has left behind it such magnificent relics, from the banks of the Euphrates to the firths of Scotland.

I was for some time so absorbed in my occupation, as hardly to perceive that some Egyptian officers and soldiers, who seemed to have made a guard-house of one of the towers, were watching my operations with considerable interest, and, as I thought, some slight degree of mistrust; indeed, the sight of a turbaned Rayah, as I appeared to be, alone, with an umbrella over his head, and a sketch-book on his knees, delineating the fortifications, was as suspicious, as it no doubt was grotesque. They came up, saluted me, looked over my work, and, after some whispering together, took their leave. Having completed my sketch, I arose to return to the house, when two of the soldiers placing their hands upon my shoulders, urged me, as I imagined, to follow them to the guard-house in the tower, for the purpose of visiting the officers. As I had no time to spare for this purpose, I civilly shook myself clear of them, and retraced my steps towards the town. Still they continued to follow, and importune me to

Antioch.

return to the tower, endeavouring to lay hold of me, and I thrusting them off from time to time with my umbrella. On receiving a rather smartish poke in the ribs, one of the fellows drew his sabre, and suddenly sliding my arm within his own, hurried me rapidly forward through the streets, which we had just entered, past the house of Girgius, as far as a building which served for head-quarters to the officers. While thus dragged ignominiously along, unarmed, and unable to speak an intelligible word, I held out my hands pantomimically to the people about, imploring them to rescue me, but they only shook their heads and turned aside. I have often since rejoiced that I had not a pistol about me, as I might perhaps have done an act which would have at least occasioned me much regret, if it had not involved me in serious difficulty.

On entering the guard-room, the soldier thrust me up on a platform; where, upon cushions, were seated two Egyptian officers, smoking their pipes; while two or three attendants were standing around. Then, addressing himself to the principal, and pointing to me, he told his story, of which I could not, of course, comprehend a syllable; but which seemed to make a great impression upon the officer, who made signs to his attendants to seize me, and administer the bastinado. This cruel process consists in laying the sufferer flat on his face, raising and laying bare his feet, and bestowing upon his naked soles a number of stripes proportioned to his supposed guilt. My blood boiled within me, but more from indignation than fear. I rushed up to the seat of the officer, drew forth my firman, and shouting out the magic word "Inglèse," almost thrust it into his bearded face. As he rapidly scanned its contents, his countenance became exceedingly blank, and he exchanged significant glances with his fellow-officer, as much as to say, "How very nearly we had committed ourselves with this dog of an infidel!" His face then became suddenly radiant with smiles, and he politely motioned me to take a seat by his side; but I could not digest my choler quite so suddenly, and without returning his salute, moved off to the entrance. Yet his mind seemed not quite satisfied, for, following me to the door, he obtained, half by force and half by entreaty, a glimpse at the suspicious sketch-book, and then courteously dismissing me, went back to his divan and his pipe.

I returned through the streets, which had just witnessed my humiliation, to the house of Girgius; who opened wide his eyes as I narrated the adventure; but to my demands for vengeance, only returned a bitter smile and a shrug. After all, as it happened, there was but little to complain of, and that little owing entirely to my own imprudence. By degrees I cooled down, but thought fit, nevertheless, to call next day with my servant, and demand an explanation of the business. This was speedily afforded. The city was near the northern frontier of Syria, and Ibrahim Pasha intended to make it a "place d'armes," and the centre or his power in this quarter. The Turkish army was encamped on the other side of the Taurus, and the sight of a person drawing the walls was suspicious; and my oriental dress, which somehow, as the Yankees say, did not look "kinder nat'ral," confirmed the impression that I was a spy in disguise, making engineering notes to facilitate some future movements. From henceforth I took leave definitively of oriental masquerading, and determined never again to sail under false colours.

Antioch, the Queen of the East, as she was called by Pliny, was built by Seleucus Nicanor, founder of the Syro-Macedonian empire, and for two centuries and a half was the seat of the Seleucidan dynasty. Its delicious situation and climate, the beauty of its environs, and the embellishments lavished on it by its princes, soon rendered it a favourite seat of luxury. Its mixed population united, as Gibbons says, " the lively licentious-ness of the Greeks with the hereditary softness of the Syrians." Its theatre formed the principal source of their enjoyment, while its temples, with their religious ceremonies, so far from advancing the cause of virtue, might rather be regarded as the deification of vice. Such as it was under the Seleucidan dynasty, it continued under the sway of the Romans, being the favourite residence of many of the emperors. The doctrines of Christianity were first brought hither by fugitives from Jerusalem, after the martyrdom of Stephen, who first addressing themselves exclusively to the Jews, but afterwards also to the Gentiles, made so considerable a number of converts, that it attracted the attention of the church at Jerusalem, who sent down Barnabas to confirm them in their new profession. Anxious for the cooperation of Paul, Barnabas went to Tarsus to seek him; and continued to labour together with the apostle for a whole year. Not only was it at Antioch that the disciples were first called Christians,— a name not given by the Jews, nor assumed by themselves but probably bestowed as distinctive by the Gentiles,—but it was there too that the first great missionary enterprise was undertaken, when Paul and Barnabas were first set apart for the work of conveying the gospel to the Gentiles; and Antioch long continued to be their head-quarters, to which they returned after their visits to Cyprus, Asia Minor, and Greece. It was here that the disputes about the necessity of circumcision, and other Jewish practices, took place, which threatened to disturb the peace of the infant church; and here, finally, Paul and Barnabas separated after the dispute concerning Mark. Luke, it should be observed, the narrator of these events, was himself a native of Antioch. The church thus planted and carefully watered, continued to increase in importance, though not, unhappily, in purity, until it was called at length the Eye of the Eastern Church. Hence, when the number of "Christians" had grown so large as to attract the notice and provoke the persecution of the Roman emperors, Ignatius, the bishop, was sent to Rome by Trajan, to be thrown to the lions in the Circus. It was here, after the triumphant establishment of the Christian faith had taken place, under Constantine, that Julian, while he satirized the hereditary luxury which the inhabitants had contrived to incorporate with their religious profession, made so ineffectual an attempt to re-establish the expiring Paganism upon the ruins of Christianity. Here, in short,—for the chronicles of Antioch would fill a volume of themselves,—the golden-mouthed Chrysostom displayed his eloquence and his virtues,. until he was translated almost by force to the superior dignity of the see of Constantinople.

Having been overwhelmed by successive earthquakes, it was rebuilt by Justinian, who gave it the name of Theopolis, or, the City of God. During the declining days of the Roman empire, it was repeatedly lost and regained by the Christians, Persians, and Saracens, from the last of whom it was taken, after infinite sufferings, by the Crusaders, under Godfrey de Bouillon. It continued to be a place of great importance during the Latin kingdom of Jerusalem, until it was finally taken from them, and ruthlessly devastated by the ferocious Bibars, sultan of Egypt. Swept as it has been, again and again, by the sword of the conqueror, and all the concomitant horrors of war, earthquakes have yet been its greatest enemy. It is said that, in A.D. 588, above sixty thousand persons perished in one of these terrible convulsions; and the only wonder is that, after such repeated devastations, any trace of its original magnificence should be left behind.

Returning, after a few days' stay at Antioch, to see our hosts at Suadéa, we hired horses to convey us to Adona and Tarsus. We were now to traverse a region comparatively wild and unfrequented, but, owing to the presence of the Egyptian army, rendered, at this time, perfectly safe for travellers. Striking across the broad plain of the Orontes, we entered the mountains, and, following the line of the ancient Roman paved way, portions of which were yet remaining, arrived, in the evening, at Beilán, one of the most romantic places in Syria, and which gives its name to this pass through the defiles of Mount Amanus, anciently denominated "the Syrian Gates." This road had witnessed the passage of the armies of Cyrus and Alexander; and, in later ages, the Crusaders and other warriors had marched along it; it had been trodden by the Apostle Paul and the early teachers of Christianity, hurrying to and fro on their errands of mercy and love; in fact, it constituted the only direct line of travel from Asia Minor and Cilicia into Syria. It is the line by which, in modern times, merchandise is conveyed from the port of Alexandretta to the city of Aleppo and the Euphrates; yet, so depopulated is the country, and so few the wayfarers, that we hardly encountered a human being on our way. It was at the head of the pass that Ibrahim Pasha defeated the advanced guard of the Turkish army, which he afterwards put to rout upon the plain of Konieh.

By a winding descent of some hours, we reached the level of the sea, at the small town of Alexandretta, the port of Aleppo, situated in a morass, so pestilential, that it had proved fatal not only to most of the European residents, but also to the crews and captains of ships in the roads. We directed our steps to the house of M. Martinelli, agent to several Aleppo merchants, and who had succeeded in cutting a small canal, and thus, by draining the marshes, had rendered the place, in some degree, more salubrious. Thence we pushed on along the coast; for the rugged ridges of Mount Amanus, coming down to the water, leave here but a narrow pathway, at a short distance from the sea. This spot was called the Cilician Gate; and the remains of fortifications show that the natural obstacles to the approach of an invader were carefully strengthened. Hence the road descends into a narrow plain, intersected by two rivulets, where Pococke supposes the battle of Issus to have been fought. We then passed a rising ground, and reached the deserted town of Payass, the ancient Issus, where we were obliged to remain for the night.

Next day we resumed our lonely course, passing over the more open plain to the north of the town, where it is generally supposed that the defeat of Darius took place. The Persian monarch had entered Cilicia by the northern or Amanic pass,

which here debouches into the plain on the sea-shore; a move-
ment whereby Alexander, who had advanced as far as the
Beilán pass, found himself dangerously hemmed in, and was
compelled to return and attack his enemy, who, on being defeated, fled into the interior of Asia by the same pass through
which he had advanced. Since leaving Beilán we had been

ARCH NEAR ISSUS.

tracing the ground which had once witnessed the marching and
countermarching of the Grecian army; and we were now passing
over the scene of that momentous and hard-fought engagement,
in which they routed, for the second time, the forces of the
Persian monarch. The spot now is utterly abandoned, and
traversed only by the Turcoman shepherd, inspiring a feeling of
deeper depression than even the desert itself, inasmuch as it

bears traces of the former presence of a considerable population. The insecurity of the route was notorious, until the recent conquest of the whole country by Ibrahim Pasha.

After surveying the battle-field, and crossing the stream supposed to be the Pinarus, we reached the extreme north-east angle of the Mediterranean, and shortly after came upon a portion of the ancient Roman paved way, resembling the Appian, across which stood a picturesque old archway, called the Black Gate, which, in connexion with some adjacent walls, closed up the passage into another narrow valley through which the road passes, and all the defensible points of which had evidently been carefully fortified.

We passed the night under a solitary tree, in the midst of a caravan, which had halted for a few hours. Long before daylight it was on its road towards Syria, while we pursued our way through the plains of Cilicia, with Mount Taurus in the distance, covered with eternal snow. Leaving Messis, we reached Adana at noon, passing over the long bridge of nineteen arches, which bestrides the river Sihoon. Here we found the advanced guard of the Egyptian army, and reached the limits of the country subject to the power of Ibrahim Pasha, without having met with a single instance of annoyance (my spy adventure alone excepted) during our passage through the whole widely-extended tract.

At noon next day, in the midst of a luxuriant plain, the minarets of the Turkish town of Tersoos, rising from amidst a grove of trees, backed by the lofty snow-covered crests of Mount Taurus, showed that we were approaching the birth-place of the great Apostle of the Gentiles, whose footsteps we had been already following from Antioch. On entering the town, it became a serious question how we were to dispose of ourselves. Mr. Barker had kindly furnished us with a letter to the English Consul, then recently appointed ; but that functionary had not yet reached the place. A miserable khan seemed to be our only refuge, when we were relieved from embarrassment by the entrance of a servant, bearing from the French Consul a pressing invitation to take up our abode at his house.

M. Gillet, our worthy entertainer, of a good family in France, had been *thrice* drawn for the conscription during the campaigns of Napoleon. The first, and even the second time, his parents had bought him off,—on the third he was compelled to serve. He had gone through the horrors of the Russian campaign, and had beheld the terrible scene at the bridge over the Beresina. While so many had left their bones amidst the snows of Russia, and others had become mere wrecks of their former selves, he had come off, apparently, with an unbroken constitution, and his cheeks were as florid, his face as unwrinkled, and his vivacity as unflagging, as if he had never quitted the banks of the Seine. He seemed to bear a charmed life. Shut up in a melancholy town in a remote corner of Syria, hardly ever sought out by the foot of a traveller, exposed to a deleterious climate, which had proved fatal to two or three of his consular brethren, he has contrived to outlive them all, and has been since translated to the more important station of Salonica.

Speaking of the unhealthy climate, I remember, some time afterwards, meeting at dinner in Smyrna a gentleman who told me he had just received the appointment of English Consul at Tarsus, and who asked me what kind of place it was. I immediately informed him that its climate bore an unfavourable reputation. "Ah!" he rejoined, "if that is all, I am already well aware of it. The last consul died of fever; but I am perfectly *acclimatée*, and do not entertain the slightest apprehension." He repaired thither, and within a twelvemonth afterwards, laid his bones with those of his predecessor in office.

It has been said that John Bull carries his country with him wherever he goes; and perhaps the same may be said, with at least equal truth, of Jean Crapaud. In M. Gillet's house, until one looked out of the windows, and saw the snowy crags of the

Taurus, one might have supposed oneself in the Chauseé d'Antin. Everything in-doors was redolent of Paris; and not the least pleasant part of the illusion was the *cuisine*. The evening passed in talking of European affairs, and in reminiscences of the "*grande armée.*" The consul's house was a little oasis of luxury in the midst of a desert of privation; and having for several nights slept on the floor, I need not inform such of my readers as have ever been in similar circumstances, what were my sensations when I stretched my unencumbered limbs between the fragrant sheets of a bed that would have done honour to a château of the old regime, or a first-rate hotel in the new.

On the next morning I turned my back on all these luxuries, to seek out the remains of what St. Paul, with a commendable degree of patriotic, or, perhaps, rather of civic pride, described as " no mean city;" but I was utterly unsuccessful—like those who had gone before me—in discovering any really important relics of ancient Tarsus, which seems to have been wholly swept away in the numerous inroads that have desolated the country since the fall of the Roman empire. The classic Cydnus, here some miles from the sea, from bathing in which Alexander the Great nearly died, and upon whose waters occurred the famous meeting of Mark Antony and Cleopatra, once ran through the middle of the city. It now holds its course half a mile east of the town, through a region of gardens, in which the intermingled foliage of the banana and the palm show that the luxuriance of the soil at least remains unaltered. The port, formed by a large basin, through which its waters once passed, is dried up; a bar is stretched across its mouth, and no barque now enters its forsaken channel. Modern Tersoos is an insignificant town; but the neighbouring plain furnishes considerable exports of corn, which, with imports destined for the interior of this part of Asia, occasion the appointment of several European consuls, who here live in a state of enforced exile from their native land, and are glad to welcome an occasional traveller, as one who reminds them of the existence of the civilized world.

Tarsus was a free city of very ancient foundation, and had not only been raised by commerce to wealth and importance, but had become so celebrated for learning and science, that Strabo gives it the preference in that respect over Athens and Alexandria. It is celebrated in history on widely dissimilar grounds. It was visited by Alexander the Great and Julius Cæsar, and was favoured by many Roman emperors. On the waters of the Cydnus, which was then navigable from the sea, and flowed through the middle of the town, took place, as we have said, the meeting between Mark Antony and Cleopatra, of which Shakspeare has given a description at once literally true and gorgeously poetical. Here the lovers began their career of luxurious revelry, and Cleopatra first essayed her influence over the enslaved Antony, by demanding the murder of her sister. And here, not very long after, as if to show human nature in its extremes, was born the great Apostle of the Gentiles. His parents were Jews, of the sect of the Pharisees, and, as we learn from himself, they brought him up in the strictest observance of their tenets. But though the basis of his education was Jewish, yet, from his early associations, he must have acquired, at the same time, such a knowledge of the Greek language and literature, as singularly to qualify him for the part he was designed by Providence to fill—that of the interpreter of Christianity to the Gentile world. His father had obtained the valuable privilege of Roman citizenship ; and thus the Apostle was " free born,"—a circumstance which proved of no small importance to him during his career. In accordance with that general and commendable practice of the Jews, which conferred independence of character and position on every member of society, he was taught a trade, in his case that of tent-making. At an early age he was sent from Tarsus to Jerusalem, where he sat " at the feet of Gamaliel," a celebrated teacher, and became thoroughly versed in the study of the Hebrew Scriptures, for his intimate acquaintance with which he was noted by his companions. No less enthusiastic in temperament than acute in intellect, he was early distinguished for his zealous advocacy of the Pharisaic tenets, and for his bitter hatred of the Christians.

Unable to content himself with a lukewarm acquiescence in any system he embraced, the same fervid zeal which he had displayed against the followers of the Cross, prompted him, after his conversion, to a life of suffering and sacrifice in behalf of the religion he had ignorantly persecuted. Yet with his daring energy and dauntless perseverance, he combined, in a remarkable degree, the qualities of prudence and self-command; and the tact of adapting his instructions to the capacity or prejudices of his hearers, without sinking, however, to unworthy compliance or dishonourable compromise. Nor less conspicuous was the native tenderness of his heart, rendered more exquisite by the rising influences of Christianity, or the largeness and expansiveness of his charity. He was a man whose heart was as open and gentle as his mental powers were comprehensive and profound; one who, even had he not been assisted by divine interposition, must have left the impression of his high personal qualities, and marked himself as one of nature's nobility, on whatever career he might have entered. But this is stepping, perhaps, beyond the province of a traveller, which is to note such local circumstances as may illustrate the events of sacred or profane history, rather than to dwell upon those events themselves.

Paul left Tarsus a Jew, he returned to it a Christian. After having been introduced to the apostles at Jerusalem, he distinguished himself by "disputing against the Grecians," who endeavoured to put him to death; upon which he was sent back from Cæsarea to his native city, where he resided until invited by Barnabas to Antioch, to assist in the care of the church, and to enter soon after upon his long and laborious course of missionary labour. There is no express mention of his revisiting it, although there can be little doubt of his having done so during his numerous journeys in Asia Minor.

It is interesting to follow in idea the great Apostle of the Gentiles when setting out upon these journeyings; to figure to the mind's eye his person and manner, and mode of travel; to realize the appearance of the great cities, the scenes of his labours, then in all their splendour; and to understand the relative position of the Jews and Pagans with whom he was brought into collision, and from among whom his converts were collected.

St. Paul tells us, that his enemies declared of him, that "his bodily presence was weak, and his speech contemptible," intimating that he possessed neither the lofty stature vulgarly associated with the hero, nor the oratorical artifices of a practised teacher of rhetoric. From ancient writers we gather that his person was small, and of a type in which the intellectual predominates over the animal nature, a sheath worn out by the sharpness of the sword within. Lucian, as Dr. Cave observes, derisively calls him the high-nosed, bald-pated Galilæan, that was caught up through the air unto the "third heaven." It would appear that his constitution was weak, and that in carrying on his arduous missionary labours, he had continually to struggle with the natural infirmity of the flesh.

The incessant journeyings of the Apostle were greatly facilitated by the frequent and easy communication between the different parts of the Roman world, both by land and sea. From the capital itself, the great paved ways, constructed with such strength that in many places they can still be traced, radiated to the extreme boundaries of the empire, and were provided with a regular service of post-horses. There was thus a ready and continual intercourse between the principal places in the Empire.

The great cities of Asia Minor, so often visited by Paul, were then at the height of wealth and populousness, were united by good roads, and further connected by a constant transit of coasting vessels. Between Rome and Alexandria a regular intercourse was kept up by means of those vessels which carried supplies of corn from Egypt to Italy, some of them being of considerable size. At no previous period, in short, had there existed such a network of communication between the various countries now united under the sway of Rome.

Of these facilities the Apostle and his companions availed themselves; sometimes travelling post by land along the high road; at others, going humbly on foot across the country; at others, coasting from port to port, or embarking on a lengthened voyage, exposed to all the varieties of hardship and peril which he has so feelingly described:—" In journeyings often, in perils of robbers, in perils by mine own countrymen, in perils by the heathen, in perils in the city, in perils in the wilderness, in perils in the sea, in perils among false brethren."

Nothing, in St. Paul's day, could have been more classically magnificent than one of the great cities, the ruins of which astonish the modern traveller. Gorgeous temples, then in all their pristine splendour, and adorned with immortal sculptures, which rose on every side; elegant though corrupting processions, as represented in works of art still existing, which filled the streets; the theatres, open to the sky, or covered with a light awning, crowded with their thousands of spectators; the long pillared avenues and porticoes, of which the remains so often still stand erect amidst surrounding desolation; the numerous and beautiful statues of the gods, in all the lustrous sunshine of an oriental climate; even the streets of tombs themselves lining the approach to the city, must have presented a dazzling and imposing spectacle to the eye of taste and refinement. Especially must the sea-ports, such as Seleucia or Cæsarea, of which the ruinous harbours are now with difficulty to be traced, have been singularly picturesque, with their crowds of oared galleys, their colonnaded piers, their temples to Neptune, filled with votive offerings. But in the mind of the Apostle, all the refinements of art were indissolubly connected with a debasing system of polytheism, which it was his peculiar office to undermine, and could only remind him the more painfully of the deep-rooted moral corruption of the Roman world, against which he had incessantly to combat.

On entering with such feelings one of these splendid cities, the Apostle and his companions would naturally address themselves first to their own brethren, the Jews, who everywhere existed a despised and detested sect. A few of them might already have heard of the wonderful events which had ushered in the new religion, and be therefore disposed to hear further of it; and with some of these, while labouring to support himself by his vocation of tent-maker, would the Apostle take up his abode. The synagogue was the first place where he would venture publicly to preach the doctrines of the Gospel. In so doing, while making a few converts, he could not fail to awaken the bitterest prejudice and hostility of the more bigotted portion of his hearers, and thus make many enemies, and expose himself to the outbursts of their indignant fury.

Sometimes, taking the law into their own hands, they would break out into acts of murderous violence; and sometimes, by artfully representing the Apostle as a despiser of the gods, they would work upon the superstition of the Pagan populace; at others, by representing the Apostle as a troubler of the public peace, endeavour to provoke the interference of the magistracy. In the last manœuvre they were but rarely successful. The narrow and unsocial spirit of the Jews was so peculiarly offensive to the more enlightened Romans, that they generally refused to interfere in what they regarded as a contemptible dispute between rival sects of Jews,—"a question of their own superstition," with which the government had nothing to do.

In seeking to overthrow the dominant religion, Paul appears to have exercised the utmost prudence, and rarely to have involved himself in any serious difficulty with the Pagan

Authorities. The toleration of indifference was at that time the principle of the Roman government. The ancient religions, effete and undermined, were, as Gibbon says, regarded by the people as equally true, by the philosophers as equally false, and by the magistrates as equally useful. So long as the votaries of different superstitions interfered not with one another, or threatened to disturb the public tranquillity, they enjoyed a general immunity and protection. In such a state of things, Christianity might gradually insinuate itself and imperceptibly grow up; nor could it attract any serious hostility, until the growing numbers of its votaries excited the apprehensions of the priesthood and the government. It was only by particular classes, as the wonder-workers and diviners, or the craftsmen of Diana of the Ephesians, that the Apostle appears to have been menaced. His bitterest persecutors were everywhere among his own Jewish brethren, to compass whose salvation he expresses his willingness to become himself a " cast-away."

It may be well to throw together a few brief notices of those cities in Asia Minor, connected with that part of St. Paul's travels narrated in the thirteenth and fourteenth chapters of the " Acts."

On the first missionary voyage of the Apostle accompanied by Barnabas, they sailed, as already observed, from Seleucia, and after traversing Cyprus, took their departure from Paphos to the coast of Pamphylia, landing at or near Perga, of which city, now utterly abandoned, there still exist considerable remains. From thence, Mark leaving them to return to Jerusalem, Paul and Barnabas next proceeded to Antioch in Pisidia. Here, as was their wont, they entered the synagogue, and preached the Gospel to the Jews, attracting also the notice of the Gentile inhabitants, who earnestly requested that the same word might be preached to themselves.

It was here that Paul, thwarted by the factious opposition of his own countrymen, declared for the first time his intention of turning from them to the Gentiles. The fanaticism of the Jewish

priests was too much for even the untiring energy of the Apostle
and his associates; they were driven from the city by their
intrigues; and, " shaking off the dust of their feet against them,"
they next repaired to Iconium.

The site of Antioch in Pisidia has lately been identified by
the Rev. Mr. Arundell as being at the modern Jalobatch, where
he found very considerable remains of its former magnificence.
It was built by the founder of the Syrian Antioch, and was a
place of considerable importance during the Seleucidan dynasty.

Arrived at Iconium, Paul and Barnabas again resorted to the
Jewish synagogue, and made a considerable number of converts,
but were driven thence, as from Antioch in Pisidia, by the
machinations of their Jewish enemies, who stirred up the
Gentiles, and would have stoned them, had they not escaped
from the city. The modern Konieh, which occupies the site of
ancient Iconium, presents but few relics of the period of St. Paul's
visit, though it is still a large and flourishing town. Its monuments are chiefly, if not entirely, mediæval.

On flying from Iconium, Paul and Barnabas retired to Derbe
and Lystra, cities in the rugged mountain region of Lycaonia,
beneath the lofty ranges of the Taurus. At Lystra occurred that
most characteristic scene, when the heathen inhabitants, excited
by witnessing a miracle wrought by Paul, exclaimed that the
" gods had come down in the likeness of men;" and calling Paul
Jupiter, and Barnabas Mercurius, because he was the chief
speaker, were preparing to offer sacrifices to them, until prevented by their earnest entreaties. Here, again, they were
pursued by the unrelenting malevolence of the Jews, who,
working on the ignorant apprehensions of the superstitious
multitude, brought about such a revulsion of feeling, that Paul,
after being stoned, was, by the same men who had so lately been
ready to confer on him divine honours, dragged out of the city
for dead. Recovering from this ill-treatment, he departed next
day with Barnabas to Derbe.

Neither the site of this city nor that of Lystra has yet been satisfactorily ascertained. From hence, disregarding their previous ill-usage, we find that they again visited the same cities, confirming and establishing in the faith the numerous converts they had succeeded in making; embarking at Attalia for Antioch, where they "abode long time with the disciples," rehearsing to them how God had opened "a door of faith unto the Gentiles."

Such was the first missionary voyage ever undertaken to propagate Christianity beyond the limits of Syria.

On leaving Tarsus, it had been my original design to proceed overland to Constantinople, by way of Konieh, the ancient Iconium, and to have visited Derbe and Lystra, and other places connected with the travels of St. Paul. A journey so long and fatiguing was judged, however, to be unsuitable in my weakened state of health; and, by M. Gillet's advice, I resolved on coasting Asia Minor, as far as Attalia, a distance of about a hundred and fifty miles, and thence proceeding overland to Smyrna.

Taking leave of my excellent host, who begged me "to bear in mind sometimes the poor exiles at Tarsus," I rode down to the port, where I found a small open boat, which had been already hired for me by M. Gillet, but which to my dismay I found, if possible, more wretched even than those I had already become familiar with. Its crew was easily mustered; it consisted of but two, one a good old Turk, the other his son, a robust fellow, about thirty. Getting our luggage and provisions on board, we took up the great stone, which served as an anchor, hoisted our sail, and began to move slowly along the coast in the direction of Attalia.

The breezes were so light and languid, that it was not till the next afternoon we reached Mezetlu, the ancient Solis, a city of Rhodian origin, and, on account of its having been rebuilt by Pompey, also called Pompeiopolis. Making fast to the ruined pier, we landed, to examine a long avenue of columns, which stretched in magnificent perspective towards the interior, but so overgrown

was the ground with brushwood, that it was impossible to pene-
trate to any distance. A ruined theatre overlooked the sea, and
the entire scene was desolate beyond description. There was no
trace of human habitation, and, save the squared stones and the
columns, everything had relapsed into the wildness of primitive
nature.

. The wind sank shortly afterwards to a dead calm. If to be
becalmed in a comfortable ship is horribly tedious; what is it in
a boat hardly twenty feet long, open to the sky, full of sand and
dirt, and without anything but a blanket hoisted on two poles,
to keep off the burning heat of the sun! Hour after hour thus
passed in weariness and suffering inexpressible. That night
I was seized with fever; I soon became delirious. For *fifteen
days* I struggled between life and death, until at length we
reached our destination. I spare the reader a detail of the
incidents of this voyage, of which, indeed, I retain but an
indistinct recollection. I faintly recall having seen, in the
intervals of consciousness, a few ruinous castles and bold headlands, around which it seemed as if we never should pass. In
the morning, some lofty promontory would loom ahead; and in
the evening, there it was again in the same position. We seemed
enchanted upon the sickly oily sea. Once or twice I remember
being carried ashore, and laid under the shadow of the trees,
while the boatmen replenished our stock of water. The pirate
town of Alaya, hung wildly upon its cliffs, also imprinted itself
indelibly upon my recollection. I can remember struggling with
my servant to go up into it, and my fighting with him for
a bunch of grapes, which he prudently forbade me to touch;
while the people, seeing my brain was affected, looked on with
evident pity. By the time we reached Attalia, the fever had
entirely spent itself, but it left me so weak that they were
obliged to carry me ashore.

Woe to the wretched traveller who is seized with sickness
in these forlorn and remote places, without any one to sympathise

with him, or show him the slightest attention; compelled to sojourn in an empty khan, devoured with vermin, and tormented with musquitoes! Attalia has since proved the grave of a talented and valued countryman, and I fully expected to leave my bones in it, to be picked by the Turkish dogs. Fresh difficulties arose also. I was here in the dominions of the Sultan; and the governor refused, on account of my Egyptian firman, to let me proceed by land. This was of little consequence, however, as I could not have borne the fatigue of the journey. On the seventh day of my stay, my servant ran in with a joyful countenance; a cutter bound for Rhodes had just come to anchor. It seemed as if expressly sent by Providence for our deliverance. In less than an hour we were on board; and in the evening, the melancholy Attalia faded on the distant horizon.

Since leaving Tarsus, we had sailed across the sea of Cilicia and Pamphylia, more than once traversed by St. Paul, who had also landed at Attalia. Perga is a little way inland, but we could not visit it. We still followed the same coast of Lycia, along which we sailed towards Cos, passing at a distance Myra, where the centurion charged with his custody "found a ship of Alexandria sailing into Italy, and put him therein." On the fourth evening we were within view of Rhodes; and on the morrow morning—oh, joyful sight!—the magnificent bulwarks of the Knights of St. John of Jerusalem rose round us in all their pride, as we cast anchor in the middle of the harbour.

On landing, I repaired to the British consulate, where I was very kindly received by Mr. Wilkinson. Exactly opposite was the Catholic convent, at which he advised me to take up my abode during my stay.

The Catholic convents of the Holy Land, and other parts of the Levant, it should be observed, are not without a certain historical interest. Many were founded by the Greek emperors, or in the time of the Crusades, and endowed by wealthy barons with ample revenues, which have been also increased by the contributions of pilgrims, and by collections made in Europe. A few are still in a flourishing condition, but the greater portion are sunk into indigence; and extensive buildings, which formerly held a considerable number of tenants, are now occupied by only one or two. Monachism, in short, seems to be everywhere on the wane.

These Levantine friars present a curious medley. Among them may be found the brightest patterns of Christian piety, and not a few consummate hypocrites and downright knaves. Many of them, too, are most amusing originals. In rambling about the East, where, from the absence of inns, the traveller is perforce obliged to take up his abode at these establishments, it is odd if he do not fall in with a few of every class.

This convent, of which I was now an inmate, was the sole relic of the once powerful Knights of St. John of Jerusalem. It was a massive stone edifice, which would have accommodated a large body of friars, but was then inhabited but by three, who were understood to be in a state of extreme poverty. I was kindly and hospitably received, installed in a small monastic cell, with a trestle bed, and took my meals with the brethren in the conventual refectory. What with the pure air and good living, I rapidly recovered my health. For poor as were my hosts, they contrived, after all, to subsist pretty comfortably in a place where forty eggs may be had for a piastre, value twopence-halfpenny, and where fine red wine was sold at a penny a bottle.

To the superior of the convent it was impossible not to become attached. He was a Genoese, a venerable man of eighty. His figure was erect and noble, his eye undimmed, his countenance open and benevolent, while his long white beard, sweeping down to his girdle, conferred on him a most reverend appearance. At an age when the human powers are generally sinking into decrepitude, he was a pattern of industry, and a bright exemplar of Catholic devotion. My cell happened to be next to his, and the first thing audible in the morning, was the old man repeating the prayers from his Breviary. He then arose, and ringing the convent bell, summoned his brethren to matins. As neither my health nor inclinations admitted of my joining in this exercise, I got up more leisurely, and met the brethren in the refectory to breakfast. This meal being over, I accompanied the superior to his private apartment, where were collected a number of children, to whom he imparted the rudiments of education. This, however, was far from being his sole occupation, for, while his pupils were conning their books, he employed himself in writing homilies, knitting stockings, curing tobacco, and carrying to completion the manufacture of the large wax candles required for the service of the church. His plan was to purchase a long wick, stiffened with a single layer of tallow, and, making the tallest of his little pupils hold it up over a basin, to then clothe it with successive coats, by basting it with melted wax, until it acquired the needful thickness; and the only symptoms of impatience I ever observed in the old man, were when, by carelessness or fatigue, the little fellow selected for this office let fall on the ground the end of the candle, thus breaking it in the middle by the sudden jerk. Besides these multifarious duties, the old man assisted in treading out the grapes, and making the convent wine; and so keen was his sight and steady his hand, that if he saw a bird flying across the garden, he would catch up his gun, and rarely fail to bring it down. As my strength returned, and I became enabled to accompany him in his pastoral walks, it was a pleasure to see the affectionate reverence with which he was everywhere greeted. The children ran to kiss his hand, and receive his benediction; and on his entering the dwellings of his flock, they seemed to vie with one another in expressions of grateful regard.

The venerable superior, as he told me, had not a single relative, save a nephew, of whom he had not heard for years. He had not a single earthly tie, yet he lived a life of cheerfulness and benevolence, useful and beloved on earth, comforted and sustained by faith in a happy futurity. Would that every adherent of his creed were an imitator of his example!

The second friar, who held the important office of conventual cook, was a much younger man, and presented, in all respects, a singular contrast to his superior. His gait was slouching and indolent, and his countenance habitually wore a half-cynical, half-sensual look. He was anything but devout, and would come yawning out of the chapel after matins, with bitter complaints as to the intolerable length of the service. Naturally keen and sarcastic, more shrewd than the superior, but totally destitute of the religious sentiment, he was compelled to pass his life in the, to him, tedious routine of services, which he evidently regarded with real, although unavowed contempt, and which had for him, as for many of his order, no sustaining or elevating influences. He hated this world without caring much for the next, and had always an ill-word for every one he met with. His only refuge from a vacant and discontented spirit, was the savoury occupation in which he had become no mean proficient; but he was not averse to imparting a knowledge of his art, for under his auspices I learned to make very tolerable " omelettes; " and so satisfied did he seem with my docility as a pupil, that he favoured me with some of his opinions, " private and confidential," one of which, I recollect, was, that " we may contrive, if we must, to get along without wives, but without good living it is utterly impossible to exist."

Such was the society in which I spent a month, partly to recover my health, and partly waiting for an opportunity of embarking for Syra. One day, while seated at the conventual board, there entered a personage, over fifty, tall, meagre, and perpendicular as a post; who, removing his broad-brimmed straw hat, gravely bowed to us, with all the formal politeness of the old school. The expression of his countenance, long and deeply furrowed by care, was rather sardonic, but wore, at the moment, what was intended for a fascinating smile. There was a touch of the *petit-maître* too, in his dress and manner; it was evident he had been somewhat of a *beau* in his younger days. His trowsers, tight, and somewhat shrunken, scarcely came down to his ankles; pink striped stockings succeeded, and shoes. His coat was short-waisted, with long thin tails to it; a huge watch-chain and seals dangled from his waistcoat; his bushy white whiskers seemed nearly to meet across his face, and his shirt collar cut up into the middle of his hollow cheeks. Entering at last upon his business, he explained that there was now a small vessel bound for Syra, in the harbour, in which he had taken his passage; and learning that there was a Signor Inglese at the convent bound to the same port, he had come to propose that we should make our provisions for the voyage in common, in which, from his great experience, he should be able to save me some little trouble. I thanked him warmly; in fact, such a proposal was just the very thing I could have wished for. Next day, the wind being fair, and our preparations completed, I took leave of the cynical cook and worthy superior. Some years afterwards, I happened to touch at the same port, and ran to the convent to greet my ancient acquaintances; but the grave had closed over the old man, and whither the other had wandered no one knew.

In voyaging by these little Levantine boats, the passengers are obliged to provide their own food, and prepare it on deck, at a small fire-place. Occupying the posts of honour, we had the first turn at the cooking-place; and it was quite a sight to see my tall friend, regularly at noon, bending his long back, and going through the operations of the *cuisine*, with a solemn gravity worthy of Quixote himself. Seated on the deck, over our soup and *bouilli*, we were the best of friends, and I soon became the confidant of some of the old gentleman's gallantries, real or apocryphal, and also of the misfortunes which caused him to wander about the Levant. He was, as it appeared, an old captain of Ragusa, in the Adriatic Gulf; who had been all

H

his lifetime beating about in quest of a quiet haven, yet had encountered nothing but foul weather and scurvy treatment at the hands of the unstable goddess, whom alone he seemed to worship; and was now as far from port as ever, while his hull was somewhat battered by time and tempest, and his rigging sadly out of order.

During the four days that we were sailing through the romantic islands of the Archipelago, not without an uneasy look out for skulking pirates, my companion beguiled the time with many an amusing anecdote and narrative; and whatever might have been my answer, had I been required to give a categorical opinion as to his religious or moral character, I must frankly confess that " I could have better spared a better man."

On reaching the island of Syra, we were immediately clapped into quarantine, for ten mortal days, in a den swarming with rats and every sort of abomination, of which I spare the reader a more particular account. On coming forth, I took leave of my entertaining fellow-traveller, in order to return to my home, little expecting that I should ever fall in with him again. In this respect, however, I was fated to be disappointed, nor was the disappointment entirely disagreeable; but as the meeting took place in a land but little, if at all, visited by those whose honoured footsteps I have proposed to trace, in this instance also I spare my reader any further details.

CHAPTER III.

HAVING, on my return from Egypt, an opportunity of paying at least a hasty visit to Greece, I took my passage in the French Government steamer, from Alexandria to Athens. Nothing of any interest signalized the voyage, unless I may except the passing off the headland of Cape Salmone, on the east end of Cyprus, mentioned in St. Paul's last voyage to Rome. We reached the shores of Greece in the night; and when, roused from my slumbers, I went on deck, I found we were at anchor in the harbour of the Piræus.

Among the miserable imitations by eastern powers, of usages that the western are just learning to throw off, is that of the establishment of quarantine. We had been put into confinement in Egypt, the very land of plague, for coming from Syria, where it was *said* that the disease was raging, although we had never encountered it, and we were now again imprisoned for coming from Egypt, although it was notorious that, at that time, there was not a single case in the country. My arrival in this glorious land was signalized by a week's solitary confinement in the Lazaretto of the Piræus.

Being at length emancipated from this " durance vile," I prepared to start for Athens, without a moment's loss of time. On issuing forth, and walking round the port, I found it wearing that look of awakening animation which then began to characterise Greece. Subjected for centuries to the desolating sway of Turkish despotism, her harbours empty, her fields uncultivated, she still wore, in general, that melancholy air of decay, so finely described by Lord Byron—

> " So coldly sweet—so deadly fair,
> We start—for soul is wanting there !"

Having, at length, after a long and exhausting struggle, succeeded, although with an alien upon the throne, in achieving independence, signs of life and hope were just beginning to appear. New buildings had sprung up; there was something of the bustle of traffic in the port, and of activity in the habits of the people. The introduction of western usages was commencing; and among other signs of improvement, was a rank of crazy-looking vehicles, intended to imitate our cabs; but, instead of a sullen fellow, in a dirty-drab mackintosh, the driver was a " gay and gilded Greek," in red jacket and cap, and white juxtonika, or more correctly, petticoats and leggings. Signalling one of these men, I entered his carriage, drove to the gate of the Lazaret, took in my baggage, and turned my back upon the Piræus, with a feeling of bitterness which not all its heroic associations—(I had enjoyed a view of the scene of the battle of Salamis for a *whole week*)—could succeed in driving away.

The Piræus is the port of Athens, from which it is five miles distant across the plain. It was connected with the city by the two parallel *long walls,* as they were called, built by Themistocles, and might thus be esteemed almost a part of the city itself. On the right of our road we had some traces of these famous bulwarks; and at the extremity of the long perspective towered the brown rock of the Acropolis, crowned with the wrecks of the Parthenon. The ranges of Hymettus and Pentelicus closed in the view. After about an hour's drive, during which time we swallowed as much dust as during any similar period in our remembrance, the cab rolled into the streets of modern Athens, and deposited us at the gate of a tolerably decent sort of French-looking hotel.

After luncheon, I sallied forth to see a little of the town, and also to make my way to the top of Mount Lycabettus, a lofty cone-shaped hill, towering up in the distance, and which, I expected, would afford an excellent view of the city and its environs. There are few places so utterly disappointing, or that so thoroughly demolish all preconceived ideas, as Modern Athens. Brimfull of classics and heroics, or striving to recall the fading traces of early lessons, as the case may be, the traveller hurries out of doors, and finds himself amid a maze of paltry streets and alleys, resembling the faubourgs of some second-rate French town, hastily run up among the tottering ruins of the old Turkish houses, which were infinitely more picturesque. Shabby *estaminets* and grog-houses—petty milliners' shops—stinking repositories for olives, salt-fish, and all unutterable things—or some English warehouse for cheese and pickles and bottled porter, kept by the inevitable Brown or Smith—compose the degrading picture. There is the same mean and mongrel look about the population, which seems, one cannot somehow help thinking, to comprise an unusual proportion of scamps ; and while everything betokens a transition from an old state of things to a new, it is by no means evident that the change is, for the present, an improvement. Advancing from the centre of the town to the suburb, the prospect brightens up a little; neat, well-built houses, with green blinds, and gardens, salute the eye, giving promise of a handsome city hereafter. But with all this, I could not help wishing that the capital of modern Greece had been fixed either at the Piræus, or in some other eligible place; and that the wrecks of the ancient city, clear of all obstruction, had been kept apart, as in a glass case, to receive the reverential homage of pilgrims from all parts of the civilized world.

With the feeling of disappointment produced by these incongruities, I found myself at last clear of the city, and at the foot

of Lycabettus, and mounted its steep ascent by a path, winding
among odoriferous shrubs.   At every step the view became more
expansive and glorious, and the panorama of classic localities and
mountain scenery more striking.

Seated on a fragment of rock, I beheld beneath me, opening
to the sea upon the south, the plain of Attica, surrounded by its
sheltering mountains.   Immediately beneath was a dark, dense
wood, of grey olives, indicating the site of the Academy where
Plato walked with his disciples.   This extended nearly up to
the city, which requires a more detailed description, and this will,
I hope, be rendered intelligible by means of the accompanying
engraving.

Nothing can be more striking, or more happily chosen, than
is the site of Athens.   In the centre of the picture rises the
oblong rock of the Acropolis, its crags of dark brown and grey
surmounted by walls, and crowned with the ruins of the most
splendid temples in the world.   The larger mass is that of the
Parthenon,—the roof and central pillars gone, but immortal even
in ruin.   To the right is seen the small temple of the Erechtheum ;
and near this spot stood on its pediment, in the days of Athenian
splendour, the colossal statue of Minerva, then towering sublime,
a sea-mark for the distant mariner, but which has long since
been thrown down from its pedestal, and lost in unrecognisable
fragments.   Terminating the craggy hill upon the right, are the
remains of the Propylea, or entrance gateway, over which is a
lofty brown tower, erected during the middle ages, when the
Acropolis was turned into a fortress.

Just under this celebrated rock is seen a long, rugged slope,
culminating to a point,—to a Christian eye, the most memorable
spot in Athens ; for this is no other than Mars' Hill, where Paul
delivered his oration.   On a gentle swell of ground at its foot, is
seen the Temple of Theseus, the most perfect, though not the
most colossal of the Athenian temples.   Behind this is another
long and rocky ridge ; its sides may be seen cut into seats, and

here is that famous Pnyx, or rostrum, from which the orators delivered their spirit-stirring harangues. In the hollow between this and Mars' Hill was the Agora, or market-place, where Paul was disputing with the philosophers, when conducted before the council of the Areopagus. This was once the very heart of Athens, and decorated with splendid colonnades and statues; it is at present merely a pasturing-place for flocks. If we turn now to the ground on the left of the Acropolis, the most prominent object of antiquity is the colossal Temple of Jupiter, erected in the time of the Romans; just on the other side of which, in a deep hollow, flows unseen the scanty stream of the Ilissus. Close by the temple appears a little Gothic church, lately erected for the English Protestants; and thence the modern city, crouching at the foot of the Acropolis, bends round as far as the Temple of Theseus, and to the edge of the olive-groves of the Academy.

The whole of the objects described were enclosed within the walls of ancient Athens, which extended as far as the foot of the mountain upon which we are standing. If every rood of this comparatively narrow circle is memorable, the same may be said of the distant landscape which forms the background of the picture.

Almost in a line with the Temple of Theseus is seen the chief port of the Piræus, with which Athens was connected, as before observed, by a double line of wall; and thus likened to a ship moored by two cables. It was on the rocky swell of ground to the right of the Piræus, that Xerxes sat to survey the battle of Salamis. Just beyond is seen the little island of Psyttalea, where he posted a body of Persians, to cut off the Greeks, who, as he expected, would retreat thither after their defeat; but where those Persians themselves were afterwards massacred by their conquerors. The Grecian ships awaited the attack of the Persians, who advanced from Phaleron, near the bottom of the gulf, at which point, from the want of space, the latter were unable to surround them with their more numerous fleet; and the engagement took place in the narrow channel between the

Piræus and the Island of Salamis, which extends its pointed peaks along the background. It was hence that the whole population of Athens, having taken refuge there on the approach of Xerxes, after he had taken and ravaged the Acropolis, witnessed, with feelings of which we can form but a faint idea, the issue of a conflict that was to be followed either by deliverance or death.

In the enjoyment of such a scene as this,—no less striking in picturesque beauty than memorable in historical associations,— it was not difficult to overlook the patchwork and incongruity with which it has become disfigured. Jerusalem excepted, there is no city on earth so interesting as Athens. If, in the former, every spot recalls to us some event memorable in sacred history, some incident dear to us in connexion with the Founder of our religion,—the latter can boast of having once concentrated within its small area all the glory and the pride of human intellect,—of leaving behind her the priceless treasures of lite- rature and art, in works and monuments which have supplied models to the world, and heroic memories which have tended to enkindle the spirit of freedom in the breasts of all succeeding generations.

It was the height of the sickly season at Athens, and most of the Europeans were " down " with fever. The air of the Attic plain in autumn is heavy and unwholesome, and during the day I found the heat exceedingly oppressive and relaxing. But the nights were glorious; the air then cooled by the sea breeze, restored the wasted energies of the exhausted frame, while the moon, being nearly at the full, left little cause for regret, that the hours of direct sunlight had passed.

On one of these nights, I wended my way from the hotel, through the streets of the town, towards Mars' Hill. The cafés and the wine-shops were full of domino players and gamblers; while the twanging of musical instruments, and the sound of voices, burst forth on all sides, showing that the volatile Greeks had lost nothing of that hereditary levity and love of amusement, which has so long distinguished them from their grave neighbours the Turks. The sound of merriment gradually died away as I left the streets behind, and ascended the solitary pathway, which, passing between the world-famed Hill and the Acropolis, leads up to the summit of the latter. Here I turned off to the right, and passing across the vacant site of the Agora, found myself in a few moments at the foot of a flight of steps, cut deeply in the stony side of the hill. At the top of these steps, and also hewn in the rock, is a level platform, with a stone bench around it; steps, bench, and all, picturesquely corroded by the tooth of time, but yet plainly indicating their original destination. By those steps, Paul had been led up from the Agora, or market-place below, where he was disputing with the Epicureans and Stoics. On that bench sat the Council of Areopagus, before whom he was summoned; grouped on the rocks around, were the listening philosophers, with doubt and derision on their countenances; and on that platform undoubtedly stood the Apostle himself, while he delivered to them his memorable oration.

The place was quite solitary; only a few goats browsing quietly about the Agora below. It was almost startling to find oneself alone, and seated on such a spot. The moon rising over the lofty crags of the Acropolis and the wrecks of the Propylea, shone brightly upon the rocky platform, defining, in the most telling manner, its every chink and crevice. The Agora was sunk in the shadow cast from the Acropolis. Everything around in the immediate neighbourhood was still and solemn; but lights gleamed in the windows of the town below, and strains of revelry rose from it fitfully, and died away again. The Gulf of Salamis was silvered over, and the dark grove of the Academy and the encircling mountains loomed faintly in the distant moonlight.

There is no spot about the identity of which there can be less doubt than this, and in none, perhaps, is so little effort required to figure the minutest details of the incident connected with it.

Paul had just landed at the Piræus on his arrival from Berea,
and after passing through the careless crowd thronging the
long connecting road, had entered the city by its seaward gate.
Athens, although she had then lost her political independence,
and become subject to Rome, yet retained the magnificent
monuments for which she had become renowned; but these were
all of them connected with that polytheism which, undermined
and tottering as it was, had been carried to such a pitch, that it
was proverbially said, "it was easier in Athens to find a god
than a man." On all sides arose temples and votive altars, with
their crowds of worshippers; "the whole city seemed given up to
idolatry." Though the great masters of the schools were departed, the porticos of the market-place were still the resort of the
philosophers; while everywhere swarmed the volatile and lively
populace, who "spent all their time in nothing else but either to
tell or to hear some new thing." The spirit of the Apostle was
stirred within him—he mingled in this restless throng, and began
to preach Christ to a curious and eager auditory. While thus
engaged, he encountered some of the Epicureans and Stoics.
"What will this babbler say?" demanded some. "He seemeth
to be a setter forth of strange gods," was the derisive reply of
others. They then hurried him up the stone flight of steps to
the summit of Mars' Hill, where the council of Areopagus were
at the time in session.

With eager curiosity, not unmingled with a shade of contempt,
they then demanded of the Apostle, "May we know what this
new doctrine whereof thou speakest is?" It was now that Paul,
"standing in the midst of the Hill," and pointing, as he spoke,
to the lofty temples of the Acropolis, shining with gold and silver,
and the great statue of Minerva, arrayed in all but superhuman
beauty, which towered above their heads; declared to them, for
the first time, the God "who dwelleth not in temples made with
hands," nor "is like unto gold and silver, or stone graven by
art or man's device" as the vulgar weakly believed,—whose nature

The spot where Paul died.

and attributes all the speculations of their vaunted philosophy had failed to bring to light; a God unlike the passive deity of the Epicurean, indifferent to the fate of his own children, or the Pantheistic principle of the Stoics, in which the Creator is confounded with the creature in one crushing system of fatality—but one who is represented as a tender Father, "in whom we live, and move, and have our being,"—who sustains us during the present life, and will receive us in that which is to come. A doctrine so stupendous, yet so simple, might well startle the pride and prejudice of the philosophers. At the mention of the resurrection, "some mocked;" others, equally incredulous, but more courteous, promised the Apostle "to hear him again of this matter." This discourse, however, was not without its fruits, and in the conversion of Dionysius, one of the Areopagites, and others, was laid the foundation of the future Church in Athens.

Such was the momentous incident narrated by the evangelist, with all those graphic touches and local allusions which convey the most vivid impression of reality, here confirmed and heightened by the exact conformity of his narrative to every surrounding object.

A basket of Attic figs was placed among the more substantial ingredients of breakfast next morning, and fully maintained their ancient reputation. A more thorough exploration of the city than we had attempted the day before, was now proposed, and under the guidance of a Greek *valet de place*, we set out on what promised to be a delightful morning's work.

The view from Mount Lycabettus, already described, will give the reader as well, if not better than a map, an idea of the course we followed. Our guide first led us to the Temple of Theseus, the most perfect in preservation of all the Athenian monuments. This building, as we learn from Dr. Wordsworth, was commenced under the auspices of Cimon son of Miltiades, four years after the battle of Salamis, just before the occurrence of

which, it will be remembered, Xerxes destroyed the city. " It is
a singular circumstance, and well worthy of observation, that one
of the first acts of the Athenians, on their return to Athens, after
their temporary banishment to Salamis and Trœzen, was to
restore their national hero, Theseus, who had been exiled by their

TEMPLE OF THESEUS.

ancestors, to his own city.   His remains were brought by Cimon
from the island of Scyros, the scene of his banishment and death,
to this place; and as the Athenians were now beginning to erect
for themselves a new and magnificent city, and to adorn it with
public buildings of great splendour, they at the same time raised
for him this noble structure, in which he is buried as a man, and
worshipped as a god."   It might be heresy; but this building did
not appear to possess any striking grandeur; perhaps the Doric
order requires a larger scale to bring out effectively the majestic
character of its architecture.   It is now converted by the Greek
government into a museum of antiquities.

Our path was up the hollow valley, between Mars' Hill and an opposite ridge of rock, formerly comprised within the city, but now covered with flocks of goats. The place looked a mere wild mountain side, nor was there anything to indicate that it had ever been otherwise, until our guide led us to a portion of the rocky hill, hewn into a large area, and cut into ranges of steps.

This was the Pnyx, or place of public assembly for the people. Projecting from the centre is a platform with steps, called the Bema, from which the orators delivered those exciting harangues which "wielded at will that fierce democracy."

Nothing could have been more grand or inspiring than the scene around. In front, towered the Acropolis, with the gorgeous Parthenon, Mars' Hill, the Temple of Theseus, the Attic plain, and its defensive mountains. Behind was the Piræus, and the Gulf and Island of Salamis, objects to every Athenian mind invested with a train of patriotic associations which at once, inspired the orator, and furnished him with a continual supply of local allusions to enkindle or inflame the feelings of his auditors. But the spot where Pericles and Demosthenes, with the electric touch of enthusiasm, heretofore moved as one man those vast assemblies, is now entirely abandoned to the shepherd and his wandering flock.

It should be remarked that we have described the Bema as it was originally placed, higher up the hill, the present site not commanding a view of Salamis, this alteration having been made in the degenerate days of Athens. Under an altered state of things, it was no longer desirable to appeal too strongly to the patriotism of the people.

After visiting the prison of Socrates,—another traditional memento of the past, situated in the same line of cliffs,—we reached the base of the Acropolis, which we ascended by a pathway winding among the remains of walls and ruinous buildings. It is difficult, at the present day, to form any adequate idea of the glorious beauty of the place in its state of original perfection. Battered by cannon, encumbered by mediæval and Turkish edifices, it was, a short time ago, hardly recognisable ; but since Greece has become independent, the government has laboured with praiseworthy assiduity to collect the precious fragments of ancient art, and disencumbering them of rubbish, to replace them carefully in their former position, thus endeavouring to obtain for the Acropolis, and its edifices, some approximation, at least, to their original state. The value of such persevering labours, may, in some degree, be judged of by the accompanying view of the Propylea.

Let us, with Dr. Wordsworth, imagine ourselves at Athens, in the days of Pericles, and "joining the splendid procession of minstrels, priests, and victims, of horsemen and of chariots, which ascended to that place, at the quinquennial solemnity of the great Panathenæa. Aloft, above the heads of the train, the sacred Peplos, raised, and stretched like a sail upon a mast, waves in the air; it is variegated with an embroidered tissue of battles, of giants, and of gods; it will be carried to the temple of the Minerva Polias in the citadel, whose statue it is intended to adorn. In the bright season of summer, on the twenty-eighth day of the Athenian month Hecatombæon, let us mount with this procession to the western slope of the Acropolis. Toward the termination of its course, we are brought in front of a colossal fabric of white marble, which crowns the brow of the steep, and stretches itself from north to south, across the whole western front of the citadel, which is about one hundred and seventy feet in breadth.

" The centre of this fabric consists of a portico sixty feet broad, and formed of six fluted columns of the Doric order, raised upon four steps, and intersected by a road passing through the midst of the columns, which are thirty feet in height, and support a noble pediment. From this portico two wings project, about thirty feet to the west, each having three columns on the side nearest the portico in the centre.

" The architectural mouldings of the fabric glitter in the sun

The Propylæa.
Athens.

with brilliant tints of red and blue; in the centre, the coffers of its soffits are spangled with stars, and the antæ of the wings are fringed with an azure embroidery of ivy-leaf.

" We pass along the avenue, lying between the two central columns of the portico, and through a corridor leading from it, and formed by three Ionic columns on each hand, and are brought in front of five doors of bronze; the central one, which is the loftiest and broadest, being immediately before us.

" This structure, which we are describing, is the Propylea, or Vestibule of the Athenian citadel. It is built of Pentelic marble. In the year B. C. 437, it was commenced, and was completed by the architect, Muesicles, in five years from that time. Its termination, therefore, coincides very nearly with the commencement of the Peloponnesian war.

" After a short pause, in order to contemplate the objects round us, we turn to explore the gallery, adorned with the paintings of Polygnotus, in the left wing of the Propylea; and to visit the Temple of Victory on our right, which possesses four Ionic columns on its western, and four at its eastern end, thus being approached by two façades, and whose frieze is sculptured with figures of Persians and Greeks fighting on the plains of Marathon."

Such was the scene of architectural grandeur which then rose on the view of the great Apostle, a scene of which, even in its present fragmentary condition, some idea may be formed, by comparing the description with the actual representation of the spot. The flights of steps, by which the gorgeous procession advanced, appear half extricated from superincumbent rubbish; the central columns, with the great doorway, and one of the wings, may be distinctly made out. The Parthenon appears in the background. On the right hand, upon a lofty platform of masonry, stands the small, but elegant Temple of Victory, sur-mounted by a lofty tower, erected during the middle ages. The history of the temple is really curious. It was visited and described by early travellers, and then suddenly disappeared, so that no one was able to discover a trace of it until after the establishment of Grecian independence. On making research about the site, it was found that the Turks had taken down the building, to make way for some other object; but with so much care, that the stones having been collected and built up, it has now resumed, to a great degree, its original character of delicate and refined beauty.

Through this noble approach we enter the interior of the Athenian Acropolis, and the Parthenon and the Erectheum are at once before us. Of these edifices, I shall not, however, attempt a detailed description, since, to add anything to the volumes already written concerning them, without the aid of numerous illustrations, would be altogether useless   Suffice it to say, that in the prime expression of intellectual beauty, the Parthenon far surpasses any other ruin in the world.

The injury caused by the explosion of a Venetian shell, is in some measure being repaired by the labours of the Greek government, who are collecting and building up again the scattered fragments, as far as practicable.   Yet, although this sort of restoration may be more satisfactory to the architect, it can scarcely be so to the Archæologist; and it may be questioned, whether it does not proportionally impair that effect of ruined grandeur, which the accidents of time and warfare have rendered so unspeakably impressive.

Our afternoon's walk was through the town, to hunt out the few but exquisite fragments of Greek art, samples of what ancient Athens must have been in her perfection, at present embedded among the maze of wretched edifices which compose the modern city. Of these last, the most detestable is undoubtedly the palace of King Otho—of huge dimensions, and of workhouse-like contour—placed in a conspicuous position, where unhappily it cannot be got out of sight, but enters into and defaces every combination of the landscape. The reader will then, it is hoped, pardon the artist for having taken the liberty to leave this

abominable eyesore out of the different views. The gems of
Athenian art to which our attention was directed, the Tower of
the Winds, and Lanthorn of Demosthenes, are so well known, and
have been so often imitated in modern edifices, that we shall not
delineate them here. Leaving the boundaries of the recent
buildings, and the small Gothic Church erected by the English
for the celebration of the Protestant worship, we gained the open
ground beyond, and paused to take a parting glance at the
remaining magnificence of the ancient city.

Our seat was upon a bold foreground, composed of masses of
rock, half buried in wild flowers; and immediately beneath was
seen the scanty stream of the Ilissus, coming down from Mount
Hymettus, which, near this spot, is joined by the fountain
Callirhoe, the only spring at Athens. Wild as it may now
appear, all this space was formerly enclosed within the walls.
A few figures are crossing the stream, and ascending the bold ridge
of ground upon which, on a lofty terrace, are the stupendous ruins
of the temple of Jupiter Olympius. This building, we learn
from Dr. Wordsworth, was commenced by Pisistratus, and remained unfinished for six hundred years, becoming a byeword for
productions of literature, which had been left unfinished by
their original authors. Thus Plato's great philosophical work,
the Atlantis, of which, in the lively and fanciful language of
Plutarch, the portico and peristyle were erected by that philosopher, but to which the cotta and roof were never added, is
compared by the Chæronæan moralist to the structure of the
vast and unfinished Olympeum, which is now before our eyes.

Sixteen only, out of upwards of an hundred columns, once
composing this vast edifice, now remain, and, standing isolated
as they do, and of dimensions so prodigious as to seem the
work of superhuman power, the spectator cannot look up to
them without a feeling of awe. In one of the gaps between
the scattered columns of this mighty temple, is seen the slender
looking façade of the arch of Hadrian, so fragile as to excite

our wonder at its having outlived the ages that have hurled so
many mighty temples into ruin.   In the background, tower the
huge grey rocky spurs, or buttresses, of the Acropolis, inaccessible on this its eastern side, and surmounted by the golden-
tinted columns of the Parthenon.   This is, perhaps, the most
impressive, though not the most historical, view of the whole.

Our glance at Athens has necessarily been brief, and confined
to its general features, especially in reference to the more salient
and well-known incidents of its history.   One subject, however,
claims a few words, and that is, the present state of Christianity
here, where it was first preached by St. Paul.   The condition of
the Greek Church is, indeed, elsewhere in the Levant, sadly
degraded, displaying less of the vital spirit of the religion than
of the narrow-minded bigotry into which its profession has so
often degenerated, in times when the moral and political state of
a people have sunk to a low ebb.   The centuries of Turkish
misrule and oppression have still left their brand upon the
character of the Greeks, while their religion has received a corre-
sponding taint, and is in that unhealthy condition which must
exist where the education of the people has been neglected.
The exertions of Messrs. Hill and King, and their wives,
(American Missionaries,) in promoting especially the improvement of the Greek women, merit the highest encomium; and,
though temporarily interfered with by the narrow and timid
policy of the priesthood, it is to be hoped the impulse given will
not be lost, especially since Greece has now received the means
of gradually working out, through manifold difficulties, her own
political and social regeneration.

My time here having expired, I returned to the Piræus,
and finding a small boat about to cross the gulf to Corinth,
took my place on board of her, in the midst of a considerable
number of passengers, mostly of the peasant class, and at sunset
was sailing out of the harbour into the open gulf.   The tomb of
Themistocles was on the left, and the hill upon which Xerxes

Coomaswamy.

sat when he witnessed the discomfiture of his fleet, on the right, while the waters through which our barque was cutting her way were the same on which the Greek and Persian armaments had closed in deadly conflict. The long island of Salamis relieved dark against the western sky; and as we ran past with the flowing sail which these Greek boats always carry, heavy gusts of wind came down from between its serrated peaks, and made us roll uncomfortably in a heap to leeward. Wrapt in my cloak, I slept, like the rest, on deck; and, on awaking at early dawn, found that we were just running into the harbour of Cenchrea.

Cenchrea was formerly the port of Corinth, on the eastern side of the isthmus, and must have been a place of no small importance; it now consists merely of a few poor houses, in one of which—a wine-shop—we recruited ourselves with bread and eggs and a cup of coffee, and then hired horses to convey us across the isthmus to Corinth. It was at Cenchrea that St. Paul, or, as others contend, his companion, Aquila, "shaved himself, having a vow." About half-way across the isthmus, a beautiful retrospective view is obtained of the port and the Gulf of Athens. Here, also, the mighty rock of the Acrocorinthus, which had been our landmark as we approached the shore, now stood out before us with the most commanding grandeur, swelling up from the plain to an elevation of two thousand feet, and casting an immense shadow completely across the isthmus. The Acropolis of Athens—a mere molehill in comparison—is indebted to art for the perfection of beauty which it once presented; but here, it is Nature herself who has reared this stupendous citadel, over which the revolutions of ages pass powerless away. Nearly three thousand years have elapsed since this natural fortress was fixed upon, under the title of the Acrocorinthus, as the citadel of the city of Corinth, which grew up around its base.

As we pursued our way, we encountered files of peasantry, the men arrayed in the gay jacket and juxtonilla, or in rough sheepskin cloaks, and the women wearing a flat head-dress of white cotton, resembling that of the Roman females. Flocks of goats were browsing about the wild expanse of brown heath; but it was pleasant to see that Agriculture was reassuming her dominion, and that large stretches of bright green corn were extending around the little villages, rising from the ashes to which their predecessors had been reduced, during the war of independence.

Corinth owed its importance to its peculiar situation, commanding the remarkable isthmus which extends from the Saronic Gulf to the Corinthian. From the citadel of the Acrocorinthus, two long defensive walls enclosed the city, and connected it with its port upon the western gulf, called the Lechæum; while a road, as at the present day, communicated with Cenchrea and its harbour in the Saronic Gulf. Commanding thus the commerce of both the east and west, and also the passage from the north to the sonth of 'Greece, it naturally became proverbial for the opulence of its inhabitants, being surnamed the Wealthy. These advantages it retained long after the fall of Grecian independence. Destroyed by the Romans, it had been again rebuilt and colonised by them; and when St. Paul repaired thither from Athens, had become, to adopt the description of Milman, "the common emporium of the eastern and western divisions of the Roman empire, the Venice of the Old World, in whose streets the continued stream of commerce, either flowing from or towards the great capital of the world out of all the eastern territories, met and crossed." Its population, attracted by the pursuit of gain, was the most cosmopolitan in all Greece; toleration, or rather indifference to religious systems, prevailed, the minds of the citizens being absorbed in the eager pursuit of gain, and the unbridled appetite for pleasure. It was here, as elsewhere, the fanaticism of the Jews that persisted in dragging the Apostle before the civil authorities of the place. They hurried him to the tribunal of Gallio, the Roman proconsul, and who, in turn, drove them contemptuously away;—one of

The Rock of Tarascon

those scenes in the Acts of the Apostles stamped with so vivid and lifelike a character that, in reading, we seem transported into the very midst of the actors. Here Paul sojourned for a considerable time, and from hence he addressed his Second Epistle to the Thessalonians. The universal depravity of morals at Corinth may be gathered from the tenour of his two epistles, afterwards written to the converts he had made in that city.

On reaching the site of Corinth, and looking around, there was nothing to delay our progress for a single hour. The town had been burnt during the war with the Turks, and a few mean buildings were just beginning to lift up their heads among the blackened ruins. The only remains of former splendour were a few Doric columns, in very bad style, forming part of a temple. We put up the horses at a small wine-house, and, taking a guide, set off to ascend the Acrocorinthus, which we found to be a more fatiguing task than we had anticipated. The eastern side of the rock being absolutely inaccessible, the path is up the western side, and passes through different gateways, until it reaches the principal inclosure, which is of very considerable extent, formerly comprising some mosques and a small town, all fallen into ruin. Recruiting ourselves with a draught from the cold and limpid fountain of Pirene, we stood, at length, upon the topmost crest.

The view was so strikingly magnificent, as amply to repay the toil of the ascent. The first object that attracted our attention was the irregular summit of the rock itself, defended by an ancient wall, which follows all its indentations and hollows. From this bulwark the eye plunges sheer down eighteen hundred feet upon the isthmus below, connecting together the two gulfs. That on the right, the Saronic, is open, and expands towards its mouth, dotted over with islands, among which that of Salamis is strikingly conspicuous, and beyond, in the clear atmosphere, may be discerned the Acropolis of Athens, backed by the lofty range of Hymettus.

The other gulf, the Corinthian, is here more narrow, resembling
a lake hemmed in by lofty mountains, but gradually opening to
the westward, where the snowy summit of Parnassus is seen, afar
off, towering above the rugged fastnesses of Delphi. The isthmus
itself, the peculiar feature of the scene, is about five miles broad,
partly level, and partly hilly; a defensive wall, thrown down,
and built up again in different ages, once ran across it; and a canal
was also commenced in the time of Nero: traces of both these
works still remain.

Like so many other scenes in Greece, the view from the
Acrocorinthus is grand, but mournful. The sea is still azure, as
of old; the mountains still rise in all their flowing beauty of
outline and purple loveliness of colour; but where are the ships
that crowded the two harbours, from the eastern and western
seas; the busy thousands, who might once have been seen toiling,
emmet-like, across the Isthmus, or repairing to its celebrated
games; the shining city with its swarming suburbs; the
numerous villages which dotted the highly cultivated plain?
All this has passed away, and there is only just that sprinkling
of life that seems rather to deepen than relieve the melancholy of
the vast and vacant area which lies outstretched in corpse-like
stillness below.

The Acrocorinthus comprising nearly all that is interesting in
this locality, there was nothing left after descending from it, but
to refresh ourselves, and continue our route. We took the road
around the head of the gulf, and passing the half-obliterated
remains of the amphitheatre, reached a little port or shelter for
boats, romantically situated near some hot springs, and commanding a splendid view of the rock.

A small vessel was leaving for Patras, our passage soon taken,
and at sunset we were sailing down the gulf. The breeze was
prosperous, and the night so soft and mild, that it was far
pleasanter to sleep on deck wrapped up in a mantle, than encounter the closeness of the cabin. Next day we were abreast

of the magnificent ranges of Delphi, surmounted by the snow-capped crest of Parnassus. Anchoring at Vostizza the next morning, our bark had reached the mouth of the gulf; and Lepanto rising on its rock, formed a striking object; recalling the famous sea-fight between the Turks and Christians, in which Cervantes was taken prisoner.

Shortly afterwards we landed on the quay at Patras. The view, as we approached, was characteristic of the present state of Greece. Under the extensive walls of a mediæval chateau, were clustered a range of buildings, some of them mere hovels, but others which, by their superior construction, betokened increasing commerce and wealth. There was a considerable quantity of craft in the roads, and much bustle on the pier; while groups of idlers flaunting in jacket and juxtonilla, or wrapped in shaggy capotes, were speculating upon the character of the new arrivals.

At Smyrna one hears of nothing but figs; at Patras, the souls of the inhabitants are buried in currants, which are grown all round the neighbourhood. Unless the traveller is interested in this subject, there is absolutely nothing else except the castle, of any interest, either ancient or modern.

Yet there is one event of interest, connected with the place; it is traditionally believed that here St. Andrew suffered martyrdom. The fisherman of Bethsaida, after labouring in Scythia, and on the remote borders of the Euxine Sea, and planting the Gospel in Byzantium, came by way of Thrace and the northern parts of Greece to Patræ, then the maritime capital of Achaia, where Ægeas was then proconsul. Here he laboured with such effect that multitudes embraced the new religion; even the wife and brother of the proconsul being among the converts. Enraged at this defection, and having laboured in vain to induce the Apostle to discontinue his teaching, Ægeas caused him to be crucified, by attaching his body to the cross with ropes instead of nails. He hung thus two days in lingering agony before he expired. The cross upon which he was crucified is said to have been in the form of the letter X, hence usually known by the name of St. Andrew's Cross. His body was taken down, and after being embalmed, was honourably interred by a wealthy lady.

"As for that report of Gregory, Bishop of Tours," says Dr. Cave, " that on the anniversary day of his martyrdom there was wont to flow from St. Andrew's tomb a most fragrant and precious oil, which, according to its quantity, denoted the scarceness or plenty of the following year; and that the sick being anointed with oil, were restored to their former health,— I leave to the reader's discretion to believe what he please of it. The body of the martyr was afterwards removed to Constantinople by Constantine the Great, and buried in the great church which he had built to the honour of the Apostles; which being taken down some hundred years after, by Justinian the emperor, in order to its reparation, the body was found in a wooden coffin, and again reposed in its proper place."

CHAPTER IV.

SOME years after my disappointment at not seeing Jerusalem, though almost within a day's walk of it, I found myself, by one of those singular chances that occur but rarely in life, actually on the way a second time performing a pilgrimage to that city.

My route this time was through Germany and the Danubian principalities, then rife with rumours even more alarming than those of war.

To run with one's eyes open into a hot-bed of "*the plague*," even the boldest must admit to be an act of somewhat culpable rashness; and yet that name of terror was sounding in our ears all the way to Constantinople. Everybody affirmed that it was still raging at Stamboul, and, what was really alarming, in the European quarter of the city, where we should necessarily have to put up. Not even the spectacle of indescribable splendour which opened around us as we anchored in the port of Constantinople could render us insensible to the obvious peril; and as we stood on the deck of the steamer, and looked upon the dense and dirty population of Galata, through which we were destined to elbow our way, we felt half-disposed to follow the example of a certain traveller, who was so enraptured with the view of the city from the water, that he would on no account weaken his impression by any rash investigation of its interior.

Overcoming this craven reluctance, we got into a caïque, and

were deposited upon the quay with our goods, which were built
up like a wagon-load upon the shoulders of a stout Turkish
porter; and pushing through the filthy street, and filthier population, from whom we endeavoured to keep clear, we ascended
to the boarding-house of Madame Babiani at Pera. The good
lady came out to receive us,—assured us that the plague was
still lingering,—enumerated certain dismal and recent casualties
in her immediate vicinity,—and urged us to submit to a pre-
cautionary process of fumigation. Accordingly, we stepped
into a sort of watch-box, at the bottom of which were bars to
stand on, and under them a pan of burning charcoal, together
with some disinfecting odour, with which, the door being closed,
we were more than half suffocated. On walking up-stairs, and
looking out of the window, we found the situation, if hazardous,
was at all events "convenient" to a neighbouring cemetery,
which had already received very numerous and recent additions,
as we perceived from the fresh clods which seemed scarcely to
conceal their foul and festering burden. A still more dismal
evidence was immediately beneath us. In the court of an
unfinished house cowered the pale wrecks of a family, from
which the scourge had swept away more than half its members,
the rest looking fearfully wan and attenuated, and as though
their recovery were hopeless. They were put into the strictest
quarantine, and appeared entirely abandoned to their miserable
fate. When we went forth into the street we were furnished
with sticks, to keep at a respectful distance any reckless passenger
with whom we might otherwise come in contact; but there was
little occasion to use them; every man seemed alarmed at the
approach of his fellow, closely hugging the opposite wall, or, as
it might be, darting nervously into the middle of the narrow
causeway. A feeling of terror seemed to brood over the plague-
haunted neighbourhood of Pera.

And thus it continued for some days after our arrival. It was
impossible to throw off the contagious melancholy with which

every one was more or less infected. At dinner, with the inmates of the boarding-house, indeed, we contrived to be gay, and keep one another in countenance. We passed round the Greek wine, and affected to laugh at our predicament; but, with our retiring to rest would come nightmare visions of horrible ulcers and sores, and pains intolerable—of a death among indifferent strangers, "who would bring your coffin," as some one says, "as unconcernedly as your breakfast,"—and a carnival feast over our ill-buried bodies by the hungry dogs of the quarter, which made their loathsome haunt in the contiguous cemetery, and kept up half the night what might well seem, in our nervous mood, a howling for the possession of our remains.

Day after day we heard of some Frank physician who had paid with his life the forfeit of coming rashly into contact with his patients. But one of them, a Doctor Bulard, seemed to bear a charmed life. He had intently devoted himself to studying the disease, and alleviating the woes of those afflicted with it during the recent plague at Smyrna, and had received the thanks of the public authorities for his exertions. Whether he had some secret for warding off its deadly contagion, or had no predisposition to take it, or whether he had made a compact with the Evil One, no one seemed to have a very clear idea; one thing was certain—he went fearlessly into the midst of danger wherever his services were required. Yet he could hardly have been a non-contagionist, for to him Constantinople owes the first establishment of a quarantine; a concession he obtained of the late Sultan, whose liberal ideas and numerous innovations, while they procured him the respect of the Europeans, caused him to be looked upon with suspicion and dislike by orthodox Moslems. A building was also appointed him for the purpose of a plague hospital, the "Tower of Leander," standing upon a small island in the midst of the rapid current of the Bosphorus, midway between Europe and Asia. To this spot I occasionally repaired with the doctor, and never shall forget the frightful

appearance of certain of his patients, as they were carried from
the boats into the lazar-house appointed for them.

This first establishment of a quarantine at Constantinople is
remarkable for one thing,—its practical infringement of the old
Turkish principle of fatalism. The Moslems are no metaphy-
sicians, nor do they puzzle themselves about reconciling liberty
and necessity. To them all things are equally from God,—and
with this wholesome conviction they have ever displayed the
utmost practical resignation to his will, and esteem it a flying in
the face of Providence to seek to ward off any of its visitations.
This, combined with their natural inertia, lent wings to the
pestilence, instead of staying its frightful course. As no sort
of precaution was observed in attending the sick, entire families,
in their fearless self-devotion, were successively carried to the
cemetery. Their infected garments, instead of being destroyed,
were taken to the bazaar, and sold; the purchasers, in their
turn, became victims; and thus the disease passed on from one
to another, until, like the raging fires that so frequently sweep
over the hills of the city, it found nothing more to feed upon.

To combat this infatuation was no easy task for the Sultan.
It was necessary to put forth a long and curious ordinance, in
which all the resources of casuistry were employed in proving to
the unwilling Moslems, that to take precautions against the
evils that Providence allows, is not irreconcilable with a true
submission to its will; and that the religion of the Koran was
neither advanced nor recommended by this wholesale and
voluntary extermination of its professors. The Turks were
silenced, but not satisfied; they obeyed, but shook their heads,
with a feeling, no doubt instinctive, that the introduction of
a new system of ideas would be the death-blow of the old; and
that the wedge of innovation once fairly introduced, the whole
fabric of the Koran would ere long totter to its foundations.

But to return. The sense of danger is soon blunted by expo-
sure to it—we began to tire of this strict precaution; time was,

moreover, slipping away, and Stamboul had yet to be explored. One fine morning, we determined to cross the harbour which separates the European from the Turkish quarters. The sun shone out so brightly upon the rippling waters and the flitting sails that animated them, the mosques and minarets glittered so sharply against the sunny sky, the thousand and one objects that make up the fascinations of this unequalled scene were all so lustrously relieved—such was the multitude of careless passengers which poured over the bridge in seemingly endless file, like that of Mirza, that we could hardly realize the fact of " the pestilence which walketh in darkness " having so recently carried off its thousands of victims, and being probably even now lurking in the closer recesses of the city. Precaution was gradually relaxed—our sticks were put less and less into requisition—we rubbed first against one and then against another, and, the ice being once broken, in a few moments plunged recklessly into the thick of the motley population.

Following the living stream through a succession of narrow streets, picturesque with mosques and fountains, we soon arrived at the bazaar. This, like that of Damascus, already described, is the gathering-place of all the moving population—the seat of traffic, and the depôt of wealth—the centre of flying rumours, and the rendezvous of secret conspiracies. To form an idea of its appearance, imagine a whole quarter of the city walled round and *covered in;* a maze of narrow alleys of one story high, with open shops below and vaulted roof above—no light being admitted upon the cool and dusky passages beneath but what falls in fitful rays through certain apertures and domes therein. No wheel carriages can enter; a few laden camels or horses pass along the principal avenue, but the remainder is impenetrable to all but pedestrians, of whom the crowd is immense, and the murmur incessant. After what one has heard of the seclusion of the oriental women, the number met with is perfectly startling. Muffled to the eyes in their white *yashmaks,* or veils, enveloped in a loose robe, and shuffling rather than walking along in large boots of yellow leather—looking one through with their dark lustrous eyes—they pass boldly along, preceded by a male servant or black female slave, and are heard chaffering and bargaining in those avenues particularly devoted to their wants and pleasures. For them the shawl or embroidery bazaars put forth their brilliant display, the terror of many an eastern husband—the shoe bazaar exposes its heaps of vermilion shoes and yellow boots, or delicate pointed slippers of every colour, in cloth and velvet, gilt and embroidered with exquisite richness and taste—or the confectionery bazaar, its delicious *kaimac*, and other tempting delicacies and sweetmeats, the consumption of which in the harems of the wealthy is almost incredible. These are among the most striking and frequented of these intricate passages; but every branch of trade has a separate one. The Bezenstein is the depôt of jewellery; of little external show, and of which the valuables are all concealed, and carefully guarded in recessed chambers, opened only to customers. The treasure thus locked up is said to be of immense value. Then there is the book and paper bazaar, to the eye dullest of all, with no " last reviews," or " illustrated novelties." The tempting tobacco and spice bazaars are redolent of musk and aromatic odours, which almost overcome the sense with a feeling of languid luxury. None, however, is so strikingly picturesque as the Tcharchi, or armoury bazaar. It is a heavy, gloomy structure, full of effects in which a Rembrandt would revel; shut in by ponderous doors, carefully closed at night, but flung open during the day, and admitting glimpses into the curious maze of surrounding vaults and columns, and the endless crowd that circulates among them. Here may be seen displayed all sorts of old armour and weapons, so marvellously antiquated and fantastic, that in looking at them, one seems carried back to the romantic ages, and to the feats of half-fabulous warriors; or to scenes of the Crusades, and the palmy days of Ottoman prowess, when their advancing armies were the terror of the West. Here is the curved scimitar and crescent-bearing buckler which Saladin might have worn, the coat of mail and heavy sabre of the Christian knight, light spears which may have glittered of old in the van of the Turkish cavalry, and weapons which were once wielded by the terrible janissaries. Here are pistols with richly embossed silver handles, in gorgeous holsters; and long-barrelled guns inlaid with pearl, and richly decorated in arabesque—rather ornamental to a collection than formidable to an enemy; while intermingled with these weapons of a bygone warfare, are others of more modern construction and of far greater efficiency. Ornamented belts and sashes, leopard skins frayed and worn half bare, housings and trappings—faded, but gorgeous, and a variety of nameless articles, make up the heterogeneous mass, slung from the walls, or piled up on the benches in picturesque confusion. Half hidden among the musty accumulation appear the grave and turbaned vendors, as antiquated as the rest of the collection; pipe in hand, they recline in dreamy lethargy, from which they are only to be roused by the arrival of some European traveller with his wily dragoman, upon whom all eyes are instantly turned with a twinkle of satisfaction, and every effort made to secure his custom, as a god-send not to be slighted.

The old-clothes bazaar—the Monmouth Street of Constantinople—with its array of second-hand caftans, jackets, and "very spacious breeches," which might not improbably have adorned some recent victims of the plague, had a fusty, ominous look about it, that gave us some uneasy feelings as to the possible result of our rash excursion. But it was too late: we had by this time shouldered half the inhabitants of Stamboul. No one could have divined the recent ravages caused by the pestilence, from the crowd in the bazaar: it may be compared with Constantinople itself, to which, as the heart of the sinking Turkish empire, while the population of the provinces is rapidly decreasing, there is a continual influx of fresh life-blood—a succession of new comers. Thus, while the remoter quarters of this great city are gradually thinned by plague and fire, while whole spaces within the walls are assuming the appearance of suburban villages, the bazaar itself exhibits no diminution of its customary throng of busy vendors, and purchasers, and idle loungers.

We returned to our quarters in Pera without, as the result proved, having contracted any taint, but were subjected by our nervous landlady to a double measure of the customary fumigation. The plague gradually disappeared; and whether it be contagious or not, this much at least is certain, that since the establishment of a quarantine, this fearful scourge, for which the inhabitants looked almost as regularly as the seasons, has never again made its appearance in the City of the Sultan.

In the evening of a lovely day, I embarked on board the Austrian steamer, bound for Beyrout, which, passing Seraglio Point, was soon in the open sea of Marmora. As the incomparable panorama of Constantinople faded gradually from view, I looked round to scrutinise the appearance of my fellow-travellers. First-cabin passengers, as it happened, there were none, myself excepted, but there were several of the second-class, while a large company of Turks had taken their passage on deck. Among the second-class passengers, I was struck with the appearance of one, whose quaint, old-fashioned costume strikingly contrasted with the flowing oriental garments around her. This was a lady "of a certain age," small and slight in figure, rather plain in countenance. She was dressed in a gown of grey serge, of pilgrim-like plainness of fashion, and wore a broad-brimmed straw hat, large enough to overshadow her whole person. Her manner, though observant, was remarkably quiet and retiring, and it was only now and then, when excited by conversation, that the kindling of her dark eye betrayed the fund of enthusiasm which formed the preponderating element of her character. I afterwards ascertained that her name was Ida Pfeiffer, that she had long resided in Vienna, and that having settled her children, she had determined to set off on a pilgrimage to the Holy Land, alone and unprotected, unless by such chance cavaliers as she might happen to encounter upon the road. She had placed herself, for the nonce, under the guardianship of an old monk, who was going to his convent in Palestine. To reach Jerusalem was, of course, her first object, as it was also my own. I promised, on landing at Beyrout, to assist her as far as possible, or, if she thought fit to accompany me, to take her under my own charge; an offer which she gladly accepted, although I was not long in discovering that, with her remarkable energy and endurance, she was perfectly independent of any adventitious succour.

The deck of the vessel was much encumbered by sundry groups of Turks and Persians, who had established themselves with their carpets and chibouques, so as to leave but little gangway for the movements of those more given to locomotion. Their picturesque appearance, however, fully indemnified us for this inconvenience. The first sight that had struck me on going on board, was a venerable white-bearded Turk, quietly going through his devotions with the customary postures and prostrations, amidst all the noise and confusion incident to a ship's clearance. This noble looking old fellow had, as we afterwards found, been buying several articles of European manufacture in the bazaars of Constantinople, and seemed to take a pride in displaying them to the gaze of his Christian fellow-passengers, upon whom he evidently looked with an eye of benevolent complacency. One morning, when we were all assembled upon deck, and standing around him, he commenced preparations for his noonday repast. First producing his little stock of provisions, consisting of Syrian cheese, coarse bread, and onions, he next carefully shredded them together, forming a sort of salad; he then gravely arose, and going to a large box which contained his store of goods and chattels, with an indescribable air of quiet self-gratulation he drew forth, by its one handle, a white earthenware vessel, whose capacious form had no doubt attracted his

K

attention as seeming admirably suited to the various requirements of his travelling *cuisine*, but which, suffice it to say, in its
original habitat, is generally kept in a state of decorous concealment. Into this, promoted at once to the dignity of a tureen,
he poured his miscellaneous collection of comestibles, adding
a little oil, salt, and pepper, then stirred up the mess, and taking
a wooden spoon, sat down and looked around upon us with a
smile of triumph, as if to announce that personally he was
neither uninitiated into the usages of European life, nor indis-
posed to adopt them. Great then was his discomfiture at the
general explosion of laughter which on all sides simultaneously
broke forth. He looked wildly round from one to another to
glean, if possible, some solution of the painful mystery, but his
comical expression of distress only added to the general hilarity.
Some of the spectators, unable to restrain their immoderate
delight, danced convulsively about the deck, as if demented;
at the same time clapping their hands to their sides, seemingly
apprehensive for their capabilities of resistance; until, exhausted
by these involuntary exertions, they sank powerless upon the
benches; yet ever and anon giving vent to their still excited
feelings, by snorting out fresh and uncontrollable guffaws. The
poor old man at length subsided into a state of quiet resignation,
but he never afterwards produced the unfortunate utensil, which
had given rise to such outrageous, and to him unaccountable
ebullitions of mirth.

We passed over the Sea of Marmora during the night, and
early in the morning entered the Strait of the Dardanelles, near
Lampsacus, where Xerxes built the bridge of boats, to transfer
his innumerable hosts from Asia into Europe. We remained
a short time between the castles which command it, and soon
after reached the point from whence it opens into the extensive
sea which we had just crossed.

As we issued out of the mouth of the Hellespont, on our left
were the low plains of the Troad, marked by the Tumulus of

Achilles, on a rising mound, overlooking the watery expanse. On the right was Tenedos, and far beyond, over the rocky island of Imbros, was seen the still loftier crest of distant Samothracia. This was a point of great interest, for directly opposite, on the Asian shore, the massive ruins of Alexandrian Troas peeped out from among a wild overgrowth of woods, above the low ground, in which are the remains of its port. It

TROAS.

was at Troas that St. Paul first embarked for the European shores, being incited to do so by a vision, in which " a man of Macedonia prayed him, saying, Come over and help us," whence he " assuredly gathered, that the Lord had called him to preach the Gospel unto them. Therefore, loosing from Troas," he continues, " we came with a straight course to Samothracia, and the next day to Neapolis," where, landing on the coast of Macedonia, he repaired to Philippi. Thus the scene of his embarkation, and even the course of his voyage, were visible at the same moment. It was at this place also he landed on his return from Greece ; several of his friends having gone before to meet him. From hence, it would appear, he went alone on foot, the nearer way to Assos, passing probably amidst its splendid tombs ; while Luke and the rest of the company proceeded thither, like ourselves, by ship. Running down the coast some twenty miles further, we suddenly turned from the open sea,

round Lesbos, a lofty headland, into the beautiful Gulf of
Mitylene, the waters of which were tranquil as a lake; and

TOMB AT ASSOS.

before long, the lofty Acropolis of Assos rose towering from the
shore, the deep Gulf of Adramyttium receding into distant
perspective.

ASSOS FROM THE SEA.

Here Paul's friends took him on board, and continued their
voyage to the southward, by the same course which we ourselves
were now steering. The scenery of the Strait of Lesbos at this
point is exquisitely beautiful. On one side of the lake-like
channel is the shore of Asia; on the other, the romantic island

of Mitylene, with the white town scattered on the side of a lofty serrated mountain hung with woods; while a bold tongue of land, projecting into the sea, is covered by an ancient fortress. At Mitylene, Paul's ship appears to have remained a short time, and thence to have sailed direct for Chios, leaving, to the left, the mouth of the Gulf of Smyrna, into which our vessel now turned; and here for a while we left the track of the great Apostle, which we had followed, New Testament in hand, and that indicating all the points of the route with the minuteness and accuracy of a guide-book.

Smyrna is the paradise of Mediterranean midshipmen, and there are few visitors that do not retain a most pleasurable recollection of its gay and hospitable European inhabitants; who, by frequent intermarriages, have come to be like one great family, whose various members vie with one another in showing the most cordial attention to the stranger. Here, too, the traveller in coming from Europe first feels that he is in the East— the land of his dreams: in the voluptuous air of soft Ionia—the novel vegetation—the palm, loveliest of trees, gently waving in the perfumed air—the clustering fig and pomegranate — the camel, symbol of the desert, here seen for the first time,—all strike upon his senses with an intoxication of novelty impossible to describe.

But Smyrna has graver associations than these: nowhere comes home more solemnly the warning, "that in the midst of life we are in death." It were, as Dr. Cave observes, "an ill-natured" (shall we say rather, impious) "interpretation of the actions of Divine Providence, to attribute the calamities that have befallen this city to the displeasure of Heaven,—yet, as described by a contemporary of St. Polycarp, by plague, fire, and earthquakes, Smyrna, before one of the glories and ornaments of Asia, was turned into rubbish and ashes, its stately houses overturned, its temples ruined." Such, even to the present day, seems to be the inalienable portion of this gay and thoughtless city, for nowhere is the recurrence of these accidents more frequent.

One of the most serious of these visitations had not long since occurred. The plague had swept off its thousands, and a tremendous fire raging unchecked among the wooden houses and narrow streets, had turned whole quarters of the city into heaps of blackened ashes. I had introductions to the American missionaries, and walked with two of them to see the Stadium—hallowed as the place of martyrdom of the venerable Polycarp. Our footsteps echoed among the burnt and blackened walls of silent streets, with their abandoned homes, prostrate mosques, and dried-up fountains, wrecks of the recent conflagration, which had raged as far as rage it could, up to the very fort of the lofty hill crowned by the ruins of the castle, and separated from the city by a girdle of gloomy cemeteries.

Here have been deposited the mortal remains of countless generations of the departed Greek and Roman, Saracen and Turk—the spoiler from the wild steppes of Inner Asia, and the European merchant from the western mart : here, too, had been but recently conveyed by thousands the victims of the plague; the ground yet heaved with its foul and fearful burden. One shrunk with loathing and with dread from the scarce-covered graves, among which the furtive lizard, and the lean and savage dog, were seen to glide and burrow in their loathsome and peculiar haunt. A forest of cypress, of gigantic growth—that gloomy tree,

> " Whose branch and leaf
> Seem stamp'd with an eternal grief,"

shrouded with its dense dark shadows the myriads of whited sepulchres and turban-headed tombstones; some gilt and fresh—memorials of yesterday's sorrow; others broken and yawning, with inscriptions faded as the memory of those to whom they were erected. These tall and mystic cones, like funeral plumes, stood silent in the sultry heat of noon, or were but momentarily

Smyrna.

swept into a low and solemn rustle by the fitful breeze in its passage from the mountains across the slumbering waters of the gulf.

Through this gloomy approach we reached the foot of the bare, brown mountain, and slowly ascended it to the castle. Saracenic walls, long since dismantled, straggle picturesquely about the crest of the eminence; fragments of Greek, and Roman, and Byzantine date, built into them, tell of successive revolutions; while the half savage Turcoman shepherd finds a good fold for his sheep and goats in the ruinous vaults, and takes his siesta, surrounded by his flock, and watched by his dog, in the grateful shadow of its hoary walls. We were standing here to recover

PLACE OF ST. POLYCARP'S MARTYRDOM.

our breath after the ascent, when my companions pointing to a green hollow in the mountain, but a short distance below, exclaimed, "That is the spot; it was there that Polycarp suffered!" We now descended to it.

The Stadium, or Amphitheatre, hollowed out in the hill side,

on a site which catches every breeze that blows, commands a wide
and glorious prospect over Smyrna and its far-stretching gulf.
Here were wont to assemble the thoughtless multitude of Asiatic
idlers—how vacant and how silent is it now! Its sides and
hollow are covered thick with turf as the surrounding hill,
through which appear here and there the marble seats, or the
orifices of the dens in which the wild beasts were confined. The
saying of the poet as to places signalized by human crime or
suffering is fully realized :

> ——"at the coming of the milder day
> Their monuments shall all be overgrown."

A few sheep are pastured about the grassy slope, or clustered
under the shadow of a lonely cypress, which serves as a landmark to vessels sailing up the gulf.

But, to the story which has invested the spot with such
undying interest. This has been told very beautifully, and at
some length, in a circular epistle addressed by the church over
which Polycarp had so long presided, to that of Philadelphia;
a document so evidently authentic, and withal so moving, that
Scaliger declared he had never, in all the history of the Church,
met with anything that so transported him, for that in reading
it he seemed to be no longer himself.

It was in the reign of Marcus Antoninus, A.D. 167, that the
persecution grew hot at Smyrna, and many having already
sealed their confession with their blood, the general outcry
was, "Away with the impious; let Polycarp be sought for."
The good man, although undisturbed by this, was yet prevailed
on by the love of his people to retire to a neighbouring village,
where he continued day and night in prayer for the Church
Universal, under her perilous and trying circumstances. "Here,
at length, he was discovered by those sent after him, whom, on
their approach, he saluted with a very cheerful and gentle countenance, ordering a table to be spread for them; so that they

wondered to behold so venerable a person, of so great age, and
so grave and composed a presence: and wondered what needed
so much stir to hunt and take this poor old man."

After a parting, and a solemn prayer, he set out with his con-
ductors, and on the road towards the city met the officer charged
with the maintenance of the public peace, who took up Polycarp
into his chariot, seeking to undermine his constancy by representing to him how trivial a thing it was to sacrifice a few grains
of incense to the emperor. Doubtless the duty of putting in
force the edicts against the Christians, must often have been
painful to men of humane minds. Sometimes, as Gibbon tells
us, they were alarmed at the multitude of the confessors, towards
whom they used every art of persuasion to induce them to
perform some act, of at least an external conformity, which
would release them from their painful office. But all persuasion
failed to induce Polycarp to comply with these suggestions, upon
which he was thrust out of the chariot with insult and violence,
so that he was injured by the fall.

" Whereat, nothing daunted," continues the story, " he
cheerfully hastened to the place of execution, under the conduct
of his guard, whither when they were come, and a confused noise
and tumult was arisen, a voice came from heaven (heard by many,
but none seen who spake it), saying, ' Polycarp, be strong, and
quit thyself like a man.' The proconsul, before whom he was
now brought, sought to persuade him to recant. ' Regard,' said
he, ' thy great age; swear by the genius of Cæsar; repent, and
say with us, " Take away the impious." ' The holy martyr,
looking about the Stadium, and severely regarding the idolatrous
crowd, looked up to heaven and prayed, ' Take away the
impious.' The proposal to blaspheme Christ, with which he
was next assailed, was treated with a noble scorn, and drew from
the venerable man this generous and touching confession,—
' Fourscore and six years I have served him, and he never did
me any harm; how then shall I thus blaspheme my King and

my Saviour?' Importuned to swear by the genius of Cæsar, he replied, 'Since you are so vainly ambitious that I should swear by the emperor's genius, as you call it, as if you knew not who I am; hear my confession,—I am a Christian!' To the threats of being thrown to the wild beasts, or of torture at the stake, the intrepid reply was, 'But why delayest thou? Bring forth whatever thou hast a mind to.' Having exhausted the arts of persuasion, the proconsul commanded the decisive proclamation to be made, 'Polycarp has confessed himself a Christian!' The cry was echoed by fearful shouts from the assembled crowd of thoughtless Asiatics and more bitter Jews. ' This is the great doctor of Asia, and the father of the Christians; this is the destroyer of our gods, who teaches men not to sacrifice, or worship the deities.' That blind and bloodthirsty rabble, already infuriated by the horrid spectacles of the amphitheatre, now clamorously requested of the presiding officer, that Polycarp should be thrown to the lions ; which being overruled, as contrary to the order of the shows, they then demanded that he should be burnt alive.

" No sooner was this consented to, than wood and fagots were instantly fetched, the Jews rendering themselves particularly active in the service. The fire being prepared, Polycarp untied his girdle, laid aside his garments, and began to put off his shoes; the Christians ambitiously striving to be admitted to do these offices for him, and deeming the man happy who first could touch his body.

" The officers came, according to custom, to nail him to the stake; but he desired them to desist, assuring them, that He who gave him strength to endure the fire, would enable him without nailing to stand immovable in the hottest flames. Clasping his hands, which were bound behind him, he then poured out his parting soul to heaven in prayer. And now the ministers of execution blew up the fire, which increasing to a mighty flame, behold, a wonder (seen," say my authors, " by us, who were reserved, that we might declare it to others); the flames disposing themselves into the resemblance of an arch, like the sails of a ship, swelled with the wind, gently circled the body of the martyr, who stood all the while in the midst, like gold or silver purified in the furnace; his body sending forth a delightful fragrancy, which like frankincense, or other costly spices, presented itself to our senses." And if our colder reason hesitate to afford implicit credence to this and other marvellous circumstances attendant upon the solemn scene, let us regard with sympathising respect, rather than with contemptuous pity, that lively faith and that excited imagination of the first Christians, which represented to them the powers of the other world as ever present for their support and consolation; and which led them unconsciously to regard a natural occurrence as no less than a miraculous interposition. The miracle, at all events, was unperceived, or unheeded by the spectators, who, finding that the flames were slow in doing their work, urged on a spearman to pierce the martyr with his weapon, on which " so vast a quantity of blood flowed from his wound, as extinguished the fire; together with which, a dove was seen to fly from his wounds, supposed to be his soul in visible form;" though these details, indeed, are considered as a subsequent addition to the original narrative. The Christians would have taken away the body, but this intention was defeated by the malice of the Jews, who persuaded the officer to have it consumed to ashes; these were gathered up by the Christians as a choice and inestimable treasure, and afterwards reverently interred. And they, moreover, resolved to meet and celebrate the anniversary of his martyrdom, both to do honour to the memory of the departed, and to prepare and encourage others to give the like testimony to the faith; in which resolution originated those *Memoriæ Martyrum*, or solemn commemorations of the martyrs, which were generally kept in the primitive church. Thus died the apostolical man, anno Christi 167, in about the hundredth year of his age; for those eighty and six years to which he alluded as having served Christ most probably commenced with his baptism. He had besides seen and conversed familiarly with the Apostle John.

My companions, though it was not of course the first time they had visited the spot, seemed absorbed in the solemn reflections connected with it. They paced the grass-grown area in silence, and I could well imagine that they breathed to Him who of old sustained the illustrious Martyr in his fiery trials, a secret prayer, that some measure of the same spirit might be accorded to themselves, under the discouragements and hindrances from which I learned they had been suffering. It was impossible not to be struck with the amazing revolution that had been wrought since the time when this half-obliterated amphitheatre witnessed the triumphant confession of the Martyr. At that time, paganism, if already indeed undermined—derided by the philosopher—the hollow profession of the great—the dreary and comfortless creed of the vulgar, was yet triumphantly established by the terrible power of the Roman empire, which threatened to extinguish in fire and blood the struggling and persecuted religion of the Cross. But after the lapse of eighteen hundred years, behold the change!—the descendants of a then barbarous and remote set of islanders,

" Penitus toto divisos orbe Britannos,"

and still more strange—the citizens of a region of the globe then undreamed of—missionaries, too, of that very religion which was here so terribly tried and so gloriously triumphant, standing on the same spot, see the last vestiges of that ancient paganism fast mouldering away—its creed forgotten—its cruel and bloody games abolished, and its monumental relics become the obscure theme of the antiquary ; while Christianity, with consolation and mercy in its train, has spread, and will continue to extend, its beneficent triumphs over a world unknown to the ancients.

Smyrna, like most of the other Seven Churches of Asia Minor,

is said to have been founded by St. John. The beloved Apostle, however, principally resided at Ephesus, where St. Paul had, many years before, settled a church, and appointed Timothy to preside over it. He was deported to Rome, and afterwards banished to Patmos; from whence, after the death of the Emperor Domitian, he returned to Ephesus, where he composed his Gospel, and lived to be nearly a centenarian. " When age and weakness," says Cave, " grew upon him, so that he was no longer able to preach to his flock, he used, at every public meeting, to be led to the church, and say no more to them than, ' Little children, love one another.' And when his auditors, wearied with the constant repetition of the same thing, asked him why he always spoke the same, he answered, Because it was the command of our Lord; and that, if they did nothing else, this alone was enough."

Prevented by the plague from visiting Ephesus, there is one scene, delineated by Laborde, (whose general accuracy leaves little doubt of its faithfulness,) so graphic, and so intimately connected with St. Paul, that, in default of an original sketch, we have ventured to copy it, and transfer it to these pages. This is the reputed site of the famous Temple of Diana, seen from the ruins of the Stadium, perhaps the same edifice, although another theatre is not far off, in which Demetrius the silversmith, who made silver shrines to Diana, by alarming the fears of his fellow-craftsmen, raised the tumult so vividly described in the nineteenth chapter of the Acts. The temple stood at the end of the port, by a morass,—a situation chosen as less likely to be affected by the earthquakes which have so often devastated the Asian cities. It was raised upon immense vaulted foundations, the ruins of which still exist, as represented in the view, and have often been explored by travellers. This wonderful edifice, as it existed in St. Paul's day, was 420 feet long by 220 feet broad; and of its columns, which were 60 feet high, one hundred and twenty were donations from monarchs; several of these now form a part of the church of St. Sophia, at Constantinople. The gorgeousness of the decorations were answerable to the splendour of the edifice. The votive offerings were priceless, and among them was the celebrated picture by Apelles, representing Alexander armed with thunder, for which he was paid twenty talents in gold, (about 38,650*l.*) It might thus well be regarded as one of the wonders of the world. Plundered by Nero, and afterwards by the Goths, the manner of its destruction is involved in obscurity.

Few scenes of desolation can be more impressive than this;— the ruinous theatre, the haunt of the partridge and the lizard— the dreary, bittern-haunted morass—the gloomy vestiges of the substructions—in the foreground and in the distance, the windings of the Cayster across the unwholesome, desolate plain, on its course to the distant sea. "The candlestick" of Ephesus *has* indeed been "removed out of its place." The site of the city is strewn with confused ruins, overgrown with herbage; not a single inhabitant is found within its confines.

After Ephesus had fallen into ruin, during the convulsions attendant upon the fall of the Roman empire, its inhabitants were removed to the neighbouring village of Aisaluck, where a castle was erected on a bold hill, and a town grew up around it; but this, too, has now dwindled down to a few miserable huts.

As is Ephesus, so also is the neighbouring city of Miletus— once so famous as to be called the head and metropolis of Ionia, the bulwark of Asia, and the mother of not fewer than seventy-five cities in Pontus, Egypt, and other parts. It was thus flourishing when St. Paul, on the voyage we are now tracing, sailing past Ephesus, landed at the promontory of Trogyllium, opposite to the island of Samos, and repairing thence by land to Miletus, called together the elders of the Ephesian Church, with whom he had that interview, the narrative of which is among the most affecting in the New Testament. A magnificent theatre, together with the remains of Christian churches, and Mahommedan mosques, speak eloquently of the succession of creeds and monuments, on a spot now forsaken by all but a few Turkish shepherds.

Next day our steamer pursued her onward course towards the shores of Palestine. No sooner were we clear of the Gulf, than we resumed the track of St. Paul's voyage, from which the reader will remember we had deviated, in order to visit Smyrna. From Mitylene, he came the next day over against Chios—the modern Scio—one of the largest islands that stud the Ægean Sea. Scio was precisely in our course, and still keeping south, like the Apostle, we passed off Samos, where he, however, landed, in order to visit Trogyllium and Miletus, to avoid lingering at Ephesus. To the scene of his leave-taking on this occasion, we have already alluded. We continued our course through the romantic islands of the Ægean, which loomed up around us in every variety of form and outline. Among these was Patmos, a long mountainous ridge, rising darkly against the distant horizon, on our right,—the sublimest prison in the world, over which the Apocalyptic visions of St. John have cast an

COS.

undying halo. At the beautiful straits of Cos, we again resume the course of St. Paul, when departing from Mitylene, after his sorrowful scene with the elders, "he came with a straight course to Cos, and the day following to Rhodes, and from thence to Patara," where he found a ship bound for Phœnicia, and took his passage on board. The sun was setting as we passed beautiful Cos, shining upon the large castle erected by the Knights of St. John of Jerusalem, and on awaking the next morning, we found ourselves, for the second time, moored in the harbour of Rhodes, under circumstances happily far different from those in which I had first reached that place.

I should in vain seek to convey to the reader the charm of this coasting voyage. It gave a singular degree of interest to St. Luke's narrative. The same cities, straits and headlands, rose before our eyes, that had saluted those of the great Apostle of the Gentiles and his accurate historian, near two thousand years ago. The journal of his course was almost like our own log. Add to this, the exquisite beauty of the scenery itself, the memorable sites that we passed, the fineness of the weather, the luxury of the atmosphere; and, I may add, too, the comforts of an excellent steamer, furnished with a well-selected oriental library, all tended to render this cruise one of those vivid passages of travel, which one sighs to think are never likely to be realized for the second time.

From Rhodes, our course lay directly across the open sea to Cyprus, and the first land we made was its eastern extremity, near the town of Baffo, the ancient Paphos. This city was famous, or rather infamous, for its temple to the goddess of pleasure; and here St. Paul, who, embarking at Seleucia, and entering the island at Salamis, had traversed it in his missionary work, until he reached this spot, rebuked Elymas the sorcerer. No spot could look less propitious to luxury and love, than this hot bare-looking coast, along which we advanced towards Larneca, the principal port on the south of the island, where we cast anchor about noon, amidst a considerable quantity of small craft, and a few vessels of larger burthen.

As we were to remain here a few hours, I resolved to go on

shore, and pay my respects to the British consul; who, in this unfrequented place, is not very often troubled with the visits of his countrymen. On landing, I was at once struck with the utter misery of all around. A few scattered white houses ranged along the tree-less shore, backed by lands that *ought* to have been cultivated, but were evidently left almost in a state of nature. I found the consul arrayed in scarlet and gold, in the act of receiving the congratulations of his brother functionaries, all of them in official costume, it being the birthday of Queen Victoria; and the attempted pomp and parade of this ceremonial painfully contrasted with the utter wretchedness of everything beside. As soon as these gentlemen had taken their departure, it was proposed that we should ride a short distance into the interior. The scene around was miserable and dreary, and I fancied that the spirits of the consul appeared depressed. He was evidently a man of education and refinement, and utterly thrown away in such a place. He had repaired to his post with highly raised expectations; there was something of romance in the very name of Cyprus, but he confessed that he had been bitterly disappointed. Still he was not without hopes of finding in the interior of the island, subjects of interesting research, with which to fill up the time that hung so heavily on his hands at Larneca. Moreover, he was shortly to be married, and the pleasures and cares of a household would contribute to fill up the vacuum. After remaining with him until the steamer was ready to start, I took leave, with many thanks for the courteous manner in which he had welcomed me, sincerely hoping that he might find reason to become more reconciled to his post, and also escape the unhealthy climate to which so many have fallen victims. It was some months afterwards, that in taking up a stray "Galignani," in a continental café, I learned the fact of his marriage,—almost the very next journal conveyed the melancholy intelligence of his death!

On reaching Beyrout, no time was lost in repairing to an

English merchant for whom I had a letter of introduction, and whose active kindness procured me a travelling servant, named Achmet, a native of the place, who was directed to lay in a stock of provisions for a two or three days' cruise, and to take our places in a boat sailing that evening for Jaffa. My lady pilgrim, of whom I had lost sight during the confusion of landing, was now sought out; nor was it long before she made her appearance at the merchant's. At first, my friend was rather shy of this part of the business, but the mature age, grave appearance, and simple manners of my new acquaintance, soon set at rest any ungenerous suspicions.

No sooner had this got wind, than we were besieged by one or two other women, who also wanted to go up under escort to Jerusalem; but this additional responsibility it was judged prudent to decline. I might otherwise have made my entry in the same style as the Protestant Bishop, accompanied by such a bevy of ladies, that when the Turks beheld it, and supposed them to be his harem, they declared he was a right good fellow who knew how to live, and not like those miserable monks, who never suffer a woman to come near them.

The evening came, and we repaired on board. The boat proved to be an undecked Arab craft, of the very rudest description, with two masts, and huge latine or triangular sails. A small cabin, about six feet square, into which it was necessary to creep on all-fours, was contrived at the stern, but it was so foul that to take refuge there except in case of a storm was impossible. The rest of the boat had a flooring of sand and shingle, and its rough ribs served for couches, and sofas, and berths, at once. The places of honour, including the aforesaid cabin, had been reserved for ourselves; the rest of the vessel was crowded with a motley collection of passengers.

Having myself roughed it before in this way, I was prepared for what I met with; but nothing surprised me more than the passive indifference of my companion. Though certainly not

" cabined," we were " cribbed and confined " with a vengeance. Wilkie, when putting up for the night in the one room of a Spanish posada, with a party of ladies and gentlemen, talks of curtains and other contrivances for decorum. I thought of the fastidious delicacy of Hood's " School-mistress " under such alarming circumstances. But there was no remedy. " Misery acquaints a man with strange bedfellows." All distinctions were literally brought to one level; and when night came on, and we were forced to lie down in the sand, which formed the sheeting of the general bed, with the canopy of heaven for a curtain, we made so tight a fit of it, that, as Stephens somewhere says, " if the bottom of the boat had fallen out, we could hardly have tumbled through."

Among our fellow-companions was a young French doctor, in the employ of the sultan, one of that wandering crew of adventurers, who, unable to find an opening at home, are compelled to seek employment in eastern lands, and contrive to accommodate themselves, far more than our own countrymen can ever do, to the manners and the humours of other nations. Our medico wore an uniform, which had become most wofully shabby, and his linen was none of the cleanest, but this did not affect the liveliness of his conversation, or the unceasing flow of his animal spirits. His stock of baggage and provisions was the slenderest possible, and, somehow or other, he always made one when the smoking platter of pilau was served up for our noonday meal. His entire equipage seemed rolled up in a mysterious blue cloak, an imposing garment, which was only assumed on occasions of ceremony, and which, like charity, concealed a multitude of defects. Apropos of this famous cloak; we afterwards heard, that having missed it at Jerusalem, he taxed his servant with having stolen and sold it. This, the poor fellow strenuously denied. The Frenchman, in a fury, drew his sabre, and threatened him with instant death, unless he confessed the theft, which the terrified creature, falling on his knees, was

compelled to do, and was put to his wit's end how to invent
a parcel of lies, in order to criminate himself. A day or two
afterwards the cloak arrived, having been rolled up accidentally
by the servant of an English traveller, a fellow-sojourner in
the same convent, who had left the city, and who returned it to
the owner as soon as discovered.

About dawn we were abreast of the ruins of Cæsarea, and
hoisting out the boat, rowed ashore to visit the remains of what
was once the principal seaport of Palestine.

CÆSAREA.

The origin of this city is thus described by Josephus : " There
was a certain place by the sea-side, formerly called Strato's
Tower, which Herod looked upon as conveniently situated for
the erection of a city. He drew his model, set people to work
upon it, and finished it. The buildings were all of marble,
private houses as well as palaces; but his master-piece was the
port, which he made as large as the Piræus (at Athens), and
a safe station against all winds and weathers, to say nothing of
other conveniences. This work was the more wonderful, because
all the materials for it were brought thither at a prodigious

expense from afar off. This city stands in Phœnicia, upon the pass to Egypt, between Joppa and Dora, two wretched sea-towns, where there is no riding in the harbour with a S.W. wind, for it beats so furiously upon the shore, that merchantmen are forced to keep off at sea many times for fear of being driven on the reefs. To encounter these difficulties, Herod ordered a mole to be made in the shape of a half-moon, and large enough to contain a royal navy. He directed, also, prodigious stones to be let down there in twenty fathom water—stones fifty feet long, and eighteen broad, and nine deep, some greater, some less. This mole was two hundred feet in extent, the one half of it to break the setting of the sea, *the other half served for the foundation of a stone wall*, fortified with turrets, the largest and the fairest of them called by the name of the Tower of Drusus, from Drusus the son-in-law of Augustus, who died young. This port opens to the northward, the clearest quarter of the heavens. Upon a mount in the middle stood a temple dedicated to Cæsar, which was of great use to the mariners as a sea-mark, and contained two statues, of Rome and of Cæsar, and hence the city took the name of Cæsarea. The contrivance of the vaults and sewers was admirable. Herod built also a stone theatre, and on the south side of the harbour, an amphitheatre, with a noble sea-view. In short, he spared neither labour nor expense, and in twelve years this work was brought to perfection." . . . . " It was finished," says Josephus, (speaking of the city,) " in the tenth year from its foundation, the twenty-eighth of Herod's reign, and in the Olympiad 192. Its dedication was celebrated with all the splendour and magnificence imaginable; masters procured from all parts, and the best that could be gotten too, in all exercises, such as musicians, wrestlers, swordsmen, and the like, to contend for the prizes. They had their horse-races also, and shows of wild beasts, with all other spectacles and entertainments then in vogue, either at Rome or elsewhere. This solemnity was instituted in honour of Cæsar, under the appellation of *Certamen quinquennale*, and the ceremony to be exhibited every fifth year."

Such was the superb seaport which Herod built, not only as a monument of his public-spirited munificence, but in the hope that it might long remain in the proud possession of his race. We need not dwell here upon the awful domestic tragedy, in which this passionate and unhappy monarch became the executioner of the best members of his own family, and the destroyer of his own hopes of the permanency of his line. The disputes of his descendants were terminated at no distant period by the sway of Rome. Herod Agrippa, his successor, and the last monarch of the Jews, had reigned, in dependence upon the Roman power, three years over Palestine, when he ordered a splendid festival at Cæsarea in honour of the Emperor Claudius. "Upon the second day of this festival," says Josephus, who gives a fuller version of the incident mentioned in the "Acts," "Agrippa went early in the morning to the theatre in a silver stuff so wonderfully rich and curious, that as the beams of the rising sun struck upon it, the eyes were dazzled by the reflection; the sparkling of the light seemed to have something divine in it, that moved the spectators at the same time with veneration and awe. Insomuch that a fawning crew of parasites cried him up as a god; beseeching him, in form, to forgive them the sins of their ignorance, when they took him only for flesh and blood, for now they were convinced of an excellency in his nature that was more than human. This impious flattery he repelled not, but while in the full vanity of this contemplation, he beheld an owl above him seated on a rope, a presage of evil to him, as it had been before of good fortune. For immediately he was seized with a fearful agony, in which he exclaimed to his friends, ' Behold your god condemned to die, and prove his flatterers a company of profligate liars, and to convince the world that he is not immortal. But God's will be done! In the life that I have led, I have had no reason to envy the happiness of any prince under heaven, but I must still be aspiring to be greater and greater.' His pains increasing, he retired into the palace; the news flew over Cæsarea, and all the people, covering themselves with sackcloth, joined in prayers and tears for Agrippa's recovery. The king in the mean time, looking down from his apartment near the top of the palace, could not forbear weeping at the sight of the mourners that lay below prostrate on the pavement. On the fifth day after the commencement of his illness, he expired."

After the death of Agrippa, his son being too young to bear the burden of sovereignty, Judæa became a Roman province, and was governed by Roman officers. The total loss of their independence, and their subjection to pagan masters, profoundly irritated the unsocial and turbulent Jews; and the Gentile population, especially the Greeks, with whom they were confounded, inflamed by their bitter insults the wounded spirit of the fallen people. The Roman soldiery regarded them with such insolent contempt, that to avoid collision between his troops and the more turbulent zealots of Jerusalem, the Roman prætor generally resided at Cæsarea. It was there that the events took place which led to a final rupture with Rome. Its situation as a port had drawn thither a great number of Syrian Greeks and other strangers; and the pagan monuments with which it had been decorated by Herod, seemed in their eyes to give it the appearance of a Gentile city. Thus they contended fiercely for preeminence with the Jews, who, from its having been built by a monarch of their fallen kingdom, on the site moreover of an old Jewish town, regarded themselves as its principal and ruling inhabitants; or at least contended for an equality of privileges. But the struggle was unequal, the soldiery encouraged the Greeks—the feuds increased daily, and the utmost influence of the moderate of both sides was found unavailing to quell it. The Roman governor, Felix, was compelled to banish the factious from the city, and upon the refusal of many to depart, he caused

them to be put to death. Commissioners were sent from both
parties to plead the cause before Cæsar, who decided in favour
of the Greeks. Upon this their insolence knew no bounds, and
the Jews were driven to despair.

At this crisis "nothing was wanting," says Milman, "to fill
the measure of calamity, but the nomination of a new governor
like Gessius Florus. Without compunction and without shame,
as crafty as he was cruel, he laid deliberate schemes of iniquity,
by which at some distant period he was to reap his harvest of
plunder. He pillaged not only individuals, but even communi-
ties, and seemed to grant a general indemnity for spoliation, if
he was only allowed his fair portion of the plunder." Such
was the man appointed to maintain equal justice between the
rival parties, and to impose awe upon the incorrigibly factious,
but by whose partiality, corruption, and weakness combined, the
dispute was inflamed to a fatal termination.

The smothered flame now burst forth. On the very day that
a Roman garrison in Jerusalem was treacherously butchered by
the insurgent Jews, the whole Jewish population of Cæsarea was
massacred, to the number, according to Josephus, of twenty
thousand. "This," he continues, "made the whole nation
mad," and the Jews, spreading through the country, made
fearful reprisals on their persecutors. "Moderate and mild-
natured men before, were now become hard and cruel." Every
passion was let loose, avarice was kindled together with revenge,
and "robbery was called victory." "It was a horrid spectacle
to see the streets encumbered with dead bodies of men, women
and children, unburied, and even uncovered." The whole frame-
work of society was a prey to convulsions, which were but the
opening act of that tremendous drama which terminated with the
destruction of the Temple and dispersion of the Jewish people.

It is refreshing to turn from these scenes of horror, these mutual
cruelties of rival nations, which heaped the streets of this new-
built city with the slain, and stained the waters of its port with

their blood, to the peaceful arrival of Paul of Tarsus. We see him, after he had escaped from the blind bigotry of his country-men at Jerusalem, sent down stealthily and by night to Cæsarea, in the custody of a body of soldiers, traversing the mountainous defiles of Bethoron, and reaching in the morning Antipatris, another city of Herod's creation. Here the foot soldiers returned, and left him to be escorted the rest of the way by the cavalry. On reaching Cæsarea he is kept in " Herod's judgment-hall." " Not many days after, came down Ananias the high-priest, with some others of the Sanhedrim, accompanied by Tertullus the advocate, who, in a speech set off by the insinuating arts of forensic eloquence, charged the Apostle, before Felix the governor, with sedition, heresy, and the profanation of the Temple. After St. Paul had replied, Felix commanded him to be kept under guard, yet so that none of his friends should be hindered from visiting him, or performing any office of kindness and friendship to him." And even here, amidst the hostile collisions of Greeks and Jews, lurked, no doubt, a few members of the proscribed sect of the Christians, the objects of their united hatred and con-tempt.

" It was not long after this before Drusilla, the wife of Felix, came to Cæsarea. Felix, Drusilla being present, sent for St. Paul, and gave him leave to discourse of the doctrines of Christianity. St. Paul took occasion to insist upon the obligation to justice and righteousness, to sobriety and chastity. But men," says Cave, " naturally hate that which ' brings their sins to their remembrance,' and sharpens the sting of a violated conscience. The prince was so moved by the Apostle's reasonings, that, trembling, he caused him to break off abruptly, telling him he would hear the rest at some other season. And good reason there was that Felix's conscience should be sensibly alarmed, being a man notoriously infamous for rapine and violence. Tacitus tells us of him, that he made his will the law of his government, practising all manner of cruelty and injustice. He

was given over to luxury and debauchery, for the compassing
whereof he scrupled not to violate all laws both of God and man.
Whereof this very wife Drusilla was a famous instance. For
being married by her brother to Azis, king of the Emisenes,
Felix, who had heard of her incomparable beauty, by the help of
Simon the magician, a Jew of Cyprus, tore her from her husband's arms, and, in defiance of all law and right, kept her for
his own wife. To these qualities he had added bribery and
covetousness, and, therefore, frequently sent for St. Paul to
discourse with him, expecting that he should have given him a
considerable sum for his release; and the rather, probably,
because he had heard that St. Paul had lately brought up great
sums of money to Jerusalem. But finding no offers made, either
by the Apostle or his friends, he kept him prisoner for two years
together, so long as he himself continued procurator of that
nation; when, being displaced by Nero, he left St. Paul still in
prison, on purpose to gratify the Jews, and engage them to speak
better of him after his departure from them.

"To him succeeded Portius Festus, in the procuratorship of
the province; at whose first coming to Jerusalem the high-priest
and Sanhedrim presently began to prefer to him an indictment
against St. Paul, desiring that, in order to his trial, he might be
sent for up from Cæsarea; designing this pretence that assassins
should lie in the way to murder him.

"Festus told them that he himself was going shortly to
Cæsarea, and that, if they had anything against St. Paul, they
should come down thither and accuse him. Accordingly, being
come to Cæsarea, the Jews began to renew the charge which they
had heretofore brought against St. Paul; of all which he cleared
himself. However, as the safest course, he solemnly made his
appeal to the Roman emperor, who should judge between them.
Whereupon Festus, advising with the Jewish Sanhedrim, received his appeal, and told him he should go to Cæsar.

"Some time after, King Agrippa, who succeeded Herod in the

tetrarchate of Galilee, and his sister Bernice, came to Cæsarea. To him Festus gave an account of St. Paul, and the great stir and trouble that had been made about him, and how he had appealed to Cæsar. Agrippa was very desirous to see and hear him, and, accordingly, the next day the king and his sister, accompanied by Festus and other persons of quality, came into the court with a magnificent retinue, where the prisoner was brought forth before him.

" Hereupon Agrippa told the Apostle he had liberty to make his own defence; to whom, after silence had been enforced, he particularly addressed himself. But who knows not that celebrated speech, from which, astonished at the fervid eloquence of the Apostle, the Roman governor considered Paul to be beside himself; while the Jewish king was 'almost persuaded to become a Christian?'

" After the conference, it was finally resolved that St. Paul should be sent to Rome; in order whereunto he was, with some other prisoners of note, committed to the charge of Julius, commander of a company belonging to the legion of Augustus. Accompanied by St. Luke, Aristarchus, Trophimus, and some others, in September, A. D. 56, or as others, 57, he went on board a ship of Adramyttium."

How interesting to realize the scene of his leaving the soil of Palestine, which he was destined never to revisit! We see the splendid city, with its marble houses and votive columns, its temples and its theatres, its port crowded with many-oared vessels, from every part of the Roman empire, from Italy, from Egypt, from the Syrian coast, the provinces, and Asia Minor. We hear the noisy din of various languages; and mark the different physiognomies and splendid costumes of the many subjects of the great Roman empire, who meet upon the crowded quay—some actively engaged in the labours of the port, others lingering idly in picturesque groups beneath the marble colonnades of Herod. The wind is fair—the "ship of Adramyttium"

is ready—the passengers hasten on board. Among them, un-
noticed amidst the busy throng, advances "the poor prisoner of
Jesus Christ," weak of body, but of spirit indomitable—the intrepid, the noble Paul. A few friends, members of the persecuted
yet growing Church of Christ, are around him; with swelling
hearts, with tearful eyes, they invoke the blessing of their common
Lord upon the departing Apostle; grieving the most, like those of
Miletus, "lest they should see his face no more." They watch
him on board; the sails swell to the southern wind, and the ship,
gliding by temples, and columns, and palaces, out of the mouth
of the harbour, soon appears a speck upon the blue bosom of the
Mediterranean.

How changed is now the scene thus hallowed by his parting
presence! As I stood with my companion upon the solitary
beach, the low, monotonous roll of the surge was the only sound
that broke the mournful stillness. Tower and palace were
prostrate—the materials hewn for the city of Herod, and since
wrought into the buildings of a later age, themselves fast
crumbling, were fallen in huge masses into the waves. The
numerous columns which once adorned the port, now scattered on
a rocky reef, are heaped with sea-weed, and chafed and worn by
the breakers of the shipless sea. It is a scene of utter ruin—of
forlorn and shapeless desolation. Yet, in the midst of the wreck,
and rising above the waves, though portions are submerged,
appear solid foundations of Roman masonry; not improbably
a part of the splendid quay or landing-place mentioned by
Josephus, which Herod built, and which the feet of Paul must
have trodden. It juts out far into the sea, a truly memorable
relic. Upon it, at its junction with the shore, stands, ruin upon
ruin, a mouldering and half prostrate edifice of Gothic construction, a memorial of the times of the Crusades. A solitary Arab
was prowling stealthily among the ruins as we landed.

Ascending from the shore, we reach the enclosed site of a
town, its every building prostrate, but surrounded with a fosse

and a wall of solid construction, which Irby and Mangles regard
as Saracenic; and that doubtless enclosed the city which, in the
middle ages, succeeded the one built by Herod, and was erected
from its materials. Little beyond a few scattered fragments were
in sight. Beyond these Saracenic walls, in the south, the same
travellers found a column of marble, with a Roman inscription of
the emperor Septimius Severus, but too much buried to allow
a copy to be taken. The Roman remains extend beyond the
limits of the above-named walls, and far to the north there are
ruins of arches, and of a wall, apparently part of an aqueduct,
for supplying the town. The city was also rebuilt and became
famous in the middle ages, but for how brief a period its deserted
site must vouch.

. This coast, with its castles, so famous in the Crusades, the
scene of many a warlike encounter between Christian and
Saracen, who have piled upon the grand wrecks of the Jews and
Romans the more perishable monuments of their temporary
occupation, will never more " echo with the world's debate."

> " There was a day when they were young and proud,
> Banners on high, and battles pass'd below;
> But they who fought are in a bloody shroud,
> And those which waved are shredless dust ere now;
> And those bleak battlements shall bear no future blow."

Yet, so long as time shall spare a single relic to point out the site
of Cæsarea, the pilgrim shall repair with reverence to the shore
hallowed by the eloquence of Paul, and to the ruinous mole
whence he departed from Jerusalem, on his last vogage, to bear
the tidings of salvation to the Western world.

On awaking the next morning, no time was wasted at our
toilette, for we were all ready dressed. The sun was rising in
glory behind Mount Lebanon. Our picturesque old bark, with
her huge latine sails, flew steadily along under the pressure of
the light breeze; and the fresh odours from the sea, with our
prosperous progress, contributed to put us into excellent spirits.

After our ablutions, Achmet was soon ready with a breakfast of coffee, bread, eggs, and fruit. We sat in the pleasant shadow of the sail; maps and guide-books were pulled out, and every point of that memorable coast successively made out and commented on. I was perfectly delighted with the intelligence of my companion, and never, surely, did any traveller, male or female, give so little trouble, and enter into everything with such a spirit of quiet, heartfelt enjoyment. And thus we sailed along, past Sidon, and past Tyre, till, as the sun's fiery ball dropped into the western waters, we reached the promontory of Mount Carmel and its white convent, looking out over the lonely, wide-spread sea. As night came on, all dropped asleep again, huddled together in the general receptacle.

On reaching Jaffa the next afternoon, a tribe of half-naked Arabs rushed shouting into the water, and bore us, lady and all, triumphantly into the town. The notion of a woman wandering about by herself was so unintelligible to the crew and Arabs, that I was, of course, looked upon as her lawful proprietor and protector; and it was rather embarrassing how to get rid of this honour, and, at the same time, to provide comfortably for my companion. Fortunately, there proved to be an Austrian consul in the place, and to his custody, as a German, I desired Achmet to consign her for the night.

Jaffa is but thirty miles from Jerusalem, and, by starting very early in the morning, I intended to get there that evening. Accordingly, long before sunrise I had ordered horses to be ready, and sent Achmet to fetch Madame from the Austrian consul's, where she had been very kindly treated by the ladies of his family. It was one of the hottest days of a Syrian summer; the half-cultivated plains, parched up by the summer heat, were destitute of shade and verdure, and haunted by myriad swarms of insects; our supply of water was soon exhausted, and had it not been for the peasant girls of the villages, who brought forth pitchers to gain a few paras from a passing traveller, we should have suffered cruelly. But not a single murmur, not even a indication of impatience, ever escaped the lips of my surprising feminine companion during the whole of this burning day. After a most blessed halt at a well, and an hour's repose under the shadow of a solitary fig-tree, we pushed into the wild defiles of the hill country of Judæa, so narrow in places that but one at a time can pass, famous of old besides for their insecurity, and as the scene of many an outrage and many a murder perpetrated upon the pilgrims to Jerusalem. Our progress through these ravines was so much slower than we anticipated, that we were benighted at a village in the mountains. We halted in the court of a ruinous mosque, and established our quarters under its vaulted cloisters. The village sheik, who had sent us a huge pilau for supper, came down for a while to visit us. At length we betook ourselves to our respective dormitories on the ground; but sleep refused to visit our eyes: we had reached, we found, to within three hours of Jerusalem. Restless and excited, about midnight, I desired Achmet to prepare for departure—our companion, I found, had been as wakeful as myself. At midnight, the camels sleeping around us in groups, we stumbled forth by star-light from the court of the mosque, and picked our uncertain way among the olive-groves surrounding the village.

The road was a mere horse-path down slippery slabs of rock into the hollow of a precipitous ravine: in the dark, it was one succession of slides and stumbles from top to bottom. I soon lost sight of Madame, who had advanced ahead of me, but hailed her from time to time with loud shouts, to which she responded in more subdued tones. At the bottom of the valley I overtook her, and we hastened onwards towards the bourne of our journey. My own excitement was beyond anything I ever experienced— the mind of my companion was no less absorbed, and thus we paced on side by side in the dim starlight, without exchanging more than an occasional syllable. At length the light broke gradually in faint red bars behind a dark wavy summit—it was

the Mount of Olives!   A long line of walls, with here and there
a tower and dome, loomed up and began to redden with the
increasing light; and as the crimson streaks became more and
more intensely vivid, with a feeling more like dreaming than
waking, we found ourselves at the gate of Jerusalem.   While
the sentinel within was unbarring it, we held a brief consultation,
when it was decided that I should remit the pilgrim-lady to her
legitimate protectors, the monks of the Roman Catholic convent,
while I sought out for myself the abode of a friend who was
then *locum tenens* for the absent consul.

It is not my intention to give here a topographical description
of Jerusalem, which I have done elsewhere, but merely to devote
a few pages to those localities particularly connected with our
Saviour and his Apostles.

The first impression of the Holy City seldom answers to preconceived expectations, either as to extent or magnificence.
Accustomed to the vastness of modern capitals, nothing seems
so startling as the narrow dimensions of cities that have played
so conspicuous a part in the history of the ancient world.   This
is particularly the case as regards Jerusalem.   Wherever the
visitor may station himself, his eye easily takes in its entire
circuit—no larger, to use a familiar illustration, than that of the
Regent's Park ; and when he scans the nature of the site,—a
lofty plot of table-land, circumscribed by deep and rugged
ravines,—it is evident that the main features of the scene remain
unchanged; and that, allowing for a considerable extension along
the level ground to the north, the city in its most palmy days
could never have been more than about four miles in circuit;
while the circumference of Syracuse is said to have been twenty
miles, that of Rome nearly fifteen, and that of Alexandria, at
one time, nearly the same.   This induces a very natural scepticism as to the immense population said by Josephus to have
been congregated in such confined limits.

No city in the world has undergone more desolating changes

than Jerusalem; her buildings have been repeatedly over-thrown, and the work of identification becomes proportionably difficult.

In a city built upon a plain, if the monuments be lost, the knowledge of its original position might be lost with them; in Jerusalem it is otherwise, the site itself being so peculiar and striking that mistake is impossible.

If we ascend any of the neighbouring heights, we cannot for a moment doubt but that all the great features of the scene, displayed like a map beneath us, subsist unaltered. The moun-tains that rise round about her, and the deep rugged glens, are the same as ever; the paths and roads indicated by convenience would naturally remain the same; no fraud, pious or mercenary, could possibly succeed. But when we step beyond this, and seek to identify the precise locality of particular buildings, all is confusion and uncertainty. So little remains of Jewish times, and with that little is intermingled so much of modern addition, that even the precise place of the temple, the most prominent edifice in the city, is yet a matter of dispute. When we de-scend to minutiæ, or reach the period of monkish tradition, we are involved in increased obscurity, and compelled to maintain a general scepticism.

It follows that the interest taken by a traveller should be pro-portioned to the above distinction. The natural features of the landscape should first engage his attention, as they will leave the deepest impression upon his memory. Let him ascend the Mount of Olives, and thence survey the outspread city—let him descend and linger amidst the ancient trees which still stretch out their gnarled limbs at its foot—let him trace the path to Bethany, and familiarize himself with the same scenery which, near two thousand years ago, saluted the eyes of the Saviour. To have seen these things alone, is to have seen Jerusalem, however interesting to the antiquary may be the study of the antiquities within its walls.

M

Of all places in the immediate neighbourhood, there is none to which so much interest attaches as Bethany. It was here that our Saviour appears to have formed the tenderest of his friendships, and to have retired from the turbulence of the city, and the pursuit of his enemies, to the enjoyment of social ties.

There is no mention of the circumstances under which his acquaintance with Lazarus and his sisters originated, but the few glimpses of his visits to their house which we obtain through the awful scenes which terminate in the crucifixion, show that a cordial and tender intimacy subsisted between them: there, as some think, Jesus lay concealed during his later and unexpected visits to the metropolis; and here, in general, he passed the nights during the week of the last Passover, seasons of retirement that seem more tranquil and precious in the midst of those terrible circumstances by which he was surrounded as "his hour drew near."

There is something in the character of the spot which well harmonizes with such associations. Eastward of Jerusalem rises from the deep valley which flanks its walls, the lofty height of the Mount of Olives, completely overlooking it, and of course cutting off all further prospect in that direction from the city itself. On the opposite slope of this Mount, and nearly at its foot, is Bethany, only about two miles from Jerusalem, and yet with an air of retirement and seclusion hardly to be expected at so short a distance.

The village consists of but about twenty flat-roofed houses, half embowered in the olive-trees, which are scattered about the Mount above. To any one approaching it, as our Saviour did, from the wild solitudes through which runs the road to Jericho, and which furnished him with the appropriate scene of the parable of the Good Samaritan, Bethany appears like a nest in a grove at the extreme verge of cultivation.

It is not probable that the place was at any time much more extensive than at present. There are a few vestiges of antiquity

about it, such as the remains of a square tower, and some large hewn stones in the houses, which formed part of more ancient edifices. The inhabitants are all peasants, and the place looks poor and neglected.

Tradition, of course, has not been idle here, and the Tomb of Lazarus, as well as the houses of Martha and Mary, and Simon the Leper, are still shown to travellers. There are traditions so palpably absurd and puerile, or so evidently improbable as to site, that it would be folly to accept of them. There are others so plainly corroborated by local evidence as to be almost incontrovertible. Perhaps that of the Tomb of Lazarus may be placed midway between these categories. A flight of steps leads down into the vault, which is cut into sepulchral recesses. And even if there be but little evidence in behalf of the identity of the tomb, yet as it conveys with the surrounding scenery a characteristic picture of this humble village, the reader may not be sorry to have a representation of it in this place.

It would appear from the historical notices collected by Robinson, that a church formerly existed over this tomb, and that a convent of Black Nuns was founded at Bethany, by Melesinda, queen of King Fulco of Jerusalem. This convent was afterwards granted to the Knights Hospitallers, but in two centuries of convulsion it had ceased to exist, and Bethany returned to its original state, that of a retired suburban hamlet.

If there is any path in Palestine which we may feel certain was trodden by the feet of Jesus, it is that leading from Bethany, across the Mount of Olives, to Jerusalem. It is incontestible that whether for ease, privacy, or enjoyment, the short, quiet, and pleasant footway would be chosen before the dusty and frequented road. Let us endeavour then to bring this path and its adjacent scenery with something of daguerreotype minuteness before the eye of the reader.

We will suppose ourselves just leaving behind the last houses of the village, low and flat roofed, built of rough materials, and

coated with coarse whitened cement, with a single door and
window. In front, Arab women, brown skinned but comely, in
long blue robes, which outline gracefully to the figure, are plying
the spinning reel, or balancing their ruddy offspring upon their
shoulders, as they gaze with keen black eye upon the passing
Frank.

We leave them, and immediately begin the gradual ascent of
the Mount of Olives. The path runs through a corn-field; it is
rugged and stony; huge blocks of rock, around which spring up
clusters of bright-coloured wild flowers, are studded among the
scanty wheat. We should not fail to notice an enormous walnut-
tree, which might attract notice even in woody England, and is
very striking in a country so devoid of large trees as Palestine.
The path now becomes more rugged, stony, and abrupt, the corn
thinner, till it gives place to the bare side of the hill; bright
green after the rains, but dusty and sad in summer. Looking
back, Bethany is seen nestling below in its dark covert of trees,
overhung by the hills of the desert, hot, brown, and indescribably
desolate,—a wilderness of jagged, red, and yellow peaks, shapeless
and horrid. Overtopping them all is the distant range of the
Moab mountains. Who, that has been at Jerusalem, but re-
members their peculiar pink and violet colouring, intense beyond
conception in our neutral-tinted country! Now come the olives,
thinly scattered over the sacred hill, some evidently very ancient;
their trunks are generally twisted about fantastically,—their straggling roots dive in between the clefts of rocks, or, void of earthy
covering, project, skeleton like, out of the stony ground. Their
foliage is thin and sombre, the oval leaf a dark dull green above,
and silvery beneath, and there is a peculiar sadness in their low
soft rustle when agitated by the gusty breeze. A shepherd or
two in a brown striped dress, and legs and face still browner, is
seated at the foot of one of these grey trunks, and a flock of goats,
with long and silken hair, of dark brown, glossy bluish black,
dull yellow, or white, is scattered about the arid, rocky soil.

We are now not very far from the ridge of the hill, some distance below the summit of which, a domed building, and a small tower peep up above the trees. This is the Church of the Ascension, so called after the event the exact site of which it is supposed to point out. This is a matter keenly controverted, and concerning which no certainty either way is attainable—suffice it to say, the very conspicuousness of the spot alone casts a degree of improbability over the tradition.

But we are now at the crest of the Mount, and Jerusalem is rolled out, map-like, below—in all its essential features, its bold hills and sunken valleys, the same as they expanded before the Saviour's eye, when he came up from the first scene of his ministry in Galilee. On a projecting knoll of the hill stands a small chapel, of monkish origin, marking the supposed spot where, in the midst of his awe-struck disciples, Jesus prophesied the impending ruin of Jerusalem; and arbitrary as may be its selection, it is probably enough at no great distance from the real one. From hence the slope of the Mount of Olives, dotted over with the trees that have given to it that name, declines steeply into the Valley of Jehoshaphat. Almost at our feet, in the hollow of the glen, appears a somewhat darker plot of these trees, within a low stone wall, which we shall presently pass; this is the traditional Garden of Gethsemane. Immediately from this plot the ground rises boldly, and forms part of the huge oblong platform of stony soil upon which the city stands, describing with its zigzag walls and battlements an irregular area of about two miles and a half in circuit. Deep as are the valleys below us, on the opposite side the ground seems rather to rise from the city; it is merely a bare bleak ridge, whitish in hue, and spotted over with grey olives.

The principal object in the city is the great enclosure which, disguised as it may be by successive revolutions and modern buildings, undoubtedly includes the site of the Jewish Temple. As Jesus passed over the Mount from Bethphage and Bethany, it would have been, as with the travellers of to-day, the first object to rivet his attention. Raised high above the valley below, surrounded by a wall of which the course, and even most of the materials, are probably the same to-day as they then were, it must have presented, with the courts it enclosed, and the façade of the Temple casting back a dazzling lustre from its golden ornaments, a spectacle to call forth the enthusiastic admiration of his disciples, and, though mingled in his mind with a feeling of sadness at its impending desolation, even that of their Master himself. To the rude Galilean peasants, wonderstruck at the first sight of their national fane, seeming as if built for eternity, and eliciting their applauding exclamation, "Master, see what manner of stones, and what buildings are here!" how awful must have been the announcement that "there was not one stone upon another, which should not be thrown down." The dread prediction is accomplished, and there exists no trace above ground of the Temple itself; but its solid and immovable foundations yet remain: some of the enormous masses of which its defensive walls were built, are still, even at this distance, plainly distinguishable from the smaller and inferior masonry above them.

Within this area, then, ignorant as we may be of the precise part of it which the Temple itself occupied, took place the scenes of our Saviour's life so vividly narrated by the evangelists, from his first arrival at Jerusalem, after quitting the scene of his labours in distant Galilee, until the hour when he was brought before Pilate in the Castle of Antonia, which most probably stood where now stands the house of the Moslem Governor at the north-east angle of the enclosure. There, too, occurred that stirring scene in the life of St. Paul, when, dragged out of the Temple-courts by the infuriated Jews, he was with difficulty rescued by the guard stationed in the Antonia, and stood on the steps to harangue his persecutors. From the ground we stand upon, the theatre of these momentous transactions is unmistakeably to be traced out.

This great enclosure is now covered with grass, and adorned

with groups of umbrageous plane-trees and cypresses. In the centre, standing where the Temple is generally supposed to have stood, is the beautiful octagonal Mosque of Omar, with its graceful dome, raised on a marble platform, to which access is had by elegant gateways of pointed arches. Another mosque even more extensive, but less beautiful and conspicuous, that of El Aksa, abuts upon the southern wall of the enclosure.

Thus far we are upon safe ground, and may believe with unhesitating conviction that we are looking upon the general scene of our Saviour's life and labours at Jerusalem. But with regard to those of his death and burial, it is far otherwise; for although no doubt these events also happened somewhere within the range of prospect before us, yet of the precise locality it would seem that no satisfactory knowledge is to be attained. Amidst the labyrinth of white and domed edifices seen beyond the Temple enclosure, midway, as it were, between that and the city wall, is a group of Gothic towers and domes, which marks the site of the Church of the Holy Sepulchre. There, for several centuries, the mass of pilgrims have been accustomed to resort with a feeling of undoubting confidence. Yet nothing has been more warmly, not to say acrimoniously, contested among the learned, even to the present day, than the genuineness of this locality. Knowing, as we do, that the crucifixion took place without the city wall, and that Jerusalem was at that time extensive and populous, our mature reflections but seem to confirm the first involuntary impression, that this can hardly be the real spot. Yet many who have scrutinised the matter most narrowly, are only the more fully satisfied. The most extraordinary theory is the recent one of Mr. Ferguson, who regards the Mosque of Omar itself as the Church which was originally built by Constantine, over what was pointed out to him as the sepulchre of Christ, and visited and described as such by early pilgrims; and when the Saracens eventually drove out the Christians from the sacred enclosure, the latter, as he believes, *transferred* the site to the present

foundation, even, as we shall presently see, some others were undoubtedly changed. Altogether this subject is at the present
moment in a state of inextricable bewilderment, very stimulating
to antiquarian curiosity and disputation, but preventive of all
sober conviction in the mind of an impartial inquirer.

Let us now descend from the height of Olivet, by the footway
which, worn among the rocks, winds down the hill-side, sometimes over the bare slope, at others beneath the chequered shade
of the foliage. As we get lower down, the interior of the city is
concealed, and nothing meets the eye but the long line of dead
walls, rising above the gloomy valley into the depth of which we
have descended. This path, which from its nature and locality
must have been often imprinted with the FOOTSTEPS OF OUR
LORD AND HIS APOSTLES, brings us out at the same group of
olive-trees alluded to as the Garden of Gethsemane. It perhaps
tends, on one hand, to establish the truth of the tradition, that
this plot of ground is close to the path we have been describing ;
but, on the other hand, unless it were enclosed within high walls,
which may well have been the case, its proximity to what was *then*,
if not now, a well-frequented public road, would seem to render
it unsuitable as a place of especial retirement, either for the pur-
poses of devotion, or as a concealment from watchful enemies.

Be this as it may, this group of eight olive-trees has upon it a
certain stamp of sadness which cannot fail to affect those who are
prepared to *feel* rather than disposed to cavil. Leaping the low
wall, we find ourselves in the plot of poor stony soil, which
has so long nourished these ancient trees. Their trunks are of
a girth enormous in proportion to their height, and their roots are
wildly gnarled and twisted, such portions as had projected from
the earth being now protected by a terrace of fresh soil, built up
with stones. In some places the grey foliage of the different
trees meets overhead, and casts a trembling shadow upon the
earth beneath. Pacing round the enclosure, and looking out
through the openings in the trees, every object is full of sombre

melancholy. On one hand towers the high dead wall of the Temple, on the other the slope of Olivet, and between them the bare ashy-coloured cliffs of the funereal valley of Jehoshaphat. It is mournful even by day ; what is it then when sunk in shadow with the last red light of evening lingering upon the top of the Mount above? There is then no one, however hardy his scepticism, who can read the event said to have occurred within these shades, and not feel himself strangely and powerfully influenced.

Let us return again to the path. Here, looking over the wall opposite to the Garden, we glance down into a court excavated in the rock, at the end of which is the picturesque "Tomb of the Virgin," so denominated by an undistinguishing tradition. A few paces on, passing under the shade of the olives, we cross the dry bed of the "brook Kidron" by a bridge. He who looks here for the bright rushing stream with which his fancy may have fondly identified it, will be sorely disappointed. The brook is nothing but a dry watercourse, filled with drift sand and whitening pebbles, brought down by the periodical rains.

We cross it, and immediately ascend to the city gate by a broken rugged path, or set of paths, straggling up the bare side of the hill, with here and there a stunted olive. Gethsemane is sunk at our feet, Olivet rises behind, with its three rounded peaks, its furrowed pathways, and its scanty foliage. We have now reached the city wall, and prepare to pass it through St. Stephen's Gate, a pointed mediæval archway, occupying most probably the site of a more ancient edifice. One or two brigand-looking soldiers, in dirty white dresses and red caps, are idly lounging under the gateway. A group of Turkish women, enveloped in loose white wrappers, which leave nothing visible but their almond-shaped, dark eyes, pass, shadow-like, under the portal to take their seat in the adjacent cemetery. They are followed by a couple of sandalled monks, in long brown robes of coarse serge, girt round with a white cord, on their way perhaps to some neighbouring convent.

We have alluded to the change of tradition at Jerusalem, and
here is a notable instance of it. The church built over what, in
the worst times of monkish tradition, not to say pious fraud, were
declared to be the bones of St. Stephen, stood on the opposite
side of the city, and the gateway adjacent to it was called after
the protomartyr's name. It was totally destroyed, however, by
the Moslems, and now we find it most marvellously transported
to the existing site. This is but a bad introduction to the
legendary localities within the walls, which we are now about to
enter.

Pass we under the deep-vaulted gateway, and a long, narrow
street is before us, bordered with edifices evidently mediæval or
modern; some lying in heaps of ruin, and others in a state of
dilapidation and decay. And when we consider the amazing
number of revolutions that have swept Jerusalem as with the
besom of destruction, there needs no other evidence of the credu-
lity or fraud which would seek to identify the houses of Lazarus
and Dives, the place where the cock crew when Peter denied
his Lord, and the many other spots where New Testament
incidents are said to have occurred, even if the very monuments
by the modern style of their architecture did not prove the
absurdity of the tale. But, all allowance made for these changes,
it is not altogether improbable, to say the least, that the streets
may yet retain much of their original direction. In a city of
such limited size as Jerusalem, and, moreover, so strongly
marked as to site, nothing is more likely, as we see at the present
day in oriental cities, than that the houses should be rebuilt very
much upon the line which convenience or necessity originally
dictated.

This consideration would seem to give some degree of plausi-
bility, at least, to the tradition that the " Via Dolorosa," (or, as
it may be freely translated, the " Path of Sorrow,") and which
is the street in which we now stand, is that along which our
Saviour, burdened with his cross, ascended to the place of

crucifixion. The scene of his condemnation, we know, was the governor's house, adjacent to the temple, upon which this street abuts. A picturesque archway—a piece of ancient and modern patchwork, called that of the "Ecce Homo," from whence Pilate is said to have displayed Jesus to the populace—here bestrides the street, which, long, winding, and narrow, hence descends into and crosses the hollow which runs through the city. High stone walls enclose this street on either hand, broken here and there by a narrow Gothic portal, a small iron-barred window, or a projecting lattice of wood-work. It is throughout gloomy, as its name imports; and, except at the season of the pilgrimage, few are the passengers that frequent it.

Leaving the street which runs along the hollow before alluded to, the "Via Dolorosa" ascends to the Church of the Holy Sepulchre. This, however, it is not our purpose to describe. All that was manifestly connected with the life of Jesus at Jerusalem—the natural features of the landscape, upon which revolution has no power—the prominent outlines of the city, which cannot be mistaken—even such traditionary localities as appear to harmonize with probability, have been already noted. It forms no part of our plan to delineate in detail the monuments of Jerusalem, nor to enter upon the interminable question as to the genuine site of Calvary and the Holy Sepulchre.

There are one or two other places of Jerusalem connected with New Testament narrative; such are the Pool of Bethesda, the Pool of Siloam, and the Aceldama, or Field of Blood—hateful memento of sordid treachery. The site of the first is extremely doubtful, as there is no indication, either in Scripture or elsewhere, of its true position, unless by the circumstance, that an angel is said to have periodically troubled the water—a popular explanation of an ebbing and flowing well. Nothing at Jerusalem at all answers, at the present day, to this description, unless it is the so called Well of the Virgin, evidently a very ancient fountain, in the Valley of Jehoshaphat, just beneath the Temple,

in which the water occasionally rises and falls, from some cause
at present not very clearly understood, though generally supposed
to be the syphon-shaped channel by which water is said to be
conducted from the reservoirs of the temple above. The position
of the Pool of Siloam is open to no such uncertainty. It is further
down the same valley, at the mouth of the deep hollow called
the Tyropeon, which separated Jerusalem into two portions, precisely as described by Josephus. That of the Aceldama is
probably merely traditional, but its selection dates at least from
the time of Jerome. It is on the rugged side of the Valley of
Hinnom, just above a remarkable group of ancient tombs. It
has been observed that the sum received by Judas was extremely
small for the purchase of a field, even of one from which the
fuller's-earth had been worked out, and which was therefore
entirely barren and unproductive. It was destined by the
Sanhedrim for the "burial of strangers." A natural cavity,
arched over, and which served in the middle ages as a charnel-
house for pilgrims, occupies what is believed to be the spot thus
ignominiously distinguished.

  Of Bethlehem I shall say but little. The identity of the town
itself is indisputable, although great doubts may reasonably be
entertained whether the traditional Cave of the Nativity, over
which is erected the sumptuous Convent and Church of Helena,
is really the birthplace of Jesus, which, however, could not, in
any case, have been far distant. With the exception of this
immense fortified convent, which gives it a certain importance,
modern Bethlehem would still be the poor and insignificant
village it was when designated by the prophet as least among
the cities of Judah.

  With regard to the flight into Egypt, tradition has not been
idle; and it must be confessed that there is nothing improbable
in the locality it has fixed upon. In directing their steps toward
the land of refuge, Joseph and Mary would most likely take the
nearest road thither, by Gaza and Pelusium, towards Heliopolis

and Memphis,—a distance sufficient to put them beyond the reach of pursuit, without being inconveniently remote from their native country. Near the site of the former city, at the village of Matarea, there is a remarkable sycamore and well, where the Holy Family are believed to have taken up their temporary abode. We rode out thither one morning from Cairo; and as this venerable tree will not last for ever, there may be a certain degree of interest in preserving a likeness of it (see title-page), since, admitting this to be merely a tradition, it must at least be admitted to be a poetical one. The old tree stands in the midst of a small grove. Its trunk is hollow, and partly rent open, and its huge branches seem ready to fall with mere age. Its bark is much broken off, and its wood mercilessly chipped with the knives of innumerable pilgrims. This hoary patriarch is surrounded by a youthful *cortége* of fragrant citron and pome-granate-trees, and sundry parasitic plants have interlaced their tendrils with its giant limbs. A few palms stand around, as if to do him honour; and it is the delight of the pigeons and vultures to sway to and fro upon their graceful and elastic fans. From the edge of the grove may be seen, at scarcely a stone's-throw off, the mounds and solitary obelisk of Helio-polis. The adjacent well is called Ain Shems (the Fountain of the Sun), reputed to be the only real spring in the valley of the Nile, from the coolness and freshness of its water, though really supplied, as Wilkinson says, by filtration through the banks of that celebrated river. According to varieties of the story, this spring was miraculously opened to supply the thirst of the wanderers, or, being originally brackish, was sweetened by their miraculous powers. There is a whole group of traditions connected with the Flight in the neighbourhood of Cairo. In Pietro della Valle's time, a house at Matarea was shown as the dwelling-place of Mary; and at the Greek Convent at Old Cairo is another of the Virgin's chambers. The Mahommedans say, that Elizabeth, with her infant John, afterwards the Baptist, also fled into Egypt.

There may be, however, no value in such traditions, except that they seem to point out the neighbourhood in which the Holy Family did really seek refuge from the violence of Herod.

During my stay at Jerusalem I saw but little of Madame Pfeiffer, but on joining some travellers who were about to go down to the Jordan and the Dead Sea,—an excursion which, though short, is both fatiguing and perilous, she proved to be one of the party. At nightfall we reached the extraordinary convent of St. Saba, among the wild deserts of the Jordan, and here I found that, lest the sanctity of the brethren should be compromised, women were never admitted within the walls, a solitary tower without being appointed as their receptacle, and that to this tower she had been conducted. Thither, as in duty

LADY'S TOWER.

bound, being desirous that she should have all the comforts their somewhat " scant courtesy " allowed, I immediately repaired, accompanied by a lay brother, who was honoured with the appointment of groom of the chamber to lady pilgrims. Stumbling

in the dark over the rocky ground, we reached at length the base
of the tower, standing, quite isolated, upon the brink of a tremendous precipice. Here the lay brother, handing me the supper-
basket, planted a ladder so as to form a communication with the
portal, which was elevated some twenty feet above the ground,
and then, ascending, I following literally close at his heels, drew
forth a key and unlocked the small heavy door which gave access
to this female asylum, or rather prison. The room we entered
was empty, and, by another ladder, we ascended to the upper
story, which was furnished with some little attention to the bodily
comforts, but also to what seemed to be more consulted, the
spiritual edification of its gentle inmates. Pictures and images
of saints adorned the walls of a small oratory, niched into
the side of the apartment, and over which a few lamps cast
a dim uncertain gleam, leaving its extremities in gloomy
obscurity. Upon a low divan sat the object of our search, with
her usual expression of calm and fearless tranquillity. Her
simple supper was brought forth, and while she was engaged
with it, I asked her whether she did not feel timid at being left
in utter solitude. In fact, the dim, dreary look of this upper
chamber, the total darkness of the lower one, and the awful
stillness of both, were well calculated to act upon a nervous
imagination, and to awaken a train of dismal and superstitious
fancies. When Captain Basil Hall and his daughters visited
the place, the ladies had refused to be thus incarcerated, and
stormed away till allowed to enter the convent walls. Not so,
however, the German pilgrim; she declared that she never was
more comfortable, and refused my offer to remain on guard in
the lower story of the tower. Accordingly, we departed, and
locked her up snug for the night.

Long before sunrise next morning, we were all, including
Madame, mustered before the gate of the convent, and descending from the elevated region of Mar Saba, reached the desolate
shores of the Dead Sea before noon, from whence, suffering

intensely with heat and thirst, we made our way across the
desert valley to the verdant banks of the Jordan, which we
reached at the bathing-place of the Greek pilgrims. The Latin
monks, their rivals in holy places, have another for their followers
further up the stream, near to a spot where there exist the ruins
of a convent dedicated to St. John the Baptist, and each party
strenuously contends for the genuineness of its respective site,
as being that where John baptized the people unto repentance,
and where Jesus himself submitted to the rite. It is enough to
know that the place was near Bethabara, the ford of the Jordan,
over against Jericho, and which tradition has pointed out as the
place where the children of Israel passed over to the assault of
that city. No spot, it must be confessed, could be more suitable
or more wildly picturesque, than that where we now took refuge
from the insufferable heat of the sun. The river, as was always
the case, pours through a sultry desert, but its banks present
a sort of double channel, the lower filled at ordinary times, the
upper when its waters are periodically swollen, thus creating
an oasis of wild and tangled vegetation, a maze of cane brakes
and creepers, with thickets of willow and other trees, amidst
which it was easy to picture the figure of the Baptist with his
raiment of camel's-hair, and his leathern girdle, dispensing
the purifying rite to the trembling and repentant crowd.

When the heat had somewhat subsided, we struck across the
desert plain to the village of Rihhah, traditionally regarded by
the monks as the site of Jericho, although no ancient remains
whatever are to be discovered there. The ruinous Gothic tower,
which is the principal building in the place, is, with as good
reason, pointed out as the house of Zaccheus, where our Lord
rested when passing through the city.

About half an hour from hence we reached the beautiful
spring of Ain es Sultan, where we had determined to halt for the
night. The copious stream bursting forth from its basin runs down
towards Jericho, creating everywhere a rich, but, in the absence

of judicious irrigation, useless growth of shrubs, which has replaced the groves of palm-trees, and the exuberant vegetation which marked this neighbourhood as one of the most fertile under heaven. About a mile from our camp, forming the western boundary of the broad plain of the Jordan, arose the precipitous mountain of the "Quarantania," so called, because it is traditionally believed that the forty days and nights of our Lord's sojourn in the wilderness were passed there; while its elevated summit, which commands a view of half Palestine, is fixed on as the spot whence the Tempter showed Jesus "all the kingdoms of the earth and the glory thereof." And whether we are to take an objective or subjective view of the Temptation, it is at least certain that no more suitable spot for retirement from the world could have been selected, than the horrid wilderness of the Dead Sea, with its voiceless ravines and its arid crags, in the caves and clefts of which, particularly here and at Mar Saba, thousands of anchorites once took up their habitation.

I have now briefly summed up all that fairly pertains to my present subject; the traditional localities connected with the life of Jesus in the region of Judæa. The conclusion is obvious —that while we find all the general features of the country still subsisting, and with so little alteration as to add life and reality to the Scripture narrative, the attempt to identify those more minute must evidently be the work of fancy or of fraud.

Next day we returned to Jerusalem, by the road "from Jerusalem to Jericho," where, in the parable of our Lord, the man fell among thieves, and was relieved by the good Samaritan. From this it would appear that the road was then as proverbially insecure, as it is at the present day.

At Jerusalem I lost sight of my earnest and intrepid fellow-traveller, Madame Pfeiffer, who lingered there some time after my departure. I had been surprised at her powers of endurance during a journey which, short as it was, from the heat of the

N

weather, and the character of the country, had tried us all pretty
severely. Some years elapsed before I could gain any authentic
information concerning her movements, except that she had safely
terminated her journey to Palestine, and had published an account
of it. Imagine, therefore, my surprise, when I chanced, through
a newspaper paragraph, to learn that she was then in the vicinity
of London, and accessible to a visit. As her host resided at some
distance from town, a meeting was appointed at his counting-house
in the city. From Jerusalem to Crutched Friars was certainly a
rather abrupt transition, and as I pushed my way through the
multifarious obstructions of our crowded streets to the place of
rendezvous, I could not help speculating as to what changes had
been wrought by the interval of time and incidents of travel that
had occurred since our previous meeting.

I reached the house, hurried up two flights of dirty stairs,
tapped at the door of an office differing in no respect from the
thousand dark and dingy ones in the city. " Come in," was
the response; and on entering, in the shadow of the room and
looking strangely out of place in the midst of a heap of ledgers
and day-books, was, sure enough, the well-remembered face of
my old fellow-traveller, who rose and received me with the most
lively expression of satisfaction. I, too, was rejoiced to find no
change for the worse in the appearance of my friend after so
severe an ordeal as a journey round the world.

After exchanging our mutual congratulations, the conversation
(which was carried on in French, Madame speaking English but
imperfectly) naturally turned upon the subject of her recent
journey. Reminding her of our original meeting on the shores
of Palestine, and of the indifference with which she encountered
fatigue and hardship on that occasion, I playfully observed
" that I considered that she had served her apprenticeship to
myself, and that I had always boasted of a pupil who had left
her tutor so infinitely behind." She admitted that it was even
so, and that her power of bearing privation, tested in that

journey, together with the taste for travelling she then acquired, had led her to meditate still more extensive wanderings.

" It was after my journey to Iceland, which followed that into Palestine—"

" *Iceland!* my dear madame!" I exclaimed, with a sudden start. "Why, I had not the slightest notion you had ever visited that country."

" Oh yes, and published a book about it," was her quiet reply; and she immediately resumed,—"After this Iceland journey, then, I left Vienna and embarked at Hamburgh for Rio Janeiro, and, after remaining some time on the coasts of Brazil, penetrated into the interior, visited the savage tribes, and crossing the continent of South America, reached Valparaiso, which, as you know, is on the shores of the Pacific Ocean. Thence I crossed over to the island of Tahiti, where, during my stay, I was upon the most intimate terms with Queen Pomare. Leaving that beautiful spot, I crossed the wide Pacific Ocean to Canton, and there penetrated the Chinese quarter, into which Europeans are forbidden to enter. Such a sight had never been seen in Canton before. The people gathered in crowds, the women held up their children as I passed along, the curiosity and amusement of the people were prodigious, and your gracious Queen, on the opening of the Exhibition, could hardly be more run after than was my poor insignificant self."

" And were you not horribly afraid?" I inquired.

" Not in the least," was the reply.

" And did you meet with no insult?"

" Not the slightest. Nothing could exceed the civility of the people. After traversing the city, my Chinese guides brought me to the house of an English merchant, who could scarcely believe that I had come off scathless from so unprecedented an enterprise. Well, from Canton I went to several of the principal ports of China, and then, touching at Singapore, made my way to Ceylon, where, not satisfied with remaining at Point de

Galle, I visited the capital, Kandy. Calcutta was the next point of my journey. I ascended the Ganges on the deck of a bungalow, went far into the interior, examined the antiquities, visited the courts of some of the native princes, by whom I was kindly received, and, satisfied with my survey of India, returned to the coast, embarked for the Persian Gulf, and then, ascending the Tigris, looked in upon Dr. Layard in the midst of his excavations at Nineveh."

Such a narrative of adventure, and from the mouth of a female, might well take away one's breath. I really seemed to be dreaming as I looked upon the frail little body before me, and heard her describe a devious career like this with far less excitement of manner than the mistress of a cockney boarding-school would throw into her account of the perils of a journey to Boulogne. "What next?" I inwardly exclaimed, as Madame, renewing her narrative, quietly went on.

".I entered next upon a *rather* dangerous journey among the countries occupied by the wandering tribes of Kurdistan. Here I more than once fell into the hands of robbers."

"You surely were not alone on this occasion?" I exclaimed.

"Entirely so," she replied; "and to that cause I probably owed my complete immunity from outrage. What could they do? They saw before them a poor unprotected woman, advanced in years, and with all she possessed in the world done up in a small bundle. They would stop my horse, gaze upon me with astonishment, ask a few questions, and then suffer me to pass unmolested. On one occasion, being exhausted with thirst, I begged for water from the leathern bottles they carry it about in, and they gave it me immediately."

"Then there are many more Robin Hoods than have ever been commemorated in song; there *is* honour even among thieves. Human nature is the same in the forest of Sherwood and the wilds of Kurdistan!"

"Well," she resumed; "after I had done with the Kurds,

I made my way through Persia and Circassia to the shores of the Black Sea, along which I sailed to Constantinople; thence to Greece, Sicily, and Italy, and so back to my own door at Vienna, after an absence of *three years.* And now guess, what do you think this journey cost me?"

Having already observed the simple and self-denying habits of my old companion, I was prepared for a rather low estimate, but when I considered the mere distance she had gone over, without allowing her anything to eat, I mentally named a figure, (a sum of several hundreds,) which some experience in travel led me to fix upon as the very minimum of her expense. What was my surprise, then, when she declared that she had performed this extensive series of wanderings into the interior of so many countries, where the means of conveyance are almost wanting, for the insignificant sum of a hundred and fifty pounds!

Far from her taste for travel having been satisfied, it seemed only "to have grown by what it fed on," and she was already preparing for a second voyage around the globe. Although scientific research was not to be expected from a solitary woman, yet her travels had not been without fruit, since she had made collections in botany and entomology which formed a valuable addition to the museum of Vienna. The Austrian Government had not merely paid her for these, but had made her a present of a hundred pounds towards the prosecution of her further adventures; while the Professors had given her instructions in the best mode of preserving specimens, and collecting objects of value to science.

Her intention was to go by the Cape to Australia and New Zealand, and thence to Borneo and the islands of the Indian Archipelago. She had already taken her passage, and was to sail during the following week.

Alluding to the manner in which I had re-discovered her, I observed, that I had previously gained tidings of her through a New York newspaper, under the head of "What is talked about," stating that she was in that city, after performing her voyage round the world. What was then my surprise to learn, " that she was never there in all her life," and that the statement was a pure mystification, like so many others in which our transatlantic brethren seem to delight. " It was this account," I remarked, " that mentioned your being wounded by a robber, stating moreover that you had valiantly defended yourself, and cut off one or two of your adversary's fingers with a knife, and that, I suppose, is also an invention of the editor's."

" On the contrary," she replied, " *that* is strictly true, and I bore away with me a lasting memento of it; " she then extended her arm, enveloped in a muslin sleeve, and invited me to make an examination of it. As I did so, my hand sunk, with a sickening sensation, into a hollow, midway between the elbow and the shoulder, the token of a deep and ghastly wound, which she will carry with her to the grave.

Reminiscences such as these filled up the remainder of our interview. I was disappointed in my hope of seeing this extraordinary woman again before leaving England. Shortly afterward she set sail upon her long and perilous enterprise, at a time of life when most persons are only anxious to repose calmly by the fireside for the remainder of their days. Notwithstanding the old proverb concerning " the pitcher and the well," let us earnestly hope that she may return safe and sound to her own home, and add another chapter to the record of her most marvellous experiences.

CHAPTER V.

DRS. ROBINSON and SMITH having identified several ancient
sites a little to the eastward of the high road from Jerusalem
to Samaria, we were induced to shape our route so as to include
them, and thus to render it, if somewhat less direct, yet con-
siderably more interesting; passing by way of Anata (Anathoth),
and Muckmas (Michmash), to Beitin, or Bethel, before regaining
the usual track.

Another interesting circuit was made to Seilun, or " Shiloh,"
where there are numerous tombs and remains of ancient edifices,
which show that it must once have been a site of some importance.

Re-entering the high road again early in the morning, we
reached, at eventide, the entrance to the valley of Nabulus, the
ancient Sichem, which turns off upon the left. The way to
Samaria and Galilee now runs up this valley to the westward,
but in all probability there was formerly a more direct road to
the eastward. Just at the point where these roads would have
intersected, is the ancient well, which, by an almost uninterrupted
tradition of Jews, Samaritans, Christians, and Mohammedans, is
said to be the same dug by the patriarch Jacob. It was by this
well that while his disciples went to buy provisions, our Saviour
sat down previous to resuming his onward course into Galilee
without turning aside into the city; and here occurred the
scene with the Samaritan woman so vividly narrated in the
Gospel of St. John.

The scene is one that, from its few and simple elements, easily

rivets itself upon the memory. In the foreground is the mouth
of the well, nearly blocked up by stones and brambles. This
orifice is in the roof of a vaulted chamber, in which is the well
itself, which is upwards of a hundred feet to the bottom, thus
answering to the description of the Samaritan woman, " Sir, the
well is deep." It now appears to be dry. Near it, upon the
mound, are the scarcely recognisable remains of a church, which
the piety of the middle ages erected upon the spot. At a short
distance appears on a little montecule, the traditional tomb of
Joseph, a Moslem edifice, built probably over the original burial-
place; and below, is the " parcel of ground," which his father
Jacob purchased of the Shechemites. This was now waving
with corn as it was in the time of Jesus, and to this he pointed

JACOB'S WELL.

when he, in his joy, metaphorically alluded to " the fields which
were already white unto harvest." Nor less vividly do the
bolder features of the landscape correspond with the Gospel
narrative.

Mounts Ebal and Gerizim, the hills of cursing and blessing,
but now rugged and barren alike, rise behind. Upon the latter,
then was, and now is, the sacred altar of the Samaritans.
To this the woman pointed when she said, " Our fathers

worshipped in this mountain," a remark which drew from our
Saviour the sublime annunciation, that "neither in this mountain, nor yet at Jerusalem" should men worship the Father, but
that "the true worshippers should everywhere worship him in
spirit and in truth."

Perhaps there is no scene in Palestine more strikingly con-
formable to the scripture narrative than this, or to which attaches
such a train of venerable and momentous recollections.

We pursued our way into Nabulus, which is not far distant,
where we took up our abode for the night. A handful of the
Samaritans still linger here after the lapse of so many centuries.
We visited their synagogue, and saw their celebrated copy of the
Pentateuch. Next morning, accompanied by a young man of
this community, we ascended to the summit of Mount Gerizim,
whence the fertile valley of Nabulus is seen spread out below,
like a carpet of verdure. The principal object of interest was the
castle that crowns the summit, and the holy place of the Samaritans. This castle, which was built by Justinian, owed its
origin to an ebullition of Samaritan bigotry. The first converts
to the Christian faith were made at the time of our Lord's visit,
and others were afterwards added by the labours of the Apostles,
until the city, which under the Romans was called Neapolis,
became an Episcopal see. The fanaticism of the Samaritans now
broke out in acts of violence; these the Christian emperors
resented by driving them from their holy mountain, and building a Christian church on its summit: as they still continued
to interrupt the worship of the Christians, Justinian built this
fortress to protect the latter from any further annoyance.

Not far from this edifice is a singular hollow, which our guide
declared to be the holy place of his people. Formerly they had
a temple on the mountain, but no remains of it have as yet been
identified.

From hence there is a very striking view, embracing the holy
place, the castle, and the "parcel of ground" which Jacob bought

of the Shechemites, with the village of " Shalim " on a small
mound, the Shalim passed by the patriarch on his route from the
banks of the Jordan, and the distant mountains on the other side
of that river.

In the afternoon we also ascended Mount Ebal, but could discover no trace of bygone generations, though the view, like that
from Gerizim, is splendid and extensive.

Pursuing our way next morning along the beautiful valley of
Nabulus, in about an hour, the bold hill of Samaria rose before
us, standing isolated in the midst of a basin of mountains, all
cultivated to their summits, a position alike strong and beautiful.
Formerly, as there is indeed monumental evidence to prove, the
cultivated terraces into which the hill-side is fashioned, were

SAMARIA.

adorned with the buildings of the city. The small village of
Sebustieh now occupies a portion of the site, and at the eastern
extremity is the church built by Justinian over the reputed tomb
of John the Baptist. This we were not permitted to enter; but
on riding over the hill, came upon the remains of a splendid
colonnade, which had once been evidently of great extent, and

which was terminated to the westward by the foundations of a gateway.

This is no doubt a relic of some magnificent edifice with which Herod adorned the city. Lower down the mountain side we found another group of columns, which seemed as though they had formed a part of some forum or public market-place. These are the only apparent remains of the splendid capital where the kings of Israel once held their court.

There is no mention of our Saviour's personally visiting Samaria—at that time in the very zenith of its glory; having been rebuilt by Herod the Great, with his customary display of magnificence, after it had been bestowed on him by Augustus, in honour of whom it received the name of Sebaste, being the Greek translation of his name. The parts about Phenice and Samaria were visited by Philip after the dispersion of the Apostles; and here a church was gradually formed, and an episcopal see established, which fell only with the triumph of Mahommedanism.

The descent from the crest of the hill of Samaria is extremely rapid, and the city, strongly fortified as it was by Herod, would seem to have been almost impregnable; yet no part of its walls are standing, and how or when they were levelled with the dust, like all the rest of the city, there are no accounts to show.

Hence our way led over cultivated hills and valleys of no remark; the isolated hill fortress of Sanur being the only conspicuous object, on the way to the edge of the great plain of Esdraelon. In traversing Palestine, even in its present state of decay, the mind is forcibly struck by the reflection that it contains much more arable land than is usually supposed, and that the evident fruitfulness of the whole region, when cultivated as it is in terraces, imparts to it a capacity of sustaining an immense population.

The evening view of the great plain as we came down upon it at the village of Jenin, was enchanting. True, its level surface was almost bare of wood, but it was covered with richly variegated crops, which caught the slanting rays of the setting sun; while the range of Gilboa, dark, dim, and gloomy, and the more distant mountains towards Nazareth, assumed a fugitive gorgeousness of effect and colouring. The white monuments and flat-roofed buildings of Jenin were below, intermingled with graceful palms. Immense heaps of corn lay in the open air, about the threshing-floors; and flocks and herds were slowly making their way towards their nightly enclosures.

The traveller in Palestine should always make some sacrifice to carry a tent, as it renders him independent of the filthy dwellings of the natives, generally swarming with fleas, and all sorts of vermin. It is almost humiliating to recal one's precautions and contrivances to obtain a comfortable night's rest. We had been horribly tattooed at Nabulus, and some of our persecutors having insinuated themselves into the clothes and baggage, a good half-hour was spent in thoroughly beating and cleansing them. The place appointed for our quarters, a raised platform of plaster outside a cottage, was then washed and scrubbed, together with the neighbouring walls: the swarming mats and suspicious cushions of the natives kicked aside before venturing to lay down the carpet and mattress which served as a nightly couch. It was a long and laborious operation, but happily crowned with entire success, and we got on horse-back early next morning with a feeling of unaccustomed exhilaration and vigour.

If the plain of Esdraelon looked beautiful the evening before, it was no less so in the bright light of morning; and there was besides an additional luxury—that of being able to gallop at will over the open ground, after being confined to the walking pace at which the ruggedness of the path generally compels one to travel. Before noon, following the track of Robinson, we reached Zerin, the site of Jezreel, recalling vividly the story of Naboth's vineyard, and the death of Jezebel; and looking from its crested height down the long valley extending to the Jordan, we could distinguish the site of Beisan, the Bethshan upon which the bodies of the fallen Israelites were displayed, after the disastrous battle in which Saul and Jonathan lost their lives, and which called forth the beautiful verses of David,—"Ye mountains of Gilboa, let there be no dew, neither let there be rain upon you, nor fields of offerings, for there the shield of the mighty is vilely cast away, the shield of Saul, as though he had not been anointed with oil." And in looking up to the gloomy mountain which towers behind Jezreel, one might almost fancy that its dark funereal-looking hollows still sympathise with the lament of the poet. At the fountain below Jezreel, they encamped before advancing to the fatal encounter.

The whole scene around was a fresh reading of the historical chapters of the Old Testament, under the light of local illustration. Upon the solitary-looking mountains opposite was Megiddo; in the plain below was fought the battle between Pharaoh Necho, King of Egypt, and the good King Josiah, in which the latter was slain. But dark and blood-stained in general are the annals of Old Testament history; and our business is with the sites and scenes of New Testament narrative.

After a short rest in the village of Zerin, we set off at a gallop, and scarcely drew bridle till we reached that of Solam, according to Robinson, the Shunem of the tribe of Issachar, where the Philistines halted before the battle on Mount Gilboa. A little beyond, we opened a second branch of the immense plain, and the rounded cone of Mount Tabor suddenly came in sight, standing up with a peculiar aspect of solitude in the midst of the corn-covered expanse. On the northern side of the mountain above Shunem, on a little acclivity above the plain, was a cluster of white houses, which, on inquiry, I found to be called Nein, the village where our Saviour restored the widow's son to life. It lies but little out of the road, yet few travellers ever deviate so far. If any place, however, could tempt a traveller from the beaten track, it is this; and we turned our horses into the narrow bridle-path leading through the rustling corn-fields up to the gentle acclivity on which the village stands.

NAIN.

We found, as we expected, nothing of the slightest consequence. Nain resembles any other of the humbler villages of Palestine—a few flat-roofed houses of white cement, before the doors of which lies, up-heaped, the corn gathered in from the exuberant plain around. A few peasants, little accustomed to the sight of strangers, gazed on our cavalcade with surprise. Women peeped out of the hovels, and a company of bright-eyed children followed our movements with eager curiosity, starting back half in play and half in fright when we happened to turn round and look at them. There was nothing in the world beside. The village is now what we have every reason to suppose it was in the time of our Saviour—a small place, where every joy and every sorrow that befals a member of the little community is sympathised with by all the others. It was easy to figure the whole of the villagers following, with genuine sorrow, the poor bereaved widow to the grave of her only son, when they encountered the Lord of life and glory as he ascended on foot with his disciples to the obscure hamlet from the neighbouring corn-fields—to picture, in short, the whole transaction, and all the feelings which it called into action among this secluded circle. We were as happy to have turned aside to Nain, as if we had discovered the site of some ancient city.

Again we descended into the plain, obtaining a pretty retrospective view of the village and mountain behind. The landscape has the serene simplicity which Wordsworth has so well characterised—

> " The mountains bare, and the bare earth,
> And grass in the green field."

Another half-hour's ride carried us over the plain, and we struck a narrow stony road leading over a space of grassy hills to Nazareth. From their summit, the secluded valley with its white village lay at our feet, possessing, without any peculiar beauty, a character of sequestered tranquillity and pastoral abundance, well suited with its associations.

> " 'Tis Nazareth in Galilee, the spot
> Where, warn'd of God, obedient Joseph fled
> With holy Mary, his espousèd wife,
> That thence the Virgin Mother's first-born Son,
> Jesus—the world's Redeemer, promised long—
> Might, as the prophets had foretold, be call'd
> A Nazarene."

> " A spot despised through Jewry in old times,
> Even as the Man of Sorrows, who thence sprang,
> Was the despised, rejected amongst men.
> ' Comes any good thing out of Nazareth ?'
> Inquired the sneering Jew."

It is now, but for the halo which will ever hang over it, and which draws the foot of the pilgrim from the most distant land, almost as secluded a nook as when it called forth this contemptuous sarcasm. It is indeed strange, and fortunate besides, that while large towns have grown up around the abiding places of mediæval saints, the village where Jesus was born has escaped this disfiguring homage, and retained its original appearance, probably, with as little alteration as it was possible for time to work. This reflection forcibly struck us as we descended the rock by a winding road into the sunny corn-fields, interspersed

NAZARETH.

with grey and venerable olives, amidst which the reapers were at work, as in the days when Joseph and Mary occupied an obscure house in this obscure hamlet, near two thousand years ago.

On arriving at Nazareth we dismounted before the convent gate, and Achmet having announced our arrival, we were shortly afterwards ushered by one of the monks into the superior's apartment. In most other parts of Palestine, the Moslem population outnumbers the Christian; the contrary of this is here the case, and thus the Nazarenes enjoy a greater degree of independence than elsewhere. The prior of the convent, who is the head of this community, is consequently a personage of importance, combining with his spiritual no small measure also of temporal influence. There was something like a consciousness of this in the manner of the man in whose presence we now stood. He was a young Italian, strikingly handsome in person, and acutely intelligent in mien, of a type of beauty that Vandyke would have delighted to paint. His conventual dress of coarse brown serge was arrayed with a certain pretension, his oval beard was carefully trimmed into shape and combed; and the fingers of the delicate white hand, which escaped from the shaggy sleeve, were adorned with rings, displayed, as we could not help thinking, with a sort of studied elegance. His reception was full of courtesy, but more like that of the man of the world than the monk; and the conversation, instead of turning upon Nazareth and its sacred associations, was altogether mundane and political in its tone. We spoke of the troubled state of the country—of the unsettled quarrel between Mehemet Ali and the Porte—of the growing weakness of the Moslems, and of the increasing power of the Christians. Should any European power be disposed to rescue the Holy Land from Ottoman misrule, the natives, he assured me, would at once arise, and receive their deliverers with open arms. "England by sea, and France by land," were, as the prior declared, irresistible; and should they combine their forces, the conquest of Syria was a matter of immediate certainty. In all this there was probably a certain reserve; the astute prior could not but be aware, that the jealousy of the European powers with regard to each other's acquisitions of territory must long defer, if it did not for ever prevent, their occupation of Palestine; and in a Catholic convent, which, like all those of the Holy Land, was placed under the hereditary protection of France, he would have been little disposed to accept the interference of any other nation, even could it add to, rather than as, in fact, it must dimimish, the virtual independence which his convent at present enjoys. But of the readiness of Syria to receive the yoke of a foreign power, we had ample evidence during our stay in the country. Our conversation terminated, he dismissed us very graciously, and ordered two beds to be made up for the Christian master and the Moslem servant—a stretch of polite attention, which we had never hitherto experienced.

The convent at Nazareth is an extensive and irregular edifice, surrounded by a strong wall, affording ample security against any sudden attack. Within its confines is the church, over what tradition has selected as the house of Joseph and Mary, in which the youth of our Saviour was passed; a tradition which, if there is nothing to establish, there is at least on the other hand as little to disprove.

This building is far less extensive than the Church of the Nativity at Bethlehem, but it is decorated in the same way, and furnished with an organ, the touching notes of which arose sweetly for vespers as we looked in upon the edifice, and disposed the mind to a train of feeling, in harmony with the sacred associations of the place.

From the window of the massive stone structure, which serves as a receptacle for the pilgrim and the traveller, I looked out upon the little valley in search of some spot where I might retire, and wear away the remaining hour or two of a very exciting day, in tranquil repose among its shades; a group of massive carob-trees, just lifted above its green level, about half-a-mile from the village, struck me as the very retirement I wished, and in a short time I was stretched beneath their ample branches.

The quiet beauty of the scene was remarkable; it was such as the Italian painters would have selected, in the midst of which to place their groups of the Madonna and infant Jesus. It is rarely the case that a locality satisfies the imagination, but in this instance there was nothing wanting. The spreading trees above bent over towards the valley, almost touching the ground, and seeming as a frame to confine the picture. The little valley lay below, encircled by hills of moderate height, alternately green and rocky, beneath which, half hidden, the white buildings of Nazareth appear to nestle for shelter; on the left, the hills drop quietly to the valley, beautifully broken by groups of trees and rocky fragments.

The sun was setting, and camels and asses laden with grain came down from all sides into the level valley, where the rich produce of the soil was deposited. The animals, relieved of their loads, were enjoying their provender; the peasants, reposing after their labours, among the heaps of corn, with their fragrant pipes, were quietly enjoying the coolness of the evening ; and beautifully shone out the whole picture as the numerous flocks slowly descended from the hills, preceded by their owners on horseback, in their bright-coloured costume, and with their glistening arms slung across their shoulders. Such, no doubt, was the landscape in the days of Joseph, and such in all respects the scene might then have appeared, had the peasants been of the same race with those who then dwelt upon the soil. But there is no Jewish population now in the valley, which is inhabited chiefly by a race of Arab blood, or rather Syrian and Arab intermingled. They are strong, well made, and fearless, clothed principally in garments of sheepskin ; bearing in their leather girdles a brace of pistols and a pipe ; their heads invested in a picturesque *bernous* or handkerchief, woven with lines of gold and vermilion, its ample folds being considered the best protection against the summer heat, and their feet shod with sandals tied by leather thongs— a costume exceedingly broad, noble, and picturesque ; probably, from its simplicity and adaptation to the climate, of very early origin ; and differing but little from that worn in the time of the patriarchs.

The monkish traditional localities at Nazareth are all so obviously and peculiarly improbable, that they may be very speedily dismissed ; indeed, I cannot say that I took the trouble of visiting them. In such a place one would rather seek to bring one's feelings into a suitable frame of seriousness, by gazing upon those same unchanged natural features amidst which the Saviour of the world grew up, than to have them disgusted or wounded by the palpable inventions of a set of interested and superstitious monks. Every one has heard of the holy house of the Virgin, which, to escape the contamination of Saracen handling, was, after resting once or twice by the way in Dalmatia and elsewhere, by angelic ministry miraculously transported hence to Loretto. As this aërial voyage rests upon testimony equally

conclusive with that of the great bulk of mediæval miracles, it
would be, as some might think, at once useless and impious to
controvert it, especially as, in order to refute any profane objec-
tions, the very spot whence it was carried away is still to be
seen under the roof of the Catholic church, the kitchen being left
behind as a memorial of the fact, and also, perhaps, as an unnecessary incumbrance. In like manner the workshop of Joseph
the carpenter, with the table at which he ate, is to be seen in
the town, duly enshrined within a little chapel. These legendary
sites are the monopoly of the Latins; but these monks, and
those of the Greek Church, each contend for the true locality
of the Annunciation, the former placing it in their convent, the
latter in their church, near to the Fountain of the Virgin.

If any of the present traditional sites of the life of Jesus and
his parents are worthy of credit, we should be disposed to select
the Well of the Virgin. It is at a short distance from the village, much frequented by women, bearing their water-jars in the
picturesque and graceful fashion of the country. The spot is
very pretty; a small white fountain stands just under the hill
behind Nazareth, and is supplied with water from a spring *under*
the Greek church of the Annunciation, a low building in the
background. It would appear that here formerly existed a subterraneous church or chapel enclosing the spring. The path of
approach to the open space before the fountain is bordered by
hedges of prickly pear; groups of women are continually passing,
while an incessant chorus of female voices rises loud at the
fountain itself; and trains of laden camels or passing travellers
give additional animation to the scene. It was not without considerable difficulty that we could get any of the women to stand
a few moments for their portraits; the eloquence of my Turkish
servant—and, to do him justice, he possessed amazing readiness and volubility—being scarcely sufficient for the purpose,
although in full play the whole time. They are generally tall,
and many possess no common beauty of face and person;

while, the figure being unfettered by certain western contrivances, their habit of carrying the jars, of course in a perfectly erect position, gives an exquisite freedom and grace to their movements. Their costume is exceedingly elegant, plying to their lithe and undulating movements with a perfection that a Parisian *modiste* would be puzzled to attain.

Nothing is more probable than that this spring should have been frequented from the earliest period; and we may reasonably picture the mother of Jesus coming with her child, like the rest of the women of Nazareth, to fetch water from the fountain. The cliff which rises steeply behind the village, too, appears stamped with every token of identity, as one of the places referred to in the few notices of Nazareth occurring in the New Testament, and as being the hill to the brow of which the enraged inhabitants led Jesus, and whence they would have cast him down, but that he, passing through the midst of them, went his way.

The evening was spent at the house of Abu Nazir, a wealthy Greek Christian, well known to the American missionaries, and who, as it was said the country was disturbed, and robbers were abroad, advised us to take an escort to Tiberias.

We set forth from his house next morning in unusual state, accompanied by his two sons and a brace of other followers, all of them armed to the teeth.

The road through the undulating and rocky hills of Galilee was pretty; the village of Reineh appeared amidst its groves of olive, and soon after we reached Kefr Kenna, anciently reputed to be the Cana of Galilee, where our Saviour changed the water into wine; but its pretensions, like those of so many other old and orthodox sites, have been of late rudely disturbed by the scrutinising criticism of Robinson in favour of another site, somewhat to the northward, called Cana-el-Jelil. Soon after leaving this village, we ascended a mountain's side, and having crossed it, obtained a very striking view of Mount Tabor, covered with wood, rising in isolated beauty, from amidst a region of oak forests, resembling, except that they are wilder, the plantations of an English park.

This was quite a new phase of scenery; the greater part of Palestine being remarkably bare of wood. In less than an hour we were at its base, and sending a messenger forward to Deburieh to bespeak our quarters for the night, we urged our horses up the grassy side of the mountain, between the scattered oak-trees. In about half-an-hour more we dismounted at the summit, which

MOUNT TABOR.

occupies a more extensive area than would be supposed at a distance, and bears traces of considerable erections, but is entirely abandoned, at the present day, to the wild boars and other animals that lurk among its thickets. The most striking of these remains is a gateway of Saracenic architecture, forming the entrance of an extensive ruined edifice, and from its lofty position well denominated the " Tower of the Winds."

The view from hence on all sides is magnificent, but the most striking feature of the scene is undoubtedly the great plain of

Esdraelon and its branches, which come up to the very foot of the mountain. Just under us was the little village of Deburieh, whither we wended our way down shady thickets of oaks, and established our bivouac at nightfall upon the roof of a house, amidst heaps of corn just gathered in from the surrounding plain.

We left Deburieh at day-break—winding through the oak glades which form so beautiful a cincture to the solitary cone of Tabor; the long waving grass which fills up the intervals of the scattered forest-trees was heavy with dew, and their branches sometimes nearly met over our heads. Though these are gene-

TOWER OF THE WINDS.

rally inferior in size to the oaks of our own island, they were yet of sufficient growth to be highly picturesque. As we passed in silence among them, we discerned on the bare topmost boughs of one of the largest, a group of eagles; the guns of my company were raised in a moment, but I would not suffer them to disturb these solitary tenants of the forest; they were startled, however, by the noise of our passage, and, spreading their broad wings, mounted slowly and majestically towards the upper region of the mountain. Not long after, we came unexpectedly upon an open grassy area, on the left of the path, surrounded by higher slopes, dotted with groups of trees, and presenting with singular exactness the appearance of an undulating English park, in the midst of which were spread out the black tents of an encampment of Bedouins. I was so struck with the picturesque beauty of this sudden apparition, that without a word I struck off the path, and made straight for their camp; when, turning my head, I perceived my servant, Mukarey, and the brace of escorts I had picked up at Nazareth, following after me with ill-disguised uneasiness.

The taste of Forest Gilpin or Uvedale Price could not have suggested a happier or more picturesque position than these Arabs had chosen for their temporary resting-place. The tents of the chief and his family were pitched upon a grassy ridge, gently elevated above the rest, and sheltered by some dense and wide-spreading oaks. The tents were composed of a strong coarse stuff, like sacking, woven in a broad mass of *black* relieved by a white line; and in general appearance there is little doubt they corresponded with those of the earliest times. Such might have been the tent of Abraham beneath the terebinth-tree. And the figures who gathered around us were truly patriarchal in aspect; an old man, whose venerable face, with long white beard, was of calm and benevolent expression, clothed in the broad and simple folds of his striped robe, and resting, like Jacob, on the top of his staff, surveyed us with quiet curiosity. Several others, dark in hue almost to blackness, were couched upon the ground, and regarded us time after time from beneath the shade of their brilliant head-dresses of striped and gilt handkerchiefs, with a less pleasing expression. They might well have personified the turbulent sons of the Patriarch. We liked not the unquiet and sinister roving of their keen black eyes. In the meantime my servant and escort were by no means at their ease; and, in reply to the numerous inquiries of the Arabs, gave them to understand that I was a Consulo Inglese, about to join the Pasha of Acre at his neighbouring encampment. This improvised fiction, borne out by the unusual state in which I happened to be travelling, repressed any disposition to take advantage of us. They rose and crowded round my sketch, laughing with childish delight as I transferred rapidly to my paper some traits of their primitive appearance. Their women, peeping from the tents, displayed harsh and bold faces, with the wild black eye and cunning expression of the gipsy; they were clothed in loose dresses of blue serge, gathered round the waist, and their attitudes would have formed a study for the sculptor. Flocks of sheep and goats were grouped around, and horses picketed by the tent sides. All this in the heart of the forest, with the towering and woody crest of Tabor above, constituted a scene of unusual interest and beauty.

The impatience of my companions hurried me away; they retreated slowly and without any appearance of alarm, but no sooner were we out of sight of the Arabs than they quickened their paces to a gallop, assuring me that this was the very worst of those half-shepherd, half-robber tribes belonging to the wild mountains beyond the Jordan, who rove with their flocks about the luxuriant pasturages of this district, and who would certainly have laid us under contribution but for the near presence of the pasha and his troops.

I was glad, notwithstanding, to have had an opportunity of witnessing a scene which brought to my mind the exquisite lines of Thomson, in which, with such singular felicity,

> "—— depicted was the patriarchal age,
> What time Dan Abraham left the Chaldee land,
> And pastured on from verdant stage to stage,
> Where field and fountains fresh could best engage.
> Toil was not then. Of nothing took they heed;
> But with wild beasts the sylvan war to wage,
> And o'er vast plains their herds and flocks to feed."

Apart from their predatory propensities, which, however, were those of their contemporary tribes, such must have been indeed the pastoral life, wandering habits, and very appearance of the names most venerated in Jewish history. In the character of these tribes themselves there is often a marked difference, notwithstanding their common descent; some being, from local or accidental circumstances, much less rapacious and treacherous than others; but, in general, their presence west of the Jordan adds to the insecurity of the quiet cultivator of the soil—who, at present placed between two evils, equally dreads the exactions of the sultan's agents, and the lawless and unchecked depredation of these roving plunderers. Thus the land mourns and languishes, and its finest portions are often left to the wild luxuriance of nature.

Shortly after this little episode we emerged from the oak forests, and saw before us two ancient castles, built in the middle ages, to command the high road to Damascus. It was here the pasha was encamped, in order to receive some dues; and there was a numerous gathering of the Arab sheiks of the neighbouring tribes. A more picturesque assemblage one would not desire to see. The greater part of these chieftains were of lofty stature, thin and sinewy in frame, clothed in long flowing robes, and their dusky bearded countenances surmounted by ample turbans. They were armed with swords slung from their sides, and huge pistols stuck in their girdles; some of them bearing their long standard-like lances, although the greater number had planted them in the ground, as rallying places for their followers. Their steeds were of the true Arab blood, fleet as the wind, slender and graceful in form, and handsomely and tastefully caparisoned. The movements and bearing of these sheiks had the ease and nobility resulting from untrammelled action and simple unchanging habits, the absence of all conventionalism; they looked, in short, like men; and the only drawback to their superb appearance was a certain sinister glancing of the keen black eye, like that of our nomad friends of the forest, which seemed to indicate that thieving was regarded among them as an ancient and respectable vocation.

Satisfied with enjoying the picturesque *coup d'œil* of the scattered groups, the castles, and the wooded cone of Mount Tabor, without stopping to pay our respects to the pasha, who seemed to have work enough on his hands, we resumed our course towards the Sea of Galilee. A high level plain extended around us, covered with crops of grain, and on the left arose the conical tops of a range of hills—the too celebrated " Horns of Hattin," the scene of that terrible discomfiture of the Christian hosts by Saladin, which led to the final evacuation of Palestine. Shortly after passing this blood-stained spot, we came to the brink of a vast hollow, and the Lake of Tiberias lay slumbering far beneath our feet.

The sun was nearly at the zenith, and diffused a flood of dazzling light upon the waters, just ruffled by a passing breeze, on which we beheld a solitary bark, a mere speck, slowly making its way towards Tiberias. That city, with its huge castle and turreted walls, a pile of melancholy ruins, lay scattered along the nearer shore. The lake, about ten miles long, and five or six broad, was embosomed in mountains; or, to describe it more correctly, was like a great caldron sunk in the lofty table-land, which broke down to its edge in steep cliffs and abrupt ravines. At one end we could see where the Jordan flowed into it, and beyond, the lofty peak of Mount Hermon covered with eternal snow. There was no wood on the hills, no villages on the shore, no boats upon the waters, no sound in any direction. If there was beauty, it was that of the intense blue sky of Palestine, reflected in the blue expanse of waters, and overcanopying a landscape of serene, but corpse-like placidity, like a countenance fixed in death, but upon which there yet lingers something of a parting smile.

On approaching the city, there was no occasion to seek for any regular entrance, for the walls, rent open by the earthquake, and nodding to their final fall, afforded so many breaches, that our only embarrassment was, which of them to choose. We made for the nearest, and urging our horses over a pile of fallen stone-work, were at once within Tiberias; a labyrinth of ruin was before us, whole streets were shaken to the earth, blocking up the passage; while a few houses, tottering perilously over the head of the passenger, seemed melancholy and folorn as the last relics of a family who have survived when the rest of their kindred have been swept away by the plague. Among these, some of the poorer inhabitants, returned to the venerated spot, were taking up their wretched temporary habitation; while some of their richer brethren had already built up again their fallen dwellings. Directed by our Nazareth friends, we picked our way through the confusion to one of these newly built houses, occupied by one of the better class of Jews. We had lighted upon him at a very interesting moment, his young second wife being engaged in celebrating the birth of her firstborn child, surrounded by a whole conclave of Jewish women, who kept up an incessant chattering. This worthy Israelite had been among the sufferers by the earth-quake; his first wife and child having been crushed to death; and "what was worse," as a friend assured me he told him, " he had lost amidst the ruins a bag of several hundred dollars, which he had never succeeded in recovering;" and it must be admitted that there was so far reason in his estimate, that it had evidently been found by him much easier to replace the former article than the latter.

As soon as we had deposited our baggage in the house, and taken some slight refreshment, I made my way through the ruined streets to the borders of the lake, with the intention of taking, if possible, a short sail in the one solitary boat—for there was but that one—which had already attracted our observation. I found it by a point of land at the foot of one of the ruined towers which overhung the water. Nothing could speak more eloquently of the decline of the country than the whole picture.

On a lake abounding with fish, and which in the time of our Saviour was crowded with Roman galleys and boats, was now

Tiberias.

none but this most miserable craft, composed of planks rudely nailed together, the mast and tackle of the most primitive description, and looking so unsafe, as if

"—— the very rats
Instinctively had quit it."

Its two or three sailors were Jews, the first and only ones we ever met with of that craft; moreover, they were fishermen, and in their garb and mien might have been no inapt representatives of the Apostles themselves. They were engaged in mending their nets, in order to " go a fishing," as soon as the evening breeze should spring up; and the offer of a small sum easily induced their compliance with my request to row me out as far as the Hot Baths and back again.

I leaped into the boat, the Jewish boatmen took up their clumsy oars, and lazily pushed off from the shore. There was not a breath of air stirring, the tattered sail hung idly by the yard, there was neither shade nor shelter, and the heat was almost overpowering. Notwithstanding, I could not but feel a singular charm at finding myself gliding along the waters of a lake the most sacred upon earth, the only one upon which the Redeemer had ever sailed—which he was in the constant habit of crossing—from which, seated on the deck of a boat, he was wont to discourse to the listening crowds upon the beach—whose waters, upborne by his power, he had trodden, and to which, in their wildest fury, he had exclaimed, with instantaneous effect, " Peace, be still!" As we receded from the shore, the ruinous walls of Tiberias, surmounted by its castle, stood boldly out, and the whole circle of surrounding mountains, terminated by the snowy summit of Mount Hermon, were reflected in its transparent basin. But all so still, so solitary, and so forsaken!

We reached the baths in about half-an-hour. They stand near the shore, at some distance from Tiberias, and have been famous from the most ancient times to our own day; Ibrahim

Pasha having but recently built a new bath-room over one of the hot springs. The whole neighbourhood was in a reek with the hot steam, and we were glad, after a short stay, to escape to our boat, and return to Tiberias for our dinner. Achmet had been diligently at work, and had been successful in procuring for us, among other things, some fish from the lake, which, on more grounds than one, was eaten with unusal relish.

After sunset I strolled down to the lake, and seating myself upon a mass of broken wall, enjoyed the freshness of the evening. The mountains were like a dark purple frame around the expanse of water, which reflected the hues of the twilight sky. There was a solemnity in the scene which was wanting under the garish light of noon. All day there had not been a breath of air, the sultry heat had been that of a furnace; but now, a cool breeze came off the lofty table-land, and rushing down the ravines that descend to the lake, began to ruffle its placid bosom, and toss up its surface into mimic waves, that broke with a gentle music upon the fallen fragments at my feet. As it grew darker, the breeze increased to a gale, the lake became a sheet of foam, and the white-headed breakers dashed proudly on the rugged beach; its gentle murmur was now changed into the wild and mournful sound of the whistling wind and the agitated waters. Afar off was dimly seen the little barque struggling with the waves, and then lost sight of amidst the misty rack. It was long before I could tear myself from the spot. To have thus seen so striking an exemplification of the Scripture narrative, was as interesting as it was unexpected. It was even thus that the storm came down upon the lake, which threatened to engulf the terrified Apostles, and called forth so sublime a manifestation of the Divine power.

Tiberias ranks with Jerusalem, Hebron, and Safet, the most holy places of the Jews, whither they resort in preference to any other part of Palestine. Yet it would appear that it is not of very ancient foundation—deriving its origin, as Robinson tells us, from Herod Antipas, who gave it this name, in honour of his patron, the Emperor Tiberius. Owing to the voluntary surrender of the city, the fugitive Jews were permitted to resort to it after the destruction of Jerusalem. Here the Sanhedrim was re-established, and, under the conduct of the most learned rabbins, a school gradually formed, whence emanated the famous Mishnah, embodying the great mass of Jewish traditional law. To this was added the Gemara, a supplement to the Mishnah, and also the Masora, intended to preserve the purity of the Hebrew text. This celebrated school has gradually sunk into decline; but the people still linger about the place, generally in a state of extreme poverty, and supported by the alms of their more fortunate European brethren. They appeared a listless, miserable set, but the women possessed much personal beauty, and were far neater in their attire than the other sex.

We left Tiberias at an early hour in the morning, and directed our steps along the border of the lake, which is overhung with mountains sloping to the water, the road being sometimes raised high above the lake, and sometimes descending to its margin. The features of the scenery were eminently suggestive of Scripture incidents; and it was easy to figure the barque which conveyed Jesus and his disciples, moored to the shore, while the strand and the hills rising behind were crowded with eager listeners. In about an hour we reached the north-east angle of the lake, and paused to take a parting draught at a spot where a little grassy promontory, adorned with tufts of crimson-flowered oleanders and quivering reeds, projected into its waters. At this part of the shore the mountains somewhat recede, and leave a little oval plain, supposed to be " the land of Gennesaret," covered with vigorous and neglected vegetation. At its entrance is the small village of El Mejdel, the identical Magdala of the New Testament. Some distance to the right of this, on the northern edge of the lake, is Khan Minyeh, where are ruins, supposed by Robinson and others to be the ancient Capernaum, which stood

undoubtedly on this side of the lake; but, "exalted once to
heaven, is now cast down into hell," so that its very site is
become obscure and uncertain.

Diverging from the shore, our road to Safet ran directly north,
up the rugged valley of Er Rubadiyeh, its enclosing cliffs split
into tremendous perpendicular crags. One of these, standing
out from the rest, seemed perforated by caverns, forming a sort
of natural stronghold. Some of the tall piles of rock, standing
out by themselves, like rude columns, present a most extraordinary appearance. The road, constantly ascending, at length
reaches the level of the high lands above the lake, and the castle
of Safet was seen before us, rising above the small village of
white houses, embowered in gardens and orchards. Achmet,
who had been here before, rode directly to the house of one of
the Jewish rabbis, at which we met with a most hospitable
reception during our short stay.

After the repose and refreshment rendered needful by the long,
fatiguing clamber from the lake, we issued forth to survey the
town. Our lungs seemed to expand with delight at inhaling the
pure, bracing air, so welcome after the furnace-like temperature
of the basin of Tiberias. The situation of Safet is really
glorious—by far the most romantic and commanding in Palestine.
From its towering position, and the fact that it is seen at a great
distance all round the country, it has been regarded as that
"city set on a hill, and which cannot be hid," alluded to, and
probably pointed at, by our Saviour, in his "sermon on the
mount;" nor, even supposing as scholars affirm that Safet
cannot be identified with any ancient city of note, does this
appear to be, in itself, improbable, as its site seems too eligible
not to have been occupied by some city or town, although it
might not otherwise have been distinguished.

The view from the heights around Safet is the grandest in all
Palestine; and, if it does not actually stretch from Dan to
Beersheba, extends over a tract but little less extensive. Far to

Saphet.

Lake of Tiberias.

the north is seen the range of Lebanon and its snowy peaks, the plain of Cœle-Syria, and the Anti-Lebanon; then comes the utmost limit of Palestine, the immense mass of the snow-covered Hermon, with the castle of Paneas at its base, and the whole valley of the Jordan, from its source down to the Laler-el-Huleh, or Waters of Merom, and through which it is seen flowing onward into the Sea of Tiberias. The southward, or that portion of the scene represented in the annexed engraving, comprises the basin of the lake, sunk among its barrier of mountains, with the city of Tiberias jutting into its waters. Above its western border extends the wide expanse of the Trachonitis; to the east, the ridge of Hattin, the isolated cone of Tabor, the wavy hills of Nazareth, and the level plain of Esdraelon, far as the purple mountains of Gilboa and more distant Samaria. The point where the Jordan flows out from the lake, may be the site of Tarichæa, and thence the desert valley of the sacred river may be traced almost to its embouchure in the Dead Sea. In short, it may fairly be said, that one-half of the sacred localities of Scripture come into view at once. Above all, here was the scene of by far the greater part of our Saviour's wanderings and teachings. Behind that screen of hills his youth was passed; on the shores of that lake he called his disciples; across its waters he was repeatedly passing; in the synagogues of its towns he preached to the people; on its mountain sides he delivered his discourses; its scenery served him for familiar objects wherewith to enforce his teaching; even its desert places, to the distant frontier of Syria, afforded him a refuge from persecution, and a solitude for prayer. The whole panorama is one vivid and enduring memento of his earthly life, who "spake as never man spake."

Conspicuous in the foreground of the view is the Gothic castle of Safet, as it appeared after the tremendous earthquake of 1837. This stronghold, to compress the interesting account given of it by Robinson, was one of the fortresses built by the Christians to protect the northern frontiers of Palestine against the incursions of the Saracens. It was given into the custody of the Knights Templars, and remained in their hands until besieged by Saladin in person, after the fatal battle of Hattin, which broke for ever the Christian power in that country. It was then so strong, that although the Sultan pressed the siege himself by night and day, it cost him five weeks to reduce it. Safet now continued half a century in the hands of the Moslems, who in A. D. 1220 caused the fortress to be dismantled. Twenty years after, it was ceded again by treaty to the Christians, and through the energetic assistance of Benedict, Bishop of Marseilles, was rebuilt by the Templars so as to be considered impregnable. But the tenure of their power was very brief, for in 1266 the [place was attacked by the impetuous and ferocious Bibars, Sultan of Egypt, and the Christian garrison, to the number of two thousand men, obliged to capitulate, were put to death, with every circumstance of atrocious cruelty. Bibars now repaired and strengthened the place, establishing a Moslem colony around it, and Safet was regarded as the bulwark of all Syria. Since this time it has gradually fallen into decay, and is now a mere ruin, an eloquent memorial of the crusading ages.

Crouching around the massive relics of this memorable fortress are seen the white houses of the town, which, owing to the steepness of the ground, are in some places built one above another, so that the roofs of those below serve as the roadway to those above. It is divided into three distinct quarters, one of them inhabited by the Jews, who regard this as one of their holiest places in Palestine, and had here formerly a celebrated school of rabbinical learning; although it does not appear that their location in it is of very ancient date. The fifteenth century seems to have been the period of its highest prosperity, since which time it has gradually declined, although the Jews still, even in their present condition of poverty and dependence, haunt the spot in considerable numbers.

Safet had been already desolated by an earthquake in 1759,

when, on the 1st of January, 1837, it was a second time over-whelmed by a similar terrific convulsion. Vast yawning fissures opened in the hill-side, the greater part of the castle was shaken down, and the entire town was overthrown. Owing to the terrace-like manner in which the houses were built, those above were thrown upon those below, and so frightful was the destruction of life, that of six thousand people, five thousand perished; four-fifths of the unhappy sufferers being Jews. Some were killed at once, others lingered in horrible suffering among the ruins, till their protracted agonies were terminated by mortification.

The scene as described by eye-witnesses was dreadful beyond description. Yet here, as at Tiberias, the Jews were beginning to rebuild their fallen houses over the spot where their unhappy relatives had perished, and it seemed as if, oblivious of this fearful catastrophe, the place would ere long assume its wonted appearance.

At Safet we were delayed an entire day before we could pro-ceed. Provided with a strong firman from the Egyptian govern-ment, enjoining the local authorities to furnish us with horses and procure us lodgings, it was still no easy matter to get forward. Such requisitions are still as odious as they were in the days when our Saviour made allusion to them. At that time, as Mr. Sharpe informs us, " every Roman officer, from the general down to the lowest tribune, claimed the right of travel-ling through the country free of expense, and seizing the carts and cattle of the villagers to carry him forward to the next town, under the pretence of being a courier on the public service. The temper of the peasants was sorely tried by this tyranny ; and difficult would they have found it to obey the command, ' Whosoever shall compel thee to go one mile, go with him twain.' " At length, with considerable difficulty, fresh horses were obtained, and we pursued our journey.

At an early hour these were waiting outside the house of the rabbi, of whom, and his interesting wife, we took leave with many thanks for the evident sincerity of our welcome. For this we were a good deal indebted to the humanity of the American missionaries, who have left in the minds of the Jewish population a deep feeling of gratitude for the kindness evinced towards them, after the great earthquake, and have consequently disposed them to look favourably upon travellers of the same race and religion.

This is the truest way to break down ancient prejudices, and to pave the way for the reception of a religion, which inculcates universal charity. A case has just appeared in the papers, of a person who refused to let his house to one of the Jewish persuasion; let that individual, should this happen to meet his eye, know how kindly the traveller was received into the house of a Jew, and profit, if he can, by the lesson.

Our road lay directly through the heart of Galilee, down to St. John of Acre. Our horses slipped and scrambled to the bottom of the tremendous hill upon which Safet is situated, and then began to clamber the opposite acclivity, till after about an hour's riding we seemed as if we could throw a stone across the valley into the town. We took a last retrospective view of the Lake of Tiberias, and descended into the Galilean vales, which, as in the time of Josephus, still teem with populous villages, and appear to be cultivated and fruitful. The whole of this region, extending to the borders of Phœnicia, was no doubt traversed by Jesus during his numerous journeys through Galilee. This part of Palestine was the remotest from the capital, and its inhabitants were considered rude and turbulent. Here took place the first act of the drama, or rather tragedy, which ended in the final destruction of Jerusalem. It was at Jotapata, somewhere in this region, that Josephus, after bravely defending the town against the Emperor Vespasian, was taken prisoner, and from henceforth attached himself to the Roman cause, perhaps, as feeling that of his country to be a hopeless one. It is singular that while so many ancient sites have of late been discovered, that of the romantic Jotapata should still elude research.

The sun was nearly setting in the sea, behind the walls of Acre, as we reached its level plain, and by urging our horses rapidly forward, we succeeded in entering the gates before they were closed for the night. The convent had no charms; the place had been already explored; the night was fine, and a light southerly breeze just crisped the azure surface of the Mediterranean; a single word to Achmet induced him to hurry down to the port, where he found a coasting vessel ready to sail for Beyrout, and only waiting, as it were, to take us on board. To him the word "Beyrout" was synonymous with "home:" there stood his neat little house among the mulberry gardens, and in that house, his pretty little wife was awaiting his return; no wonder, then, that he displayed an unusual alertness. As we jumped into a boat which was to convey us on board the vessel, a Turkish soldier, the first time such a thing had happened to us in the East, muttered something about "Passaporta," but we contented ourselves with replying to him by a look of ineffable contempt. In five minutes more we were outside the reef of Acre, and the following afternoon, after a delightful sail, cast anchor abreast of the hospitable *comptoir* of Mr. Heald.

CHAPTER VI.

VOYAGE AND SHIPWRECK OF ST. PAUL—EMBARKATION AT CÆSAREA—COURSE
TO MALTA—SYRACUSE—REGGIO—PUTEOLI—ROME.

In this concluding chapter, dedicated to the voyage and shipwreck of St. Paul, it will be necessary to depart from the plan
hitherto pursued, giving instead a connected outline of the whole
voyage, and afterwards filling in the details from personal reminiscences of the different localities it embraces.

It is unnecessary to recal the circumstances already described
of St. Paul's examination at Cæsarea before Festus and Agrippa,
and his determination to appeal to Cæsar. Hereupon the Apostle
was delivered into the custody of one Julius, a centurion of
Augustus' band, and, accompanied by Aristarchus, Trophimus,
St. Luke, and, as some suppose, by the historian Josephus, put
on board a ship bound for Adramyttium, in Asia Minor. The
wind being fair from the south, they arrived next day at Sidon—
still a city of considerable commerce—where the vessel remained
a short time; and Paul, who was "courteously entreated by
Julius," received permission to go on shore and refresh himself.
From Sidon, their course, had the wind been favourable, would
have been direct towards the Straits of Cos; but as it happened
to be contrary, they were compelled to make a circuitous course,
and to sail under Cyprus; that is, to the eastward of it; and
thus to traverse the sea of Cilicia and Pamphylia, between that
island and the coast of Asia Minor. They next reached Myra, a
city of Lycia, whose magnificent remains testify to the importance

which it once enjoyed. So far they were on their course, although an indirect one, for Italy; but as the "ship of Adramyttium" would now pursue her voyage to the northward, it became necessary to leave her and to embark in another. One of the vessels then engaged in carrying supplies of corn from Egypt to Rome, also driven out of her direct course by contrary winds, was then in the harbour. These ships were of the largest class, carrying often several hundred people, and commanded, no doubt, by the most expert mariners to be found in the Mediterranean. From a representation of one of them on a coin of Augustus, it would

COIN OF SHIP.

seem that they carried but one large mast, on which was hoisted the mainsail to propel the ship, while a smaller sail at the bowsprit assisted in steering her, a peculiarity which should be remembered in reading the subsequent account.

Owing to the westerly wind generally prevalent in the Mediterranean, their ship appears to have worked her way very slowly as far as Cnidus, where, unable to make a course direct west, which would have carried her to the northward of Crete, she was compelled to bear to the southward, and with difficulty doubling Cape Salmone, the eastern point of that island, came to an anchor in the roads called the Fair Havens; supposed to be a harbour on the southern side of Crete. So much time had been already lost, and the stormy season was now approaching so near, that Paul strenuously urged the centurion to remain

where they were for the winter; a plan overruled by the master
of the ship, on account of the incommodiousness of the harbour.
As there was another haven called Phœnice, at no great distance along the coast, which offered superior advantages, they
waited until there sprung up a gentle south wind, which promised to waft them to their destination in a few hours, and then
set sail, keeping close along the shore.   They had not proceeded
far when they were suddenly caught by "a tempestuous wind,
called Euroclydon," blowing off the land directly athwart their
course, and so furious that, being unable to bear up against
it, they were compelled to let the vessel drive before it to the
south-west, passing under the small island of Clauda, and using
their utmost efforts to secure their boat, which had been hitherto
towed after them.   The gale blowing heavily from the north-

CAPE SALMONE.

east, would, had the vessel been suffered to scud on directly
before it, have inevitably driven her into the Syrtis, or Great
Gulf, on the coast of Africa, where she would have gone
ashore; they were, therefore, obliged to put the vessel about,
so that she might drift to the northward.   Deeply laden, and
encumbered with the huge and heavy yard required for the great
sail, she laboured so heavily as to strain open the seams, to
avoid which they "undergirded" the ship; that is, passed a
thick cable round her, threw overboard part of the cargo, and on

the third day—the tempest continuing with unabated violence—
to lighten her still further, " threw over with their own hands the
tackling of the ship,"—that is, in all probability, the ponderous
mainyard and its appendages. They had now done all that it was
in the power of good seamanship to do, towards averting the fate
which threatened them; yet the gale still blew with such fury, and
the sky was so utterly obscured, that they might shortly expect
either that their overlaboured ship would founder, or go ashore
upon some unknown coast, especially as, since the vessel was put
about off Clauda, they had continued to drift in the same course.
Despair was seizing upon their spirits, when Paul, gently re-
proaching them for not listening to his advice, now told them
he had received a miraculous assurance, that although they must
suffer shipwreck, not a hair of their heads should perish.

On the fourteenth night, as they were doubtless on the look-
out, the shipmen deemed that they drew near some land;
detecting perhaps in the breeze the fragrance of gardens on
shore, or faintly discerning at a distance the looming of the
tremendous breakers of the coast of Malta. They now sounded,
and finding the depth of water gradually decreasing, they cast
four anchors out of the stern, and, in the emphatic language of
the Apostolic narrative, "wished for the day." The practice of
anchoring by the stern was usual in ancient seamanship, as Mr.
Smith has proved by a representation of a vessel having holes
for the purpose; but they were also sometimes, to keep them in
a fixed position, anchored both fore and aft. And thus we find
that, under pretence of throwing out the anchors forward, but in
reality with a view to save themselves, the sailors were preparing
to take to the boat; but on Paul's assuring them that if they
did so the whole would perish, the soldiers cut off the boat-ropes,
and let her fall into the sea. We may judge by this of the
powerful ascendancy gained over the minds of all on board by
one who had embarked with them as a prisoner. When the day
dawned, Paul besought the fasting sailors, who during the storm

had been prevented from taking their usual allowance—as is often the case in modern times under similar circumstances—to recruit their sinking spirits with a hearty meal. He stood up in the midst, took bread, and giving thanks to God, himself set the example, which was followed by the two hundred and seventy-six persons on board, who afterwards awaited the catastrophe with cheerful confidence in the Divine mercy. As the vessel was labouring heavily at her anchors, they lightened her by throwing overboard the remainder of their cargo. The day now broke, and disclosed a shore unknown to them; but they perceived an opening in the iron-bound coast, and determined to run the ship into it. They cut their cables, hoisted their artemon, or foresail, and with mingled feelings of hope and apprehension, committed themselves to the Divine guidance.

The controversy that has so long been maintained respecting the identity of that "Melita" upon which the Apostle was wrecked, would have been easily settled had the details of his course been scanned with the eye of a seaman as well as those of a scholar, when the assumption that it was the "Meleda" of the Adriatic Sea would have plainly appeared to be utterly inconsistent with the whole course so indicated, both before and subsequent to the shipwreck. This scientific examination of the subject has recently been made by Mr. Smith of Jordan-hill, to whose work we are indebted for the brief outline which will there be found completely filled up. His researches tend to confirm in the strongest manner the popular tradition, that the spot at Malta called "St. Paul's Bay," is really that where the Apostle was driven ashore.

Having in another work given a particular description of St. Paul's Bay, as well as of the island of Malta, but a brief notice of it can properly be given in this place. Suffice it to say, then, there is every ground for believing that tradition—in so many instances doubtful or obscure—is here in exact conformity with the requirements of the Scripture narrative. The bay, on the shore of which the ship is believed to have grounded, is on the south-east side of the island, precisely in the line of her drift from the western shore of Crete. At its mouth is a bold rocky island called Salmoon, upon which has lately been erected a colossal statue of St. Paul. Between one end of this island and the mainland is a narrow inlet, through which the sea would force its way from without, thus crossing the main current setting in through the mouth of the bay. There, it is presumed, is the spot where the two seas met, and where the vessel, running head foremost upon the mud, stuck fast, while the hinder part being exposed to the heavy seas, was broken to pieces. The bay is studded round with objects recalling the tradition. Here

ST. PAUL'S BAY.

is the " Fountain of the Apostle," of which he first drank after going ashore, and a small chapel and fort bearing his name. About two miles inland is a grotto, where he is said to have retired; while at Citta Vecchia, which in the Apostle's day was the capital of the island and the residence of the governor, are further memorials of his abiding there; and although some of these sites are probably fanciful, the main fact of the shipwreck may now be considered as fully established. After remaining three months in the island of Malta, Paul and his companions departed for Puteoli in a ship of Alexandria which had wintered in the isle.

The first place where he landed was Syracuse, on the eastern coast of Sicily, where he remained three days. This city, founded by a Corinthian colony, had attained a state of great magnificence. It is memorable in history for its two great sieges, the first by the Greeks, and the second by the Romans. During a war with the people of Leontini, the latter implored the assistance of the Athenians, who availing themselves of this pretext to besiege Syracuse, as the first step towards the conquest of the whole of Sicily, assembled accordingly a large fleet at Corcyra (Corfu), and thence repaired to Rhegion (Reggio). Having been disappointed of the succours promised by the other Sicilian cities hostile to Syracuse, the Athenians were compelled to undertake the siege of this great city by themselves. The original seat of the Corinthian colony was the island of Ortygia, at the mouth of one of the finest harbours in the world. This island, surrounded by fortifications, was afterwards joined to the peninsula forming its northern angle, which received the name of Acradina, and was defended by a second wall. As the city continued to increase, two suburbs were thrown out and enclosed within additional defences. Still further inland they extended along a boldly rising ground as far as the Labdalon and Euryalus, while on the opposite side of the harbour was the fort of the Olympeion.

The famous siege of Syracuse by the Athenians would, of itself, fill a chapter; suffice it to say here, that after a long and desperate struggle, both by land and sea, the great harbour having become the scene of several sea-fights, the Athenians were at length decisively beaten, and compelled to abandon their ships, and attempt escaping by land towards Calonia, but were overtaken by Gylippus, and forced to surrender at discretion.

Syracuse continued to increase in extent and splendour until it was besieged by the Romans under Marcellus. The whole of the high ground extending to the Labdalon, had by this time been enclosed with a wall; the new quarter of Neapolis, also fortified, had arisen, so that there may be said to have been five cities now united together. Its different walls are said to have extended twenty-two miles in length, and to have contained upwards of a million of inhabitants. Archimedes, the greatest mechanist of the age, was among the defenders of the city, and by his stupendous machinery, completely defeated the utmost efforts of the Romans. Vast beams of wood, with grappling hooks at the end, were made to descend upon their vessels, and, raising them out of the water, to dash them with their crews upon the shore, or sink them; while others were set on fire by burning-glasses. The paralysed besiegers declared that they were fighting against the gods, and Marcellus was compelled to turn the siege into a blockade; nor was it until, taking advantage of a festival of Diana, when the people incautiously gave themselves up to revelry, that he succeeded in making himself master of the Epipolæ. The island still held out, and it was only by the treachery of the mercenary troops, that the city was at length compelled to surrender, and was reluctantly given up to pillage by the Roman general.

During the attack, Archimedes, it is said, was deeply engaged over a problem, when a soldier broke in, and killed him by mistake, to the great concern of Marcellus, who had offered a large reward to any one who would bring him alive into his presence. The city was then rifled of its innumerable objects of art, which were borne away to Rome, where they contributed greatly to form that taste for art which afterwards prevailed among the people.

Notwithstanding this declension from its original splendour, Syracuse was still a great and magnificent city when St. Paul and his vessel entered its harbour, and probably conveyed to its inhabitants the first tidings of Christianity which had ever been heard in Sicily. Whether he made any converts is not, however, recorded. From this period, the city, like the Roman Empire itself, gradually declined, and after suffering from Arabian inroads and domestic feuds, has dwindled down to an insignificant modern town, confined exclusively to that portion originally settled by its founders, namely, the island of Ortygia.

"At the present moment," says the judicious Mrs. Starke, " Syracuse is chiefly famed for its excellent hotel *Il Sole*, the Sun," and those who may think such an announcement too trivial for notice, would form a different opinion if they knew the filth and starvation of Sicilian inns in general. It was therefore with feelings of lively satisfaction that, as we ascended the rugged ground of Acradina, and saw the ancient island of Ortygia and the town of Syracuse, surrounded by the strong walls built by Charles V., we looked forward to somewhat better quarters than at the wretched hovel of Lentini, in which necessity had obliged us to take refuge the preceding night. We found " Il Sole " fully bearing out its reputation, a perfect oasis of comfort in the surrounding desert of misery, and were the more surprised at it, since it is not now on a line of high road, and the travellers who visit it are comparatively few and far between.

On sallying forth from this delectable hostelry into the streets of Syracuse, everything bears an air of decay and misery. A squalid population vegetate in a state of moral and industrial torpor, although under a sky of cloudless serenity, and in one of the most fertile islands of the world. Such is the superstition of the Sicilians, that even the Neapolitans cry out against them. One of the latter assured me that instead of contenting themselves with the wooden effigies of our Saviour commonly made use of in Italy, they have been known to hire a poor wretch to submit to be fastened up in the painful attitude of crucifixion, in order to stimulate more powerfully the feelings of the devout. Their ferocity is in proportion to their superstition. I was assured by the vice-consul that, on the appearance of the cholera, which they ignorantly attributed to some machinations of the

Syracuse

Neapolitan authorities, they seized upon the governor, who was already unpopular, and who happened at the time to be almost unprotected, and after putting him to death with every circumstance of cruelty, cut up his mangled body into small portions, and sold it for dogs' meat in the public streets. Such is the depth of abasement to which a bad government and a system of superstition have succeeded in degrading humanity, in the beautiful lands cursed by the sway of the most bigoted and despotic of the Bourbons.

Little now remains of Syracuse within the island itself. Part of a temple is incorporated with the principal church; the Fountain of Arethusa, so celebrated by the poets, is now become a tank for washerwomen. Without the walls of Ortygia, however, the traces of former magnificence are striking and extensive. As the distance to be traversed is considerable, I hired a mule and a guide, and set off after breakfast to make the circuit of the walls. On our way we examined the extensive quarries which served as prisons to the defeated Athenians, and where the greater part perished by disease and hunger. Connected with these is the celebrated Ear of Dionysius, the tyrant of Syracuse, a small chamber in the rock, up to which every sound in the prisons was so conveyed by a natural channel, that he is said to have amused himself with listening to the conversation of the prisoners. Not far from this is a splendid and very perfect amphitheatre; and still further, the remains of a theatre, whence a passage, cut in the rock, and lined with tombs, conducts to the high ground of the Epipolæ. Riding along the ridge, we pursued our way until we reached the utmost limit of the fortifications, and obtained the annexed view, which will serve far better than any description to convey a correct idea of the position of the city and of the immense circuit of its walls, surpassing that of Rome, Jerusalem, Athens, or Alexandria.

Nothing can exceed the luxuriance and beauty of the wild plants and shrubs, which spring up among the ruins, and attest the astonishing richness of the Sicilian soil. Flowers that, at home, form the cherished ornaments of the garden or the hothouse, here, among the fallen blocks of Fort Labdalon, flourish in wild luxuriance. From hence the walls, carried along the edge of the high ground, are seen extending past what was the Epipolæ, as far as the island, the only part now fortified. Part only of Acradina appears to the left. The valley of the Anapus below is still as marshy and unhealthy as when it proved fatal to the Punic troops. The papyrus flourishes in its waters. Adjacent to the harbour was Neapolis, the last built and most extensive quarter of the city. On the rising ground opposite Ortygia the Greeks encamped, and the great harbour was the scene of their final discomfiture by the Syracusan fleet. It is not, perhaps, generally known that, in consequence of an order obtained by the influence of Lady Hamilton from the Queen of Naples, Lord Nelson was permitted to water his fleet in this harbour, and was thus enabled to go in quest of the French fleet, which he soon afterwards surprised and destroyed in the Bay of Aboukir.

After this hasty glance at Syracuse, we proceed to trace the course of the Apostle towards Rome. On leaving Syracuse, the narrative informs us, they "fetched a compass," and came to Rhegium, just within the entrance of the Straits of Messina. In sailing along the coast, or, as is probable, even at some distance out to sea, the lofty cone of Mount Etna, covered with eternal snow, would be the prominent object to arrest attention, until they reached the rugged mountains of Calabria. Rhegium was a city of Grecian origin, and had undergone many vicissitudes, having been devastated by some of those tremendous earthquakes which, from the earliest ages to the present day, have repeatedly overwhelmed the "cities of the strait." When St. Paul's ship touched there, as we should infer from the narrative, in consequence of the wind being contrary, it was just arising from its ruins, having been made a naval colony by Augustus.

Rigps

Nearly opposite to Reggio, the ancient Rhegium, on the Sicilian side, is the city of Messina, the heights above which command a sublime view of the whole length of the strait through which St. Paul sailed, and of his further course along the Italian shores. The path from the city to these heights, is bordered with hedges of aloe and cactus; and, on attaining the aërial summit, we look down upon a wilderness of conical-shaped hills, of volcanic appearance, almost all cultivated to their tops, sinking gradually to the white buildings of the city, which repose gracefully along the margin of the strait. The shape of its harbour, as seen from hence, fully explains the appellation of "the sickle," originally bestowed by the Sicilians upon it. Just beyond the entrance is the formidable whirlpool of Charybdis, which, with the opposite rock of Scylla, at the northern extremity of the strait, formed the proverbial terror of ancient mariners. On the other side of the strait, and near its mouth, Reggio is seen upon a narrow plain, crouching at the foot of the stupendous mountains of Calabria, which are deeply indented with gloomy ravines, and rise into dreary snow-capped peaks; while the sea, which the barque of Paul must have traversed on the course from Syracuse, expands to the southward horizon.

On looking down upon this scene, at once awfully magnificent and serenely beautiful, few would imagine the fearful events that have occurred within its confines. The earthquake that desolated Reggio has been already alluded to. Another convulsion, of a still more tremendous character, occurred in 1783, by which great part of Messina was laid in ruins. On the Calabrian shore, a vast number of people fled to the beach, when the waters of the straits suddenly arose, and swallowed them up. The quay of Messina was destroyed, and the ships in the harbour were engulfed or dashed to pieces.

But let us follow the Apostle on his voyage from Reggio. "After one day," says the narrator in the Acts, "the south wind blew, and we came the next day to Puteoli." This would give a run of about four-and-twenty hours from the Straits of Messina to the Bay of Naples; exactly the time in which the writer performed the voyage in a sailing vessel.

On issuing from the straits, Scylla appears upon its craggy precipice, overhanging the waves, and soon after, the "lone volcanic isle" of Stromboli rises grandly from the sea; while the rugged shores of Calabria continue in sight all the way to Naples. Here, at the mouth of that unrivalled bay, stands, as it stood when St. Paul's vessel sailed past it, the bold romantic island of Capri, like a huge breakwater, to stem the force of the southern

MISENUM.

swell. It was at that time, or shortly after, the retreat of the Emperor Tiberius, who chose this secluded spot in order to indulge unobserved in a career of horrible licentiousness. Vesuvius now comes in sight, and distant Naples, ranging along the shore its glittering palaces, while the white buildings of Torre del Greco mark the site of Herculaneum and Pompeii, before they were destroyed by the tremendous convulsion described by Pliny. But the vessel of St. Paul leaves these objects in the distance, for, steering across the mouth of the gulf, she directs her course towards the graceful and sheltered Bay of Baiæ.

Passing the bold headland of Misenum, she steers direct for
Puteoli, or Dicæarchea, and anchors within the shelter of the
mole, amidst a crowd of corn-ships, bearing supplies from Egypt
for the citizens of Rome. " Here," says St. Luke, " we found
brethren, and were desired to tarry with them seven days."

At the time when St. Paul first landed on the shores of Italy,
Rome had attained the highest degree of power; her foot was
upon the neck of prostrate kings, and she was gorged with the
wealth of vanquished empires. Corruption of their early simplicity of manners, and luxuriousness of habits, had followed in
the train of conquest. The ancient religion was despised by
the philosopher and man of the world; the doctrine of a future
life was treated as an idle dream;—in short, practical atheism
was the creed of the more polite part of the community. Yet
there were, no doubt, many who sighed for something more
consolatory than either the vulgar superstition of the plebeian, or
the dreary scepticism of the patrician; and to such Christianity
would not appeal in vain. At what time, or by whom, the
doctrines of the Gospel were first promulgated in Italy, appears
uncertain; but, at the period of St. Paul's visit, a little band of
disciples had been formed at Puteoli, and by these the Apostle
was received as an angel of God, and pressed to take up his
abode with them for a few days.

The city where he thus sojourned for a week, otherwise called
Dicæarchea, was the principal station for the corn-fleets from
Egypt, and the usual landing-place of travellers desirous of
repairing to Rome. Its harbour was spacious, being formed by
sinking vast masses of stone, cemented by mortar of a peculiarly
adhesive nature, formed by calcined nodules of limestone and
sand, now called *Pozzolano*, from Pozzuoli, the modern name of
the place, and closely imitated in our " Roman cement." It
possessed a conspicuous lighthouse, and was adorned with the
usual number of temples, the remains of which are still to be
traced among the mean buildings of the modern town.

But Pozzuoli possesses in its quay a relic incomparably more interesting than these. Let us ascend the heights above the town, where the graceful round-topped stone pine rises among masses of " opus reticulatum," and where huge aloes, and citron and olive-trees entwine their roots among the obscure ruins of the Roman villas. From the spot where we stand the beautiful Bay of Baiæ sweeps round in a gentle curve, terminated by the bold headland of Misenum. On its shore, almost at our feet, is seen Puteoli, projecting its mass of modern Italian houses into the waves; and at its extremity appear the wrecks of that ancient quay, upon which St. Paul must have landed. This massive mole was a work of great antiquity, supposed to have been originally formed by the inhabitants of Cumæ, and afterwards strengthened by the Roman emperors. Its wave-worn fragments of dark-brown stone, stained with the green sea-weed, and encrusted with marine shells, stretch out some distance into the sea, and some of the rings are yet remaining upon them by which the vessels were moored. Beyond the pier, the sea expands to the southward, and the island of Capri rises boldly on the horizon, on the very track by which St. Paul approached the port.

At the period when he landed, the adjacent Bay of Baiæ was the favourite resort of the more wealthy and tasteful Romans. Its graceful curving shore, open to the southern breeze, was surrounded by costly villas, furnished with warm baths and every appliance of luxury, and was studded with temples, exhibiting the utmost perfection of classical elegance and refinement. The neighbourhood, too, was full of poetry. At Parthenope, now Naples, Virgil lived, and sung, and was buried; and here he has laid many of the scenes of his Æneid. In short, this was the most favoured region in all Italy—the especial delight of the more intellectual as well as luxurious patricians. How insignificant to them, should they have chanced to hear of it, would appear the arrival of a poor Jew in bonds, from a distant

Bay of Bacan

The Mole of Puteoli — (Pozzuoli)

and despised country; and how little could they have anticipated the day when the religion he came to teach should fill the land, and that its stately shrines would stand triumphant, when the sea should wash over the tesselated relics of their luxurious villas, and splendid temples!

Leaving Puteoli, St. Paul and his companions directed their steps towards Rome, whence a band of disciples, who had received the joyful news of his arrival, were hastening to give him the meeting. Baiæ and Puteoli communicated with Rome by a branch road, which entered the Appian Way near Minturnæ. This famous highway, the Via Appia, called the queen of Roman roads, was constructed with large stones, so well prepared and fitted, that they adhered for ages without the aid of cement. It was well furnished with inns and post-houses, being the most frequented outlet from the capital. The modern road from Rome to Naples runs, for the most part, upon its foundations, and displays, in many places, the most enchanting scenery, especially at Mola, Fondi, and Terracina; but upon this our plan forbids us to dwell in detail. The road had not long been traversed in the opposite direction, by a very different sort of traveller—the poet Horace, who has given the facetious account of his adventures, so familiar to classical scholars, and so truthfully presented to the English reader by the gentle Cowper.

In what way the Apostle and his friends may have travelled, we are left very much to conjecture; but, across the Pontine Marshes, between Terracina and Torre Treponti, supposed to occupy the site of Appii Forum, ran a canal, along which Horace was conveyed during the night, and of which some vestiges are still to be traced. At Appii Forum Paul met the first detachment of his sympathising friends, and the remainder at Tres Tabernas, or the Three Taverns, the next station towards Rome, situated near the modern town of Cisterna. The sight of company after company, thus prepared beforehand to welcome him, must have been cheering indeed to the Apostle, after his long and arduous journey; and, to use the brief but expressive words of the sacred narrative, "he thanked God, and took courage."

The whole party now proceeded together towards Rome, crossing the romantic hills of Aricia and Albano, till the wide expanse of the Campagna opened before them, terminated in the distance by the glittering buildings of the Eternal City. Far different from what it now is, was then the approach to Rome. The throng of chariots and horsemen must have pressed eagerly along the narrow causeway, lined with those splendid sepulchres, of which the ruins are now scattered over the dreary and deserted plain, where the solitary herdsman pastures his droves of buffaloes. But where shall we find the scene, such as it must then have been, so vividly portrayed as in the well-known lines of Milton?—

> "What conflux issuing forth, or entering in,—
> Prætors, proconsuls to their provinces
> Hasting, or on return, in robes of state;
> Lictors and rods, the ensigns of their power;
> Legions and cohorts, turms of horse and wings;
> Or embassies from regions far remote,
> In various habits, on the Appian road,
> Or on th' Emilian; some from farthest south,
> Syene, and where the shadow both ways falls,
> Meroe, Nilotic isle, and more to west,
> The realm of Bacchus, to the Blackmoor sea;
> From th' Asian kings and Parthian among these,
> From India and the golden Cheronese,
> And utmost Indian isle Taprobane,
> Dusk faces, with white silken turbans wreath'd;
> From Gallia, Gades, and the British West,
> Germans and Scythians, and Sarmatians north
> Beyond Danubius to the Tauric pool."
>
> *Paradise Regained*, b. iv.

The modern road from Rome to Naples, diverging from the Via Appia, enters the city by the Porta S. Giovanni. Paul and his companions continued, of course, to follow the Appian Way, and leaving on the right the beautiful round sepulchre of

Cecilia Metella, entered the city through the gate of Drusus, the remains of which still bestride the original causeway.

ARCH OF DRUSUS.

Arrived at the metropolis of the world, Paul appears to have been, although nominally a prisoner, yet admitted to bail, and allowed to live for two years in his own hired house. Here he largely increased the number of the Christian converts, which it would seem was already so considerable as to have excited the hostility of the Jews; thus giving rise to dissensions which had caused both parties to be banished for a while from the city. It was not long after his arrival that Paul was called upon to appear before the tribunal of Nero, on which occasion he was deserted by most of those whom he had expected to stand by him. For the present, however, he escaped the cruelty of the tyrant. After his first sojourn at Rome, he set out again on his missionary travels, probably going as far as Spain, and revisiting also the churches in Greece and Asia Minor, generally accompanied by

Luke, and sometimes by other of his friends. " The indefatigable activity of this one man," to use the words of Milman, " had planted Christian colonies, each of which became the centre of a new moral civilization, from the borders of Syria as far as Spain, and to the city of Rome."

During this absence of the Apostle occurred that terrible fire which laid Rome in ashes, and for which the unoffending Christians were punished by the infliction of the most unheard-of tortures, being enveloped in wax cloths, and set up for torches in the public gardens. This circumstance seems to prove that they could be no longer an obscure insignificant body, but must have become sufficiently numerous to attract the notice, and to fix the suspicions of the government. Paul at length went back to Rome, but only to obtain the crown of martyrdom. His Second Epistle to Timothy, written shortly after his return, alludes to his recent journey into Asia Minor and Greece, and declares that he " was now ready to be offered, and that the time of his departure was at hand."

Whether St. Peter was ever at Rome, and after being a fellow-labourer with St. Paul, suffered martyrdom about the same time, is a question warmly disputed to the present day; suffice it to say, that such appears to have been the general belief of the early Fathers. According to this belief, St. Peter was crucified upon the Vatican Mount, at the spot whereon Constantine afterwards erected that chapel, which became the nucleus of the most magnificent church in the world. Whatever may be the genuineness of this tradition, there can be little or no doubt that St. Paul, after being some time confined in prison, was led out to execution at the Aquæ Salviæ, three miles from the city, where, as crucifixion was too infamous for a Roman citizen, he was put to death by beheading, and afterwards buried in the Via Ostiensis. The church raised over this spot by Constantine, was one of the most splendid of Christian basilicas.

To give the history of Rome from the time of St. Paul to the

Rome.

present day,—to trace the growth of that spiritual power, which from being small as a grain of mustard-seed, at length over-shadowed the whole earth, would of itself require volumes, and is, of course, wholly out of place in a work of this nature. Nor is it possible here to delineate the different legendary sites and objects connected with St. Peter and St. Paul; all that can be done is to cast a glance over the site of what was the most impor-tant part of Rome in the Apostle's day, and shortly afterwards, and to dwell briefly upon its most remarkable monuments.

From the tower of the Capitol, the view southward embraces by far the most interesting portion of ancient Rome. The half-deserted area of the Forum is just beneath, with its triumphal arches, temples, and scattered columns; their bases, deep below the modern level of the soil, dug out, and exposing the pave-ment of the Via Sacra. In the centre of the Forum is seen the solitary column of Phocas, and further on those three celebrated pillars of the Comitium, which have served to after ages as a canon of the Corinthian order of architecture. On the right, the dark irregular mass of the Palatine Mount, the abode of the Cæsars, rises from the Forum, its mouldering vestiges of imperial splendour matted together and overgrown with the cypress and the vine. The Arch of Titus is seen in the centre of the view—that of Constantine behind it. Beyond the walls, where the Church of St. John Lateran is the most conspicuous object, the melancholy Campagna, dotted with tombs and broken aqueducts, is seen extending to the distant mountains of Albano and Frascati. In the centre of this wide area of ruin, one huge pile of red masonry rises darkly above the rest; and, though shorn of much of its original grandeur by time and havoc, it is still no less than imperial in aspect—the proudest and the most enduring of all the monuments erected by the great mistress of the ancient world. Since the eighth century, when the " sublime prover-bial expression," as Gibbon calls it, " While the Coliseum stands Rome shall stand; when the Coliseum falls Rome shall fall; and when Rome falls the world shall fall;" was called forth by the "rude enthusiasm" of the pilgrims of the North, great inroads have been made upon the fabric; yet, when the spectator stands beneath its triple range of arches, towering almost into the sky, and sweeping round in a majestic circle, his feelings of awe and wonder will be hardly less than theirs.

As this edifice arose in the most palmy state of imperial greatness, when, with the decline of liberty, the stern qualities of the old Roman were giving way to the thirst for luxury which followed in the train of conquest; so its history is that of a debased people—its colossal proportions commensurate with the wide and growing corruption of the age. But, as a spectacle, nothing could possibly be grander than its pristine appearance. "It was a building of an elliptic figure, 564 feet in length and 467 in breadth, founded on fourscore arches, and rising, with four successive orders of architecture, to the height of 140 feet. The outside of the edifice was encrusted with marble and decorated with statues. The slopes of the vast concave, which formed the inside, were filled and surrounded with sixty or eighty rows of seats, of marble likewise, covered with cushions, and capable of receiving with ease above fourscore thousand spectators. Sixty-four vomitories (for by that name the doors were very aptly distinguished) poured forth the immense multitude; and the entrances, passages, and staircases were contrived with such exquisite skill, that each person, whether of the senatorial, the equestrian, or the plebeian order, arrived at his destined place without trouble or confusion. Nothing was omitted which, in any respect, could be subservient to the convenience and pleasure of the spectators. They were protected from the sun and rain by an ample canopy occasionally drawn over their heads. The air was continually refreshed by the playing of fountains, profusely impregnated with the grateful scent of aromatics. In the centre of the edifice, the *arena* or stage was strewed with the finest sand, and successively assumed the most different forms. At one moment it seemed to rise out of the earth, like the garden of the Hesperides, and was afterwards broken into the rocks and caverns of Thrace. The subterraneous pipes conveyed an inexhaustible supply of water, and what had just before appeared a level plain, might be suddenly converted into a wide lake, covered with armed vessels, and replenished with the monsters of the deep."

Here, and in the Circus, the Roman people were gratified by the sight, and subsequent slaughter, of animals brought for the purpose from every part of the wide confines of their empire; and we read of the almost incredible massacre of an hundred lions, an equal number of lionesses, two hundred leopards, and three hundred bears. From this it was but a step to human blood; and the passion for gladiatorial combats became so strong that, beside the wretched compulsory victims of this savage taste, voluntary performers were not wanting, and even women, in the end, appeared upon the arena. So deeply rooted in the popular mind was the thirst for this accursed excitement, that it survived more than half a century the fall of Paganism; and was finally put an end to by the self-devotion of the monk Telemachus, whose interference cost him his life, but led to a decree, by the Emperor Honorius, of final suppression. Few, we should think, can stand within this area, once slippery with human gore, and re-people the mouldering seats of the amphitheatre, tier above tier to the very sky, not only with the populace, but with all that was great and beautiful in ancient Rome—with the most refined patrician, and even with woman—gazing with one feeling of eager delight, not only on the skill, but on the very blood of their victims—without a shudder. " But Time, the beautifier," has thrown over the scene of such horrors a solemn charm, difficult to describe; feeding, " like dull fire upon a hoary brand," on the stupendous ruin; in which now, worn with the rents and weather-stains of ages, the huge broken vaults and buttresses all overgrown by a wild garland of ivy and bird-haunted foliage, it has

half-obliterated the dark page of history, and withdraws the mind
from its past purpose to its present beauty.

> " There is given
> Unto the things of earth, which Time hath bent,
> A spirit's feeling ; and where he hath leant
> His hand, but broke his scythe, there is a power
> And magic in the ruin'd battlement,
> For which the palace of the present hour
> Must yield its pomp, and wait till ages are its dower."

Neither the Coliseum nor the greater part of the monuments
now seen from the Capitol, were erected till after St. Paul's death.
Of these there is one which, to the Christian or the Jew, must
ever be the most interesting at Rome, marking, as it does, the
final downfal of the Jewish state, and preserving upon its triumphal tablets the only authentic representation in existence of the
implements of the temple worship. This is the Arch of Titus,
erected, after his death, to commemorate his capture of Jerusalem,
and which is, perhaps, the most simple and beautiful at Rome.
The ruined frieze bears the triumphal procession of the conqueror ;
and, sculptured on the wall *within* the archway, is a procession
of captive Jews, bearing on their shoulders the spoils of the
temple at Jerusalem,—the eleven-branched golden candlestick,
the jubilee trumpets, the tables of the shew-bread, and other
details, copied, no doubt, from the originals themselves, which,
deposited in the temples, are said to have been finally carried
away by Genseric into Africa. This sculptured tablet, and the
edifice which it adorns, form, perhaps, the most vivid page in
monumental history to be met with in the whole world.

Another memento of the same calamity also remains. Although
at that period bulletins and gazettes were unknown, and what we
now term "the press" was unthought of, yet there existed presses,
which at the imperial bidding could throw off their ten thousand
impressions, and which, circulating through the remotest ramifi-
cation of the empire in a form almost universally accessible and

intelligible, proclaimed the event to which they related; and more than one of these still exist in the coins struck upon this occasion, a copy of one of which is here introduced.

COIN—JUDÆA CAPTA.

Here we must bring to a close these scattered pages, in which an attempt has been made to convey to the reader, by the combination of travelling sketches and historical notices, some idea of the present condition of spots which must remain hallowed as long as the world endures, in many of which the last monumental vestiges of apostolic times are fast mouldering away, so that the pilgrim of the next century will vainly seek to trace their form or to fix their site.

THE END.

Breinigsville, PA USA
18 March 2011
257977BV00003B/31/P